MW00325288

We Heal From Memory

We Heal From Memory

Sexton, Lorde, Anzaldúa,

and the Poetry of Witness

Cassie Premo Steele

palgrave

WE HEAL FROM MEMORY
Copyright © Cassie Premo Steele, 2000.
All rights reserved. No part of this book may be used or reproduced in any manner whatsoever without written permission except in the case of brief quotations embodied in critical articles or reviews.

First published 2000 by
PALGRAVE™
175 Fifth Avenue, New York, N.Y. 10010 and
Houndmills, Basingstoke, Hampshire, England RG21 6XS.
Companies and representatives throughout the world.

PALGRAVE™ is the new global publishing imprint of St. Martin's Press LLC Scholarly and Reference Division and Palgrave Publishers Ltd (formerly Macmillan Press Ltd).

ISBN 0-312-23342-6 hardback

Library of Congress Cataloging-in-Publication Data
Steele, Cassie Premo, 1967–
    We heal from memory : Sexton, Lorde, Anzaldúa, and the poetry of witness / Cassie Premo Steele.
        p. cm.
    Includes bibliographical references (p.) and index.
    ISBN 0-312–23342-6 (cloth)
    1. American poetry—Women authors—History and criticism. 2. Women and literature—United States—History—20th century. 3. American poetry—20th century—History and criticism. 4. Anzaldúa, Gloria—Criticism and interpretation. 5. Lorde, Audre—Criticism and interpretation. 6. Sexton, Anne—Criticism and interpretation. 7. Victims of crimes in literature. 8. Witnesses in literature. 9. Violence in literature. 10. Victims in literature. 11. Healing in literature. 12. Memory in literature. 13. Women in literature. I. Title.

PS151 .S74 2000
811'.54099287—dc21

                                                                00-040488

A catalogue record for this book is available from the British Library.

Design by Westchester Book Composition.

First edition: October, 2000

10 9 8 7 6 5 4 3 2 1

Printed in the United States of America.

for Meili, my witness

Contents

Acknowledgments

Grateful acknowledgment is given to the following for permission to reprint:

The papers and manuscripts of Anne Sexton at the Harry Ransom Humanities Research Center at the University of Texas at Austin. Reprinted with permission.

Excerpts from THE COMPLETE POEMS OF ANNE SEXTON. Copyright © 1981 by Linda Gray Sexton and Loring Conant, Jr., Executors of the Will of Anne Sexton. Reprinted by permission of Houghton Mifflin Company.

Excerpts from BORDERLANDS/LA FRONTERA: THE NEW MESTIZA. Copyright © 1987 by Gloria Anzaldúa. Reprinted by permission of Aunt Lute Press.

Excerpts from "A Litany for Survival." Copyright © 1978 by Audre Lorde. "Chain." Copyright © 1978 by Audre Lorde. "To My Daughter the Junkie On A Train," "Afterimages," from COLLECTED POEMS by Audre Lorde. Copyright © 1997 by the Estate of Audre Lorde. Used by permission of W. W. Norton & Company, Inc.

Earlier versions of parts of this book appeared or are forthcoming in the following:

"When Pain Precludes the Possible: Audre Lorde and the Poetry of Witness." *Witnessing and the Rhetoric of Pain*, ed. Martine Delvaux. Forthcoming.

"Remembering the Great Mother of Us All: Audre Lorde's Journey Through History to Herself." *Gendered Memory*, ed. Helga Geyer and John Neubauer. Forthcoming.

"Leading from 'You' and 'I' to 'We': Contemporary American Women's Poetry of Witness." *A Leadership Journal: Women in Leadership—Sharing the Vision* 2:2 (Spring 1998): 67–80.

"Mutual Recognition and the Borders Within the Self in the Writing of Cherríe Moraga and Gloria Anzaldúa." *Critical Studies on the Feminist Subject*, ed. Giovanna Covi (Trento, Italy: University of Trento Press, 1997): 229–243.

Introduction

We Heal From Memory: Sexton, Lorde, Anzaldúa and The Poetry of Witness

Halfway through the fall semester, sitting in my basement office at a Southern college, there is a presence at my door. It is Alicia, one of my students. She has missed the last two weeks of class and she has come, I assume, to give me an excuse. I put my papers to the side of the desk and ask her to come in. She sits and starts talking. She wants me to know she has something to tell me. She warns me that I will think she is making it up. She sometimes thinks it didn't happen. She has told no one. No one.

What she tells me, what I have been prepared to hear as a result of writing this book, is that two weeks ago she was kidnapped and raped. She was out late. He abducted her in the parking lot across the street from her dorm. He took her to his house. He had a knife. And a gun.

She tells me the whole story. I listen. I nod. I tell her I believe her. I feel sick. I remember to breathe. I tell her again that I believe her. Despite my desire not to believe her. Despite my desire not to know that this has happened to her. That it happens all the time. That it could happen to me. All of the power of my deep need to deny that this is true fights against the deeper impulse in me toward compassion. This compassion, I realize, must come from the head *and* the heart, for my heart is telling me to run away. My head tells my mouth to speak the words that she needs to hear. Later my heart will know I did the right thing by staying. And believing. Witnessing.

This book is about the poetry of witnessing. It is written for Alicia. And Anne and Wendy and Maria and all the others. But it is also, and perhaps more crucially, written for those on the other side of the desks, professors and politicians and social workers and all those who are in a position of power, a position to witness. To witness means to decide to participate—not only with the head but with the heart—in the experience of another, an experience so painful that it must be shared in order to be confronted. Those in positions of power in our society have a tremendous ability to bring others from pain to possibility. And the beginning lies in poetry, for poetry provides distinctive access to pain.

What I aim to do in this book is to describe, explain, and show how the poetry of three American women writers—Anne Sexton, Audre Lorde, and Gloria Anzaldúa—may teach us how to witness to our own and bear witness to others' traumatic histories. The poetry of Sexton, Lorde, and Anzaldúa shows vividly how our culture has hurt women—through child sexual abuse, through the ownership and enforcement of women's sexuality, through the transmission of violence through generations, and through the destruction of non-white cultures and their histories. In showing us the pain that such violence inflicts, these American women writers help us to realize that not only women, but all of us—men, women, and children—are hurt by the horror of such violence. They also allow us to hope that we do not have to continue to be either the victims or the perpetrators of such violence if we follow their lead, if we heal from memory.

In the poetry of Sexton, Lorde, and Anzaldúa, it is memory, as both a problem and a promise, that forms and allows us to form our individual and collective identities and histories. As my readings of their writings will make clear, it is precisely in understanding the memories of a past marked by traumatic violence as a problem that, paradoxically, these memories hold the promise of becoming a solution for the future. In order to examine the problematic way in which memory operates in the formation of "experience," I will use the theoretical work done on "trauma," studies that are psychoanalytic, historical, and philosophical.[1]

Rather than being something "bad" that happened in the past, an event or experience—as the general public sees trauma—scholars of trauma (myself included) define trauma precisely *not* as an experience or event but as the paradoxical structure of an experience that was missed, was not experienced. Trauma, as this understanding holds, marks the painful after-effects of a violent history in the body and mind of the survivor. Hence, it is not the event itself (rape, incest, accident, slavery) that determines whether it is traumatic; it is the way that the survivor survives such violence by not experiencing it in the normal way we experience and remember. And while such violence is not and cannot be experienced consciously at the time, it nevertheless repeats itself later from the inside through dreams and repetitions.[2]

This is because a trauma is not recorded in the usual, narrative way we remember experiences. Instead, the survivor's mind and body skip over the event temporally in order to survive. Traumatic memories are encoded not narratively but in images and feelings, both emotional and physical. Thus, the traumatic experience cannot be directly referred to but must be remembered, reconstructed, and worked through indirectly in an address with another.[3] This is why poetry allows us to witness as survivors to having survived and to witness to others' survival: poetry, like trauma, takes images, feelings, rhythms, sounds, and the physical sensations of the body as evidence. My readings of the poetry of Sexton, Lorde, and Anzaldúa show that poetry allows us to witness and to heal from traumatic events, whether individual or collective, events as disparate as incest, sexual assault, spousal abuse, slavery, and colonization, because the "evidence" is not to be found in the events themselves but in the survivors' painful reactions to having survived.

One example may help illustrate this. As we will see later in my reading of one of Lorde's poems, "To My Daughter the Junkie on the Train," the speaker is on a subway, confronted with a young woman, an African American drug user, whom the speaker wants to avoid. This young woman, the "daughter," is one of the children of generations of African Americans who hold within themselves the aftereffects of slavery. These children are, as the poem indicates, "unavoidable." Yet these children are also "dreams we avoid." The fact that the children, the generations who try to escape the painful aftereffects of having survived slavery, are both avoided and unavoidable stems from the paradoxical structure of trauma itself. The avoidance, which comes in the form of escape mechanisms like repetition compulsion, drug abuse ("the junkie on the train"), alcoholism, etc., is itself one of the signs of bearing witness to an unacknowledged traumatic past. This past, at the same time, is unavoidable, and inevitably returns in nightmares, flashbacks, and physical sensations, which, if witnessed to, if given language through poetry, may be healed from.

Further, the difference between narrative and poetry is crucial in this book and in our ability to witness. Trauma is not recorded narratively, but, as many researchers have found, is recorded as images and feelings. It is poetry—with its visual images, metaphors, sounds, rhythms, and emotional impact—that can give voice to having survived. Narrative—what is commonly thought of as "telling the story of what happened"—may be possible later, but is not possible for the survivor at first. This is one reason why silence among trauma survivors is so pervasive and why the aftereffects of trauma then often get passed down, are left to future generations to witness: there simply is no story, no narrative memory of the event that was skipped over in order to survive. Poetry begins the process of healing by allowing survivors to give voice to the non-narrative memories, called by researchers "traumatic memories," of having survived.

While this book does not pretend to present new findings on the psychoanalytic study of trauma, trauma theory does provide a lens through which previously unexamined yet important aspects of literature can be seen.[4] First, the study of trauma gives us insight into the questions of "experience," so often deadlocked between praise from humanist feminists and rejection from poststructuralists.[5] Second, as I examine the role of memory as both a problem and a solution (what we "heal from"), trauma theory illuminates our connections to the past, showing both how we connect to the past and how the past connects to us. Finally, trauma theory makes visible the problems and possibilities of our connections to each other. As we read these three writers in the light of these questions, we will see how our individual and collective identities are shaped by the implicit and explicit ways in which we continually confront memory.

Indeed, it is one of the signs of the importance of a study like this one that there are many people, particularly in academia, who want to disprove trauma, or dismiss its existence.[6] Part of the reason for this, quite simply, is the enormity of the horror of the histories that a study of trauma unearths. It is much easier, psychologically, to deny that witnessing needs to take place on such a grand scale than to begin. This is why studies such as Allan Young's *The Harmony of Illusions: Inventing Post-Traumatic Stress Disorder* tend to receive praise and acceptance so easily.[7] Young charts how PTSD has been invented for men in order to allow payment of therapy for veterans, while he completely ignores the existence of female PTSD. Yes, the reviewer will nod, we knew it was a scam all along, so now we can go back to business as usual. Meanwhile, as this book will demonstrate, the great blindness toward the histories of the majority of Americans continues.

What will become clear in the course of this study is that trauma cannot be adequately dealt with on an analytical level—through psychoanalysis, social science, or even the field of history. What keeps these disciplines from being able to incorporate true understandings of trauma into their schemata is the absence of feeling, of subjectivity, in the analysis of a subject. What poetry can do that social science cannot is to engage the hearts and souls and imaginations of readers, to allow the "other" into oneself, so that the "other" becomes part of the self, engaged with the self. This is what happens in the witnessing process, and this is what happens in poetry, and this is why the poetry of witness is a "solution" in a way that social science is not.

In addition to showing the ways that poetry allows us to witness to traumatic histories in ways social science cannot, this book breaks new ground in other ways, as well. Clearly, it breaks the critical silence about the traumatic aspects of the three writers' work. While Sexton's work has received much critical attention over the years, no critic has definitively argued that Sexton was indeed a survivor of childhood sexual abuse. A recent essay in *Signs* traces the lack of critical attention to incest in Sexton's poetry but does not lay out an argument that Sexton herself was a survivor.[8] Nor does any critic discuss the implications of reading Sexton's poetry as a poetry of survivorship and healing.

Certainly similar omissions exist in the scholarship on Audre Lorde.[9] While Lorde has been widely praised and cited as a spokeswoman for valorizing difference, most critics have shied away from an engagement with Lorde's entire corpus and with her multiple identity.[10] Very few critics place her work in its proper historical context.[11] And there has been complete silence about her narrative of sexual abuse in her autobiography.[12] My reading of Lorde's work fills in all three of these gaps by addressing Lorde's multiple identity, her work's historical context, and her experiences of sexual abuse.

Gloria Anzaldúa, like Lorde, is praised and quoted widely as a spokesperson for the positive possibilities of "living on borders" between cultures; however, no critic has demonstrated how Anzaldúa's "border" can be read as a traumatic wound in history.[13] Further, critics tend to cite Anzaldúa's work in a sociological context, as a case history or as an example of "border identity," while I read Anzaldúa's work as literature and show that it is *through literature* that we may heal from traumatic histories.[14] As we will see, it is the transformation of "real experience" into literature through image, metaphor, and re-imagination, that turns the trauma of history into a poetry of witness.

Moreover, this book breaks new ground by comparing the work of a white woman to two women of color. Currently, studies of women writers tend to cluster around women of color or white women authors. In showing the ways in which Sexton, Lorde, and Anzaldúa are all dealing with the legacies of different kinds of historical violence, we can see more clearly both the differences and the similarities between women's experiences. We see how American culture inflicts violence on women regardless of color yet how the manifestations of this violence arise out of different histories. It is indisputable that women of color experience daily realities of violence and oppression far more damaging than do white women. As this book demonstrates, these daily realities are a result of traumatic histories of violence against people of color in our nation. And yet, the failure to recognize, to admit, or even to see these realities of oppression also stems from white people's own participation in these traumatic histories. On the one hand, white women have played a specific historical role as wives, daughters and mothers of white men, positions that connected them to power and protected them from harm, and on the other hand, white women themselves have been the victims of the same kinds of violence toward women that is at the heart of a patriarchal society. What the poetry of witness enables, as this book demonstrates, is that we may begin to listen across our differences, that we might begin to reconstruct these skipped histories, claim them, and heal from them. This comparative approach opens the possibility of witnessing to these different histories, and this, as we will see, is necessary in order to heal from these histories.[15]

This book addresses two types of readers: the academic and the general. The first reader is one who works in the disciplines of comparative literature, feminist theory, psychoanalysis, history, or philosophy, or one who teaches and studies the work of Anne Sexton, Audre Lorde, or Gloria Anzaldúa. For this reader, I have placed the focus of the book at the crossroads of these disciplines, taking care not to immerse the writing unnecessarily in the language of any one discipline. The first section of the book is most directly addressed to this reader as, in the text and in extensive footnotes, I trace the scholarship underlying my argument.

The more general reader is someone who is interested in the issues of trauma, memory, and healing because these issues have personally affected her life. I ask this reader to be patient in the first section and to continue on to the second section, which turns more toward an examination of the practical ways in which one may heal from trauma. By the third section, the two readers begin to approach each other, as by this time the general reader has gained an understanding of the theoretical issues at stake in the study of trauma, while the academic reader has begun to examine her own past and her own memories which, as the many readers of Sexton's, Lorde's, and Anzaldúa's writing will attest, is something their writing asks us to do. In the third section, then, the individual readers become a collective "we," as together readers compare their dreams and desires with those of Sexton, Lorde, and Anzaldúa, as together readers create their own visions of healing for the future.

Interestingly, as we move from the explorations of trauma to the visions of healing in each writer's work, we see more clearly the similarities among all three. These similarities further reinforce one of the arguments of the book: that the splits between individuals and communities are themselves the historically produced effects of traumatic violence. When these histories are recognized as traumatic and are healed from, the splits themselves may also heal, and this, finally, is the promise of what it means to heal from memory.

This study will be structured around three questions, answered through comparative readings of the three writers' works. These three questions are, What is the trauma for each writer? How does each writer deal with the trauma in her writing? And, what does it mean to heal for each? In answering the first question, I will not be searching for an event or cause but rather reading their work for those gaps in knowledge or experience which provide clues to a traumatic event, a threat to bodily and psychic survival. As Bessel A. van der Kolk and José Saporta write, "Regardless of the circumstances, traumatized people are prone to have intrusive memories of elements of the trauma, to have a poor tolerance for arousal, to respond to stress in an all-or-nothing way, and to feel emotionally numb."16 In the first three chapters, then, we will be tracing these "aftereffects" for clues to how histories of traumatic violence continue to affect the survivor, regardless of the survivor's conscious awareness of trauma.

Section I will examine the signs of having survived trauma in each writer's work. Whether the trauma is individual or collective, the responses to trauma are similar, marked primarily by the intrusions and repetitions of the past upon the present. In this section, then, we will see that to heal from memory means, first, that we must shake off the waking sleep of denial, addiction, and harmful repetition that consumes our lives. We do this by perceiving these patterns as signposts, by seeing them as signals that something is very wrong in our culture, by recognizing them as reminders that we have survived. The writings of Sexton, Lorde, and Anzaldúa show that if we follow these signposts, they will reveal a past that we are hiding from, a past that we would rather forget. It is the past of a history of traumatic violence.

Sexton's work provides us with a picture of the consequences of childhood sexual trauma. In chapter 1, "'My night mind saw such strange happenings': Anne Sexton and Childhood Sexual Trauma," I provide an introduction to trauma theory through close readings of the life and work of Anne Sexton. In this chapter I bring together my own research on Anne Sexton's biography gained from my reading of her papers, early poem drafts, and correspondence currently available at the Harry Ransom

Humanities Research Center, as well as the more extensive research done by Diane Wood Middlebrook for her definitive biography of Anne Sexton. I present the evidence in Sexton's writing, then, which reveals signs of a history of child sexual abuse. In chapter one, through close readings of the figures in the poems, "Kind Sir: These Woods" and "Music Swims Back to Me," I explore the processes of traumatic memory. My readings of these poems teach us how traumatic memory works and how poetry may be a way to turn wordless images and feelings of pain into the beginnings of witnessing.

In chapter 2, "'We are sisters and our survival is mutual': Audre Lorde and the Connections between Individual and Collective Trauma," I take the insights about individual trauma from chapter one and turn toward an examination of intergenerational trauma, the effects of trauma which are passed down through generations. I show how Audre Lorde's work follows the tradition of other black women writers, such as Ida B. Wells-Barnett, Angela Davis, and Darlene Clark Hine, who address the links between the history of silence about black women's sexuality and the history of slavery in America. Lorde's work shows how these traumatic histories continue to affect black women both individually and collectively.

The precise link between individual and collective experience is made more clear in Anzaldúa's work, as she connects her individual history with the collective history of colonization in America. In chapter 3, "'Una Herida Abierta': The Border as Wound in Gloria Anzaldúa's *Borderlands/La Frontera,*" I draw from the psychoanalytic writings on collective, historical trauma to show how Anzaldúa's text moves from an exploration of the border as a literal site of trauma to a representation of the border as a figure for the possibilities of healing from the effects of a traumatic history.

In Section II, I explore how each writer deals with trauma in her writing. To do so, I will provide an overview of the processes of healing from trauma: reconstructing, witnessing, and mourning. The processes of remembering, reconstructing, and working through trauma are evident in the work of all three writers. In this section, we will see that to heal from memory means also to connect our dreams to our histories: to see how the images and fears of our most personal visions are related to, and constructed by, collective histories.[17] In remembering and reconstructing these dreams, we engage in healing not only from personal memories but from collective histories of violence.

The reconstruction of traumatic memory—with another who shares in the witnessing process with us, with another who shares in the feelings of the process with us—may allow memory to be turned from a problem into a solution. This reconstruction, as we see in the writings of Sexton, Lorde, and Anzaldúa, puts an end to the escape mechanisms of denial, addiction, and repetition as it allows memory to work for us and not through us. Further, as we witness to the past and as we serve as witnesses for others, we may begin to see how the cords of one story link to the cords of another. This recognition of how our histories are woven together enables a reconnection between people in the present. As we witness to our past, we open the possibility of allowing ourselves to be healed from the past through a healing relationship with another in the present. While Section I will focus more on what is called "intrapsychic reconstruction," the process of turning dreams and flashbacks into verbal reconstructions, Section II will move toward an examination of how these reconstructions are then shared with another through the process of witnessing.

"Intersubjective witnessing," then, is the term used for the "working through" portion of Freud's remembering-reconstructing-working through trinity by those who work with trauma survivors, such as Holocaust survivors.[18] To witness, one needs a listener who will hear the story of the event. Until the repetitions of the event are turned into memories and reconstructed in some way, the survivor is left to suffer in silence. This silence becomes a fear that invades all aspects of the survivor's life. A silent survivor who has not remembered or reconstructed the trauma is one whose silence contaminates her life, distorts the memory, makes it—the memory, the life—evil. This can manifest itself in various ways, such as feeling a lack of relation to others, feeling a sense of lack, feeling one has a heart of stone, or finally, feeling that one is responsible for the atrocities one survived. This silence, this aloneness, is ended by speaking to a listener, one who cares enough to participate, together with the witness, in the reliving of the event. In this way, the survivor can regain the sense that there is an internal listener. The dialogic relation between witness and listener becomes a dialogic relation internal to the survivor. And this sense of an internal witness, a "you" inside yourself who cares for you and watches over you, is essential to healing from a traumatic event. As Bessel A. van der Kolk and José Saporta write, "Recent studies have indicated that learning to express the memories and feelings related to the traumatic event can restore some of the psychophysiological and immunological competence in people with traumatic histories."[19]

Witnessing not only makes the promise of such healing possible, but it also acknowledges the breaking of the promise, the hope, that things can return to the way they were before the trauma. Successful witnessing, then, leads to an acknowledgment of many losses: the loss of the experience, the loss of others through death, the loss of a life untouched by trauma, and the loss of the memories and histories of civilizations. Mourning these losses constructs us as individuals and as cultures.[20] In mourning, through a delicate balance of incorporation and negation, we find the means to recognize difference in ourselves and in others. Thus, the ultimate result of dealing with trauma is the birth of the possibility of recognition.[21]

Chapter 4, "'This Kind of Hope': Anne Sexton and the Language of Survival," shows how very difficult the processes of remembering and reconstructing a traumatic past can be. In this chapter we see that while Sexton lacked the intersubjective support necessary to be able to witness or to mourn, she was able to work intrapsychically to invent a language of survival. Sexton's language of survival is a poetic language in which her images, motifs, and metaphors parallel the intrapsychic mechanisms associated with melancholia. I argue that Sexton's poetry shows us how healing must take place both intrapsychically *and* intersubjectively in order to heal from traumatic memory.

In contrast to Sexton, who tried to heal from a disorder that had no name in the 1960s, Audre Lorde's witnessing took place in the context of the feminist and civil rights movements, which gave her more of the societal support necessary to make her entire life's work a project of survival and healing. In chapter 5, "'To Speak Remembering': Audre Lorde and the Poetry of Witness," I show how Lorde's poetry moves beyond the intrapsychic realm to enter into the intersubjective space of witnessing. In so doing, Lorde's poetry makes it possible for readers to remember, reconstruct, and bear witness to our culture's history of violence toward women and African Americans. Lorde shows us that, if we do not want to contribute to the perpetuation of violence, witnessing is a necessary choice for all of us who inherit this history.

Anzaldúa, like Lorde, also is conscious of her work as a project of survival and healing. In chapter 6, "Healing from Awakened Dreams: Anzaldúa as Individual and Collective Witness," I examine how Anzaldúa's writing demonstrates that witnessing can occur on both the individual and collective levels. In a reading of her poem, "that dark shining thing," we see how the witnessing process takes place as two individuals mutually experience the reconstructions of traumatic memory, and in so doing, move toward a mutual recognition of their collective identity. Then in a reading of Anzaldúa's poem, "Matriz sin tumba o [Womb without tomb]," we see how Anzaldúa acts as a shaman who witnesses to the collective history of a people in order to discover ways to heal from this collective past.

As Sections I and II show the necessary connections between individ-

ual and collective histories, so does Section III show the necessity of mak-
ing connections between what is conceptually and historically split in our
culture. Section III demonstrates that all three writers' visions of healing
entail not only a reconnection between individuals but also a reconnection
of sex and spirit within individuals. In this section, we see how we heal
from memory in another sense as well, as we use memory to create visions
for the future. Healing from memory means re-membering the split aspects
of our existence, re-claiming the goodness of our bodies and our spirits,
and re-storing to us the ability to use creativity as power: the power to cre-
ate and not to destroy, the power to empower and not to oppress, the power
to envision and not to blind. As Diana Hume George wrote in her study
of Anne Sexton, "[P]oets are among the few whom our culture still invests
with a ritual function."[22] Sexton, Lorde, and Anzaldúa create rituals of
healing in their reclamation and recreation of mythologies, and these in
turn enable new visions of women as creative, powerful, sexual and spiri-
tual beings.

Chapter 7, "'I wish to enter her like a dream': Anne Sexton and the
Prophecy of Healing," shows how her poetry presents a vision of "femi-
nist spirituality" a decade before such a term came into being. I will show
that, throughout her entire career, Sexton's poems of sexuality can be read
as depicting healing rituals, while the "spiritual" poems in which she
searches for God, Mary, and the goddess end ultimately in a vision of sex-
ual/spiritual healing. Sexton's later poetry explores the possibilities of a
spirituality that celebrates female sexuality as a resource for a connective
ritual of healing.

Chapter 8, "Drawing Strength from Our Mothers: Tapping the Roots of
Black Women's History," explores the historical split of sexuality and spir-
ituality in black women's writing and shows how Lorde's writing presents
a vision of healing this split through a reclamation of history and myth. In
this chapter I show how Lorde's essay, "Uses of the Erotic: The Erotic as
Power," can be read as a keynote to her vision of the connection between
sexuality and spirituality, and I examine how this essay resonates through-
out her work and is given its full dramatization in the final scenes of *Zami*,
through the figure of Afrekete.

Anzaldúa, like Lorde, has an "embodied mythology" that revisions the
mythologies of Aztec goddesses and Chicana female figures such as La
Malinche and Guadalupe to provide the connection between sexuality and
spirituality. Chapter 9, "Grinding the Bones to Create Anew: Gloria
Anzaldúa's Mestiza Mythology," continues to address the connection of
history and myth as I show how Anzaldúa rewrites the myths of La Mal-

inche and the Virgin of Guadalupe to make visible their connections through the ancient goddess, Coatlicue. Anzaldúa's revisioning of these myths offers ways for women to recognize and to heal their own "splits." Anzaldúa also goes beyond such revisions and creates her own goddess, Antigua, a goddess of healing for our own times.

It is my hope that these readings may demonstrate that we are neither only victims nor only oppressors, but that all of us inherit the legacies of a history of violence. This history is both a problem and a solution, as my readings of Sexton, Lorde, and Anzaldúa show. History is a problem when it is not remembered and worked through but is repeated and used to inflict further violence. History may be a solution if we remember, witness, and mourn our traumatic past. The recognition of the problem of memory—that our seemingly most personal, individual memories are not only connected to the collective past but are also shaped by it—is the necessary first step toward our being able to say that, indeed, we heal from memory. The tremendous hope of these writers' visions, then, comes from their courage in remembering the enormous horror of their pasts. To create from horror, to regain the power of hope: these are the promises that arise when we heal from memory.

PART I

I think that writers . . . must try not to avoid knowing what is happening. Everyone has somewhere the ability to mask the events of pain and sorrow, call it shock . . . when someone dies for instance you have this shock that carries you over it, makes it bearable. But the creative person must not use this mechanism anymore than they have to in order to keep breathing. Other people may. But not you, not us. Writing is "life" in capsule and the writer must feel every bump edge scratch ouch in order to know the real furniture of his capsule. (Am I making sense? I am trying, but I have never expressed this before.) I, myself, alternate between hiding behind my own hands, protecting myself anyway possible, and this other, this seeing ouching other.

—Anne Sexton, in a letter dated May 6, 1960

Chapter 1

"My night mind saw such strange happenings": Anne Sexton and Childhood Sexual Trauma

T o read Sexton's work and life approximately twenty years after her death shows how much has changed in our society in one generation. Born to a wealthy family in Newton, Massachusetts, in 1928, Sexton's life looked—from the outside—like a version of the American dream. She attended a private high school, was beautiful—even modeled for a time—then married and settled down to take care of her house and to have children. Even Sexton herself had wanted to be married from age 13 and thought that children would make her happy.[1] After the birth of her second daughter, though, the illusion started to crack; Sexton became increasingly depressed and, on the day before her twenty-eighth birthday, attempted suicide.[2] Soon after, at the suggestion of her therapist, Sexton began to write poetry.[3]

While we could read Sexton's poetry for what it can tell us about her life, we will see that reading the poetry not only teaches us about her life but also tells us what her life could not. Reading Sexton's poetry today, after more than 20 years of research concerning the signs, aftereffects, and possibilities of healing from childhood sexual abuse, we can see that there is ample evidence that Sexton was a survivor of traumatic childhood sexual abuse. In her biography of Anne Sexton, Diane Wood Middlebrook notes that Sexton's "dissociative states . . . sexualizing of significant relationships . . . and the fluidity of boundaries . . . fit the clinical picture of a woman who has undergone sexual trauma" (57); however, Middlebrook never confirms for the reader that this trauma did indeed take place. Other critics have denied the trauma or resisted confirming it, while only one has gone so far as to say that the "incest may be true."[4] Given the unwillingness of critics to discuss this, then, it is only now that a critic is willing to come forward to draw the parallels between the patterns of behavior found in research on survivors of sexual abuse and Sexton's behaviors. I will argue, using my own research, readings of the poetry, and secondary sources, that Sexton's life and work can be read for signs that she survived childhood sexual trauma.

As I shall examine, it is not only the fact of abuse which is at issue, but also the lack of a social context in which the abuse could be recognized and treated. Sexton lived in a time when marriage and children seemed to be her only options for fulfillment, and one critic goes so far as to call her a victim of the American dream.[5] Certainly as a young wife in her 20s, Sexton seemed to fit the media ideal of a woman who was completely fulfilled as a housewife.[6] Perhaps it was this ideal of complete fulfillment that helped contribute to her silence and conformity for much of her married life, even in the face of domestic violence.[7]

Moreover, her writing, which was her only outlet for healing, as we will see, was not supported by those around her. Throughout her life, she wanted more time for her poetry than being a wife and mother in the society allowed. She wrote at a time when it was considered selfish for women to do anything else but take care of their children. This was also a time when women writers in America did not often identify themselves as feminist, a time when to be a good writer usually meant to write like a man.[8] It was also a time when psychiatry was a predominantly male profession, and when women's concerns were not respected even on the therapist's couch.

For the most part, Sexton saw her gender, not as an impediment to her career, but as extraneous; in a letter dated March 25, 1970, Sexton writes, "[I am] not a political poet . . . not even a very social one" (Middlebrook 297). Yet at other times, she seemed to be conscious of her social roles. In her journal dated June 16, 1967, Sexton shows her awareness of her situation as a married woman who is not supposed to disagree with her husband publicly: "I hate killing of any kind, and protest the war in every way, and my husband thinks we ought to win the war. I live a lie. . . . We just don't talk about the war. A lie" (Middlebrook 296). Indeed, as a woman poet in a society when feminism was not yet a household word, her ambivalence about being a woman is understandable.

Instead of focusing on the pain, complexity, and ambivalence in Sexton's life and work, however, many critics have chosen to focus their debates on whether Sexton's work should be read as feminist.[9] This diversion reveals the tendency in the work of many white feminists to be ahistorical; that is, to read the past only through the lens of the present. This mistake allows white feminists to ignore not only historical context but other factors such as race and class. In short, this tendency to ignore the past reveals an unwillingness to claim that past as one's own, often because the past is filled with the same types of pain, complexity, and ambivalence that many readers would rather ignore: our own pain from the past, our own failure to witness, and our own complicity in the present with the conditions that make possible the painful repetitions of women's lives. This tendency to leave behind or to forget the past is, as we will see in the next section, not uncommon to survivors of a traumatic history.

Repeating: the game

The survivor of a traumatic event survives by leaving the event behind. Leaving the event is necessary when something happens that so severely threatens the life of a person—her bodily or psychic integrity—that to stay present, or fully conscious, during the event would lead to death. In *Moses and Monotheism,* Freud describes this structure as "an accident that one walks away from, apparently unharmed, only to discover later a series of grave psychical and motor symptoms, which can be ascribed only to his shock or whatever else happened at the time of the accident."[10] These "symptoms" manifest themselves later as repetitions, or repeated acts, through which the survivor returns to the skipped event of the past. Early in his career, Freud surmised that this "repetition compulsion" was an attempt by the survivor to achieve mastery over the past.[11] However, this explanation contradicts what we now know of traumatic experience: namely, that its repetitions are involuntary.

Later in his career, Freud recharacterized the repetition compulsion as a game: Fort/da is Freud's name for the game that he found a young boy playing after his mother had left.[12] This game in which the survivor involuntarily reenacts the "scene" of trauma is itself the sign of having survived—not experienced consciously and not remembered—a traumatic event. This game of repetition often manifests itself as acts which are destructive to others as well as to the self. The survivor, who has no memory of the event, recognizes her problem only in the painful and repetitive actions of the present. The destructive quality of the repetitive game continues until the event is remembered, which begins the process of healing from a trauma.

Remembering a trauma is often characterized as an awakening. This is because "traumatic memory" is different from ordinary memory in much the same way as dream consciousness is different from waking consciousness.[13] As Elizabeth Waites writes,

The shock of trauma produces states that are so different from ordinary wak-
ing life that they are not easily integrated with more normal experience. As
a result of this discontinuity, the traumatic state may be lost to memory or
remembered as a dream is sometimes remembered, as something vague and
unreal.[14]

In addition, traumatic memory, unlike ordinary memory, is not struc-
tured narratively. Rather, traumatic memory tends to consist of frozen
images, which are wordless or contain stereotyped phrases, and which flash
before the survivor in vivid sensations and images.[15] Further, these images
often come during dreams which "wake the survivor to the fact of having
survived."[16] These figures of trauma—repetition and game, departure and
return, dream and awakening—that make up the attempt to capture the
nature of traumatic memory in psychoanalytic writings, are found in Sex-
ton's poetry as well. To examine this, let us take a closer look at a poem
from her first book, *To Bedlam and Part Way Back,* entitled, "Kind Sir: These
Woods" (4–5).[17]

The poem is ostensibly a memory of a childhood game played by the
speaker during summer vacations at the grandfather's cottage in Maine.
However, there are several figures in this poem that allow us to read the
poem as a representation of traumatic memory. Most important is the fig-
ure of the game, which resembles the repetition compulsion in three ways.
First, the game is one that is repeated: "This is an old game / that we played
when we were eight and ten." The habitual nature of the game is implied
by the word "old," as well as by the verb "played," which implies a repeated
action, instead of "have played," which implies a discrete event. Further, the
even numbers, "eight and ten," imply a pattern. Secondly, the game is not
only repeated but is repetitive, which is shown in the descriptions of the
game's motion; turning around is described three times in the poem. It is a
repetitive game that continues: "Still." Thirdly, the game is dangerous, as the
repetition compulsion is often dangerous to the self and others. The dan-
ger is conveyed by adjectives: "cold . . . white . . . strange . . . white . . .
strange." It is also announced by the sounds of a crow crying, the coast cry-
ing, and the bell buoy's bell.[18] Finally, the danger is communicated with
symbols of the devil, who has the power to change nature and who fre-
quents the New England woods in Puritan stories.[19]

The game, with its qualities of repetition and danger, points to a refer-
ent which is not known to the players: "we did not know." The referent
itself is missing, even as the players search for it through the game: "know
you were lost"; "Lost"; "I search in these woods and find nothing." All that

the players have is a profound knowledge of loss. This is because the experience has been lost or missed or skipped while the player had her eyes closed: "eyes tight"; "with my eyes sealed." While the eyes are closed, it is the "night mind" that registers the event, and it is only with the night mind, or dreaming mind, that one can see the event: "my night mind / saw such strange happenings, untold and real." The event seen in the dream has not been told to anyone, and yet it is "real." The "reality" of traumatic memory is experienced not through waking consciousness but through dreams.

The dream thus performs the function of bringing the traumatic experience to consciousness, to reality, as the dreamer awakens: "And opening my eyes, I am afraid of course / to look." Waking from the traumatic dream allows the dreamer to feel the fear of the event for the first time. This fear arises as a result of the realization that the nightmare is "real," and this fear helps to begin the process of integrating the event through the remembering and reconstructing processes, as we will examine later.

Interestingly, in an early draft of this poem, there is a third stanza that signals more clearly the important temporal role of the dream in the poem.[20]

> Kind Sir: This is a strange dream.
> I am thirty, but I walk in the old woods
> and things are not what they seem.
> I know I am ten. I hear the same sounds,
> the ball and the crows. The trees unfold
> their arms like some children who die young.
> I remember growing up. But I am not old.

The connection between the game and the dream in the poem's drafts suggests that in both processes—traumatic dreaming and the repetition compulsion—time is both "old" and "present" at once. That is, the past, that which has been skipped over in order to survive, returns in the present in such a way that the past and present collide in the survivor: "I am thirty. . . . I know I am ten." This collision can be the beginning of a witnessing process, if there is a witness to help the survivor through the "trees."

Finally, in both the early and final versions of the poem, the speaker addresses a male listener, "Kind Sir," an authority figure, which is marked by the polite address, the capital letters, and the term, "Sir." This male authority could be Sexton's literary precursors, Thoreau or Hawthorne, or a male therapist, or the male superego. As we will see later, the listener plays an essential role in the healing process of a survivor of a traumatic event. The listener is someone who must not only be able to listen to the survivor's story, but also be able to participate in the retelling of the story in order to help the survivor turn the traumatic "memories"—the images and repetitions—into remembrance and reconstruction. However, in this poem, as in Sexton's life, which we will examine next, there were no figures—male or female—who would play the role of this listener. Thus when the speaker of the poem opens her eyes, she finds no one there: "Still, I search in these woods and find nothing worse / than myself, caught between the grapes and the thorns." There is no one there to help her reconstruct the traumatic memories that the game and the dream might be signaling. As Rosaria Champagne has written of incest survivors' memories: "What is important is that aftereffects take on a life of their own. The bearer of the mark does not connect these somatized memories as memories at all; without analysis, these memory traces cannot become memory proper."[21] Without help, she is alone, caught, unable to find anything but herself, stuck.

Reading the life

Seen from our perspective today, there is something in Sexton's life that points to having survived a traumatic event, an event that was lost, an event that leaves the survivor at a loss. As we turn from Sexton's work to her life, we will trace the evidence we now have that shows that she was a survivor of childhood sexual trauma. I do so not only out of a concern to prove Sexton's status as a survivor but also to highlight the differences between her time and ours. Indeed, this reading of Sexton's life would have been impossible during her lifetime. Later we will return to the poetry to examine what it shows us that her life cannot.

In what might be seen as a tragic irony, the earliest feminist research on the after-effects of sexual trauma in childhood was conducted near Sexton's home in the Boston area during the early 1970s.[22] I will rely upon this research conducted by Judith Herman and Lisa Hirschman, published in 1977, to compare the patterns of the survivors in their study to the behavior of Anne Sexton as documented in Diane Wood Middlebrook's biography. Herman and Hirschman's study shows that the survival of sexual trauma in childhood leads to identifiable patterns of behavior in the lives of the adult survivors. There are several direct links between the survivors in the study and Sexton: a craving for the love of a parent-figure, promiscuity, dissociation and lack of memory, a witch/bitch/whore self-image, and a lack of boundaries which leads to the repetition of dysfunctional family behaviors.[23]

First, there is the "underlying craving for an adequate parent [which] dominated the lives of these girls" (Herman 739). Sexton's aunt, whom she called Nana, moved to Wellesley to live with the Harveys when Anne was 11. After Nana arrived, Anne felt she had a parent who loved her unconditionally, as they lay "together under Nana's blue bordered quilt," stroking and talking (Middlebrook 14–15). Anne believed she "betrayed" Nana, during a session of kissing and touching with her father, which Anne believed Nana saw. The betrayal of Nana during an episode of father-daughter incest is depicted in Sexton's unpublished play, *Mercy Street*.[24] After the incident with her father, Anne started to hear a "tiny voice . . . shouting from far away" telling her to kill herself (Middlebrook 16). Anne would from then on long for those "safe" days with Nana, trying to recapture them with lovers throughout her life, just as the women in Herman and Hirschman's study "overvalued men and kept searching for a relationship with an idealized protector and sexual teacher who would take care of them and tell them what to do" (Herman 750).

This search for an ideal parent-protector often manifests itself in promiscuous behavior: there is a "strong association between reported incest history and the later development of promiscuity or prostitution" (Herman 739). The abuse survivor may show a "pattern of many brief unsatisfactory sexual contacts" (Herman 750). As early as 1945, when she was 17, Anne was sent to a boarding school after her family noticed her "boy crazy behavior" (Middlebrook 19). Three years after Anne was married, in 1951, she began having an affair, and her mother, Mary Gray, shouted at her, "You're just like me and I know it!" (Middlebrook 27). By 1955, Anne wrote in her notebook to her therapist, Dr. Orne: "My sexual life is in reality a hideous mess and I don't understand it and furthermore I don't want to discuss it or understand it" (Middlebrook 36). In 1956, she told Dr. Orne in a session that her only talent might be for prostitution (Middlebrook 42). As Freud in *Moses and Monotheism* writes, "A girl who was seduced in early childhood may orient her later sexual life towards provoking such assaults over and over again" (119). This, combined with the fact that as a child a girl in our culture (even more so in Sexton's era than today) learns that "she may acquire power only indirectly, as the favorite of a powerful man" (Herman 74), helps to explain why, in mid-June 1966, in addition to numerous other affairs, Anne started an affair with her therapist, Dr. "Zweizung," a situation which is considered an abuse of the therapist's power over the patient (Middlebrook 258).

In addition to cravings for parental love and patterns of promiscuity, adult survivors often show patterns of forgetfulness, in the form of "passive resistance and dissociation of feeling" (Herman 750). As Herman writes, "They learned to deal with the sexual approach by 'tuning out' or pretending it was not happening. Later, this response generalized into other relationships" (747). Indeed, Sexton often went into "trance-like episodes" after which she would remember nothing. Middlebrook notes that Sexton suffered from "profound dissociation . . . and lesions of memory" throughout her life (39). Sexton's therapist, Dr. Orne, comments that in the fall of 1961 "She was really trying to work, and she was severely handicapped by the inaccuracy of her memory" (Middlebrook 137); this led him to ask Anne to listen to their taped sessions so that she could remember what had happened and maintain a thread of continuity. What originated as a tool for survival during the abuse continues in the adult life until the survivor can begin to stay conscious during episodes which cause her to remember aspects of the traumatic event.

Survivors also have "a sense of being different, and distant, from ordinary people" (Herman 749). In their research, Herman and Hirschman note that "Almost every one . . . described herself as a 'witch,' 'bitch,' or 'whore'" (Herman 751). Sexton, too, held this negative self-image in her daily life. She started calling herself Elizabeth in her therapy sessions in 1957: "a flamboyantly naughty role . . . a fantasy or memory, narrated in a trance, about an incestuous experience with her father" (Middlebrook 55). Her father had called her "a little bitch" when he was drunk and spanking her (Middlebrook 56). Sexton also used the term "Rat" as one of her metaphors for her sick self (Middlebrook 124); "Diminutive and helplessly evil, this inner creature had a life of its own that Sexton longed to destroy" (Middlebrook 217). This hateful self-image becomes painfully clear in Sexton's notes from January 13, 1962: "I am so scared that my fingers hurt, my arm hurts, my stomach hurts. I pass out, for one thing, to get rid of my body. . . . I want my mother, I hate my mother. Nana was safe. Nana was crazy. Daddy was drunk. I am a little bitch" (Middlebrook 174).

All of this paints a picture of an Anne who did not know where she ended and the abuse (Elizabeth/the bitch/the rat) began. She was afraid to go anywhere alone and had to be accompanied everywhere: "Somebody sees me, and I see myself through them," she said in therapy on March 9, 1961. Finally, the fact that Anne had her "physical boundaries repeatedly trespassed by the adults in her family" (Middlebrook 59) had repercussions for her children as well. Her eldest daughter, Linda, bore the burden of Anne's reenactment of the scenes of trauma: from placing her head on

Linda's stomach, "making Linda be the mommy" (Middlebrook 204), to masturbating in bed beside Linda (Middlebrook 223), to rubbing and kissing the sleeping Linda at puberty (Middlebrook 325), Sexton's behavior demonstrates the fact that abuse certainly can affect generations.[25]

Why weren't these links obvious to the therapists with whom Sexton worked? Admittedly, the feminist-based research of studies such as Herman and Hirschman's were only recently underway. In his 1972 study of the survivors of the Buffalo Creek flood in 1972, Kai T. Erikson cites Irving L. Janis' *Stress and Frustration* from 1971, in which Janis summarizes the dominant view of the treatment of trauma at the time:

> Most persons who develop the symptoms of acute traumatic neurosis following exposure to accidents or disasters spontaneously recover quite rapidly, usually within a few weeks; and (2) the persons who fail to recover spontaneously are more likely than others to have a history of emotional disorder.[26]

Further, Herman and Hirschman provide us with another reason why Sexton's symptoms were not met with more understanding: "Consciously or not, the male therapist will tend to identify with the father's position and therefore will tend to deny or excuse his behavior and project blame onto the victim" (Herman 753). It is interesting to note that when Anne turned to a female therapist in 1969, after first seeing Dr. Orne, who said he was "virtually certain [the abuse] never occurred" (Middlebrook 58), and then Dr. "Zweizung" who had sexual relations with her while treating her, the new therapist "made it a condition of treatment" that she not see her former therapists again (Middlebrook 317).

And while in hindsight we can match the behaviors studied by Herman and Hirschman with Sexton's own, those around Sexton at the time were not able to recognize such patterns. Indeed, the *patterns* themselves did not exist until researchers demonstrated their existence. Further, this research did not appear in print until three years after Sexton's suicide. Thus, Sexton herself was left to make an individual and unsupported attempt to make a pattern out of the pain of her life. This attempt manifests itself in her writing.

Dancing a circle

As we turn back from Sexton's life to her work, we should remember that, as recent debates in literary studies attest, language cannot simply be read as proof of the truth value of an empirical event. For there is in literary language the imperative to interpret, to analyze, and to find meaning. It is for this reason that when we turn from Sexton's life to her poetry, we must read the poetry, not for what it can tell us of her life, but for what it can tell us that her life cannot. Now let us examine another poem from Sexton's first book, *To Bedlam and Part Way Back,* which allows us to look more closely at the process of remembering (6–7).

In "Music Swims Back to Me," which may be read on one level as the remembrance of a patient's night in a mental hospital, we can see a representation of the remembering process that is the start of the Freudian trinity: remembering, reconstructing, and working through. The figure of music in the poem behaves like water, which is an image of the unconscious. It is the music, the unconscious, that sees and remembers, remembers more and better than the "I," the conscious self. The music swims back from the past, from what has been forgotten. In so doing, the music pours over the sense, allowing the survivor to experience both psychically and physically the forgotten event: "I have forgotten all the rest."

At the beginning of the poem, before the music has helped the survivor remember, the conscious self dances in a circle. This implies a limit, a turning, and a repetition: we can read this as another representation of the repetition compulsion. Before memory of the event, there are "no sign posts" and "no signs to tell the way." The survivor is lost: she is lost because she has been left and also because she has left the event behind.[27] Thus her sense of being lost is both spatial and temporal. The traumatic event is an event out of time, out of our ordinary experience, not because traumatic events happen rarely, but because we experience them as out of the ordinary in order to survive them. But by dancing to the music, which swims *back* from the past, by hearing the unconscious, traumatic memory, one can move from dancing in a circle to dancing a circle. To dance a circle is to slip the yoke of the repetition compulsion, the repeated game of "Kind Sir: These Woods," in order to move from being an object of the game to a player through the artistic ordering of the event.

This poem does not present an altogether happy ending, however, for we are left with some questions: first, about fear. The line that appears near the end of the poem, "I . . . was not afraid," may seem like a good thing, but in terms of trauma, it means that the event is not being felt or experienced, so that it cannot be integrated into the life. Also, there is the "Mister?" at the end. At the beginning we could read the "Wait Mister" as the need for a male listener, a male such as a therapist, father, or husband to tell the way. But does the "Mister?" at the end mean that he is gone and that she has been abandoned? Diana Hume George reads the end of this poem in this negative way: the Mister "cannot help or protect her, as the final and one word plea indicates."[28] Or does this final "Mister?" mean that she is in effect questioning the role of "Mister" itself, the role of the male authority figure who cannot hear her pleas? Indeed, the original title of this poem, as seen in early drafts, was "Hey Mister," which shows how Sexton herself might have linked it more concretely with "Kind Sir" as a poem of request for a witness.[29] Certainly, the desire for a "Sir" or "Mister" to listen, to understand, to feel compassion, is a great concern throughout Sexton's poetry. Her request for such a witness and the request's denial becomes a repeated motif in the poetry and in her life until the very end. As we will see in chapter four, Sexton remained unable to find the "Kind Sir" or the "Mister" who could help her heal from her traumatic past. In chapter seven we will see how she finally turned from waiting for an answer from "Mister" to inventing an answer for herself. But at this early point in her career, because of the absence of societal recognition of child sexual abuse, Sexton's writing provided the only music for her dance.

Chapter 2

"We are sisters and our survival is mutual": Audre Lorde and the Connections between Individual and Collective Trauma

Audre Lorde was, as she described, "a black woman warrior poet" who lived from 1934 until her death in 1992, after a 14–year struggle with breast cancer.[1] Lorde was, in many ways, a survivor who worked tirelessly to end the many silences in black women's history. As we turn now from tracing Sexton's individual trauma of childhood sexual abuse to examining the connections between individual and collective experiences of trauma in Audre Lorde's life and work, we will see that it is the context of a collective history that makes the critical difference in reading an individual's life and work. At the individual level, "Unless childhood trauma is resolved through reparative experiences, including psychotherapy, components of the trauma will be incorporated into the pattern of family life in the next generation."[2] We have seen a concrete example of this in the first chapter; now in this chapter, we will see how Lorde's work further dramatizes the effects of a traumatic history passed down through generations.

In this chapter, I will explore how both a collective silence about black women and an individual silence within black women are results of traumatic histories. I will trace the historical roots of these silences and show how Lorde's work both follows from and reacts to this legacy in black women's history. To date, the criticism on Audre Lorde has not usually been done with sufficient attention to the multiple aspects of Lorde's existence.[3] For the most part, certain aspects of Lorde's writing are highlighted, and others are left in shadows while the critic focuses on a singular aspect of Lorde's identity, as a woman who is lesbian, feminist, black, or a cancer survivor.[4] There are critics who do engage with the multiple aspects of Lorde's self; however, they do not explicitly connect these elements with their historical contexts.[5] Only three critics place Lorde's work in a historical context.[6] Taking its lead from the work of black women themselves, my reading of Lorde's work is founded upon the importance of recognizing the multiple aspects of the black women's work and of placing the work in historical context, both within dominant tradition and within the tradition of black women's thought itself. As Maria P. P. Root writes of the necessity for historical contextualization: "Similarly to American historians' neglect to record the atrocities suffered by ethnic minority groups of people, psychiatry's and psychology's theoretical foundations have limited contexts and tend to be ahistorical, in a sociopolitical sense, making invisible the experiences of large segments of the population who have been historically oppressed" (258). To acknowledge the multiplicity of black women's existence and to fit this existence into its history and tradition is to work against the historical silencing of black women.

This chapter will focus primarily upon the historical causes of this silence: the silence imposed upon black women from the outside, the silence imposed from within, and the possibilities of ending silence. In the section below, I will examine how a history of oppression engenders a collective silence. As Bruno Bettelheim has written, "What cannot be talked about cannot be put to rest; and if it is not, the wounds continue to fester from generation to generation."[7] In the following section, I will show how a history of trauma engenders an individual silence, a silence within the individual, a silence at the heart of the identity of the individual. Lorde's work shows how these silences are connected and how it is fundamental to one's survival to end the silences. As an example of how Lorde's poetry witnesses to the silence, let us examine the poem, "A Litany for Survival," from 1978.[8]

We can read this poem as a call to witnessing to trauma, the experience of knowing "we were never meant to survive," which is repeated twice in the poem. Until the event is told, the silence becomes a fear which invades all aspects of the survivor's life, as in Lorde's poem. A silent survivor who has not told her story is one whose silence contaminates her life, distorts the memory, makes it—the memory, the life—evil. This can manifest itself in various ways, such as feeling a lack of relation to others, feeling a general sense of lack, feeling one has a heart of stone, or finally, feeling that one is responsible for the atrocities one survived.[9]

In Lorde's poem, we see the effects of trauma (which is here not only personal but also collective as in the history of African Americans): living both inward and outward, before and after, as the trauma shifts the inside and the outside, both spatially and temporally, so that the event becomes the ever-present now within the survivor. We also see the effects of silence: the fear that leads to lack: lack of love, lack of food, lack of nurturance. It is a fear that becomes generalized, projected onto the world as the speaker fears even the sun will not rise again. It is a fear that perpetuates the silence unless we "speak/remembering": speak our remembering, and "speak/remembering/ we were never meant to survive": speak the stories of what threatened, and continues to threaten, one's survival.

This silence, this aloneness, is ended by speaking to a listener, one who cares enough to, together with the witness, participate in the reliving of the event. In her poems, then, Lorde invites readers to witness to the truth of the destruction that has been survived. For Audre Lorde, ending silence is the first and most important step in ending both the political oppression as well as the psychological oppression of black women. Lorde provides a model for coming to speech—even in the face of fear, even in the face of fatigue, even in the absence of memory, even in the absence of feeling.

History and silence, or silence from without

We might wonder about the significance of the silence of Lorde's critics regarding black women's history. Their silence is connected to a corresponding silence regarding black women's sexuality.[10] Both of these silences—the silence about black women's history and the silence in black women's history—point to the profound connection in history between black people's sexuality and racism in America. Dating from slavery, black women's sexuality was owned and used by white slave owners in two main ways: for the reproduction of wealth and labor through enforced pregnancies, and for the depositing of white men's desire in a system where white women were seen as chaste under the "cult of true womanhood." Thus, enforced mating, pregnancy, childbearing, and rape were routine experiences for black women under slavery. Furthermore, marriages between black men and women were outlawed under slavery, making it impossible for black women to be "respectable women."[11] The following account by historian Winthrop D. Jordan makes this clear:

> In the West Indian colonies especially, and less markedly in South Carolina, the pattern of miscegenation was far more inflexible than in the other English settlements. White women in the islands did not sleep with black men, let alone marry them. Nor did white men actually marry Negroes or mulattoes. Yet white men commonly, almost customarily, took Negro women to bed with little pretense of concealing the fact. Edward Long of Jamaica

described the situation: "He who should presume to shew any displeasure against such a thing as simple fornication, would for his pains be accounted a simple blockhead; since not one in twenty can be persuaded that there is either sin; or shame in cohabiting with his slave." Negro concubinage was an integral part of island life, tightly interwoven into the social fabric. . . . Sexually, as well as in every other way, Negroes were utterly subordinated. White men extended their domination over their Negroes to the bed, where the sex act itself served as the ritualistic re-enactment of the daily pattern of social dominance.[12]

Even after slavery ended, the Reconstruction prohibition of relations between whites and blacks and the systematic lynching of black men, women, and children contributed to the continuation of "the daily pattern of social dominance."

As the only black woman to address frankly the issue of sexuality in her time, Ida Wells-Barnett believed that "existence was a phenomenon in which belief and action could not be separated," (Braxton 137), and to this end, Wells-Barnett addresses lynching as a feminist issue in 1900 with her essay, "Lynch Law in America."[13] Wells-Barnett analyzes lynching as an institutional threat to the black community, a threat that covers over the reality of real sexual violence of white men upon black women. As a way of upholding the cult of true womanhood, the law held that "no white woman shall be compelled to charge an assault under oath or to submit any such charge to the investigation of a court of law" (72). Thus whenever white women claimed sexual assault, black men (and the women and children who refused to tell white mobs the location of their relatives) were lynched routinely in America. Underlying this practice, argues Wells-Barnett, is the truth of the matter: "The negro has suffered far more from the commission of this crime against the women of his race by white men than the white race has ever suffered through *his* crimes" (74). Here Wells-Barnett alludes to the history of sexual exploitation and rape of black women by white men both during and after slavery. It is this history that resulted in the repression and silence surrounding black women's sexuality.

In a pattern typical of such a history of oppression, the "true" story of the event is left behind and is replaced by an "official" story that obscures the violence, the force of the history.[14] Angela Davis' essay from 1971, "Reflections on the Black Woman's Role in the Community of Slaves," attempts to refute the "official" story by reading through the silence about black women's lives under slavery.[15] In her essay, Davis refutes the Moynihan Report, which argues that black women "assented to slavery" by being "related to the slaveholding class as collaborator" (201), as one example of an "official" story of black women under slavery.[16] By paying attention to this silence in the "official" story, Davis is able to reconstruct the "true" story, a story that documents the violence surrounding black women's sexuality under slavery: "she had to surrender her child-bearing to alien and predatory economic interests" (202); she was subjected to "the slave master's sexual domination" (212); and she was ultimately imperiled by "the most elemental form of terrorism distinctively suited for the female: rape" (213). As remarkable as this essay was—it was the first such attempt to read through the silence of black women's history, and it was written while Davis was in prison—it did not gain a wide audience. The nation—in 1971—was quite simply resistant to giving up its belief in the "official" story of black women under slavery.[17]

The silence surrounding the history of violence regarding black women's sexuality was only recently given its proper theoretical context in Darlene Clark Hine's 1989 essay, "Rape and the inner lives of Black women in the Middle West: Preliminary thoughts on the culture of dissemblance."[18] Hine argues that because of the historical threat of rape and sexual violence toward black women, a culture of dissemblance has developed in which black women keep matters of sexuality silent and private so as not to be abused by the larger society that would construct it in other, more harmful, ways. In order to protect themselves, black women "created the appearance of openness and disclosure but actually shielded the truth of their inner lives and selves from their oppressors" (380), and often, I would add, from themselves. As a result, "stereotypes, negative images, and debilitating assumptions filled the space left empty due to the inadequate and erroneous information about the true contributions, capabilities, and identities of black women" (383). It is for this reason that the stereotyped dichotomies of Mammy and Jezebel, representing the split between spirituality and sexuality, so persistently haunt the forms of subjectivity for black women in America.

Trauma and silence, or silence from within

Thus far we have seen that the history of violence and oppression for black women in the United States is accompanied by silence. This silence is imposed upon black women from the outside—through the force of institutional law, educational authority, and cultural norms. Yet these external forces are not the only reasons for silence. There is another silence, a silence from within, that further enforces the perpetuation of black women's silence. This silence is, as we will see, a traumatic silence, a silence resulting from trauma. While black women indeed have endured multiple oppressions in American history, the trauma at the core of their oppression is sexual. The enforced use of black women's sexuality under slavery, compounded by generations of sexual violence, together mean that black women must not only struggle against multiple oppressions from outside, from the exterior, but that they must also contend with a legacy of silence at the interior of their being.

Beverly Guy-Sheftall, in her essay "The Women of Bronzeville," remarks that the images of black women as "matriarch, whore, bitch" persist in literary works by both white and black writers, which might lead to the question of whether there is something deeper at work in these images than simply negative stereotypes.[19] In their research on incest, Herman and Hirschman write that survivors have "a sense of being different, and distant, from ordinary people," and they also note that "[a]lmost every one . . . described herself as a 'witch,' 'bitch,' or 'whore.'"[20] Similarly, researchers find that among survivors of sexual abuse there is a legacy of silence caused by "passive resistance and dissociation of feeling" (Herman 750). We might wonder if these images of black women in our society and the corresponding silence regarding the origins of these images are so persistent precisely because they originate in deep, historical ways from the psyches of the survivors of rape and sexual abuse themselves. It is precisely this connection between the silence imposed from without and the silence imposed from within that Lorde's work examines. As we will see, Lorde shows us that the collective, institutionally enforced silence for black women is accompanied by an individual, psychically enforced silence within black women themselves.

Audre Lorde's autobiographical narrative, *Zami: A New Spelling of My Name,* tells the story of a black lesbian woman coming to consciousness of herself through her history: a history of traumatic violence toward black women.[21] The main character, Audre,[22] becomes conscious of her race in the second grade (58–59), which teaches the reader that identity-formation is a process that develops over the course of a lifetime.[23] Later, Audre learns to connect her identity with history when, as a young adult working in Stamford, Connecticut, her friend, Ginger, tells her about Crispus Attucks, the "first cat to die in the Revolutionary War, in Concord, Massachusetts. A Black Man" (131). This causes her to ask, "What did that mean about the history I had learned?" (133). As Janet Brice-Baker writes, "Maintaining the slavery system depended upon creating a distorted image of Africans, concealing their true history, and presenting the distorted version to both Black and White Americans."[24] With her question, Lorde begins her quest to end this concealment of black history.

Yet, Lorde has to contend with the silence not only of black history, but also of women's history and lesbian history: "It was hard enough to be Black, to be Black and female, to be Black female and gay" (224). Lorde's project is to write the myths and histories that were invisible to her as a "Black female and gay" woman coming of age in the 1950s: "There were no mothers, no sisters, no heroes. We had to do it alone, like our sister Amazons, the riders on the loneliest outposts of the kingdom of Dahomey" (176). The invisibility of these myths and histories, as we will see, is a result of individual and collective trauma.

While we will see later in chapter eight how Lorde finds positive spiritual and sexual roots through her mother and the history and myth of Carriacou, her own personal history contains much pain. In curiously non-introspective ways throughout the narrative of *Zami,* Lorde relates incidents of sexual molestation and impropriety. While Lorde's lack of self-reflection about the incidents has led critics to ignore their importance, we can see this lack of self-reflection as itself one of the results of a legacy of a sexually traumatic history.[25] Lorde narrates seven such incidents in which black women are sexually violated or threatened by men—four white men, one black man, and two men of unspecified race. In so doing, Lorde shows how the silence about sexual trauma can and must come to an end—simply by beginning to speak.

The earliest scene occurs during one of the "summers of my earliest days" (48) between Audre and a man in a comic book store, a "fat white man with watery eyes" (49): "His nasty fingers moved furtively up and down my body, now trapped between his pressing bulges and the rim of the bin. By the time he loosened his grip and allowed me to slide down to the *blessed* floor, I felt dirtied and afraid, as if I had just taken part in some filthy *rite*" (49, italics mine). In describing the incident as being lifted up and back down again into blessing, as a baby being baptized, Lorde connects the incident with religion. However, the blessing comes not from above as in traditional Christian thought, but from below, from the earth. Later Lorde will describe sexuality as a blessing from below, from the earth, as well.

Lorde again connects abusive sexuality with religion as she tells of witnessing the practice of the principal of her Catholic elementary school, Monsignor John J. Brady, a racist priest who tells Audre's mother that "he had never expected to have to take Colored kids into his school" (60): "His favorite pastime was holding Ann Archdeacon or Irene Crimmons on his lap, while he played with their blonde and red curls with one hand, and slid the other hand up the back of their blue gabardine uniforms. I did not care about his lechery, but I did care that he kept me in every Wednesday afternoon after school to memorize latin nouns" (60). The fact that she says, "I did not care," shows her own inability to deal with the feelings surrounding these incidents. But despite her lack of feeling, Lorde shows that speaking is the necessary first step. The numbness and silence surrounding the abuse will have to end, as we will see, in order for Audre to heal from these events.

Subsequently Lorde foregrounds the scene of her first menstruation during her fifteenth year by telling of her knowledge of sexuality: "But four years before, I had to find out if I was going to become pregnant, because a boy from school much bigger than me had invited me up to the roof on my way home from the library and then threatened to break my glasses if I didn't let him stick his 'thing' between my legs" (75). This threat to break her glasses is significant for two reasons. First, it shows the relation between class and the threat of sexual violence, as we are led to conclude that Audre's mother may not be able to afford another pair of glasses and certainly would be angry if they were broken. Second, it shows the importance of reading for Audre, even at the age of ten: she is returning from the library in this scene and she eventually goes on to become a librarian.

What happens after the threat is not narrated; instead, Lorde connects her fear of her mother with her own loneliness as a way of explaining what happened: "I was afraid my mother would find out and what would she do to me then?" is followed by "I was always so lonely in the summer, particularly that summer I was ten" (75). After the incident she gets home late, "washed myself up" and "got a whipping for being late" (75). She spends the rest of the summer trying to find books in the library that might tell her if she is going to be pregnant. So when her period finally comes four years later, at the age of 15, she is relieved that she is not pregnant.[26]

The most emotionally charged incident of sexual abuse occurs in high school, when Audre's best friend, Gennie, shows up at Audre's house late at night with a scratched face after fighting with her father who had been drinking. As Gennie tells Audre, "And when [my father] drinks he doesn't know what . . ." (94–95). Audre refuses to ask her strict parents if Gennie can stay with them, and so Gennie leaves alone to deal with her "good for nothing call himself father" (96) who is "using that girl for I don't know what" (101), as Audre's mother phrases it.[27] One of the intergenerational effects of traumatic violence is silence, which is here marked by Audre's mother's silence, by her inability to say the words for what Gennie is experiencing.[28] These silences inflict themselves on subsequent generations from within, and such internalized silence leads to devastating consequences: Audre hears of Gennie's suicide the next day.

The incidents continue in Audre's young adulthood. After she moves out of her parents' home, her landlady's brother "closed the door to my room and said I was a nice girl and I wouldn't have to pay him for moving me if I'd just be quiet and stand still for a minute." Here there is a paragraph break, and then Lorde writes, "I thought it was all pretty stupid, and he got cum all over the back of my dungarees" (105). In the paragraph break is the silence that stands in for the emotions surrounding the incident. Also after Audre gets pregnant by Peter, a white boy she'd met at a Youth Labor League party with whom she had slept "since it was expected" (104), she has an abortion which leaves her "with an additional sadness about which I could not speak" (119). And later, she writes, as an adult she "got out of being raped although not mauled by leaving behind a ring and a batch of lies" (182) to a "Black brother" (181), a "bastard . . . stronger than I was" (182).

The results of these incidents manifest themselves in the inability to feel feelings and the inability to speak about them—and these results affect her in other ways as well, such as at her father's death when she feels numbness instead of grief (147). And in Mexico, she tells her older woman lover, Eudora, that she doesn't like being made love to (169), another sign of blocked feeling caused by sexual trauma. Audre starts therapy in the fall of 1955, when she is 21, because "There were things I did not understand, and things I felt that I did not want to feel, particularly the blinding headaches that came in waves sometimes. And I seldom spoke" (214). The pain, whether physical or emotional, and the silence go together, along with the lack of understanding and the feelings. Thus while *Zami* is the story of an individual, this story is also connected to a larger, intergenerational, collective context. In telling her story, Lorde is also telling the collective history of African women under colonization and slavery, as well as the collective history of all women and girls, like Gennie, who live through or die from sexual abuse. In speaking out about her silence, she is providing a model for collective and individual healing.

Testifying: speech in the face of silence

Let us examine Lorde's strategy of speech more closely to show how these individual and collective silences are connected. As we have seen, the collective silence regarding black women's sexuality has been enforced through a history of institutional force. At the same time, we have seen how the silence of black women themselves has been enforced, not from an outside force, but from within the individual woman herself. This is because, for the survivor of a traumatic event, silence is not simply a command from the other but the very condition of the possibility of survival. In other words, the individual survives precisely because she does not consciously experience the event; this means she does not remember the event in a narrative way, but only through flashbacks and dreams, and therefore, *she cannot speak of it, she cannot tell the story.* How then, does Lorde move from this state of silence to speech?

The answer lies partly in the work of black feminist lesbians who, in the late 1970s, provided the context in which these silences could begin to be broken. In April 1977, the Combahee River Collective wrote "A Black Feminist Statement" in which they state, "Our politics evolve from a healthy love for ourselves, our sisters, and our community which allows us to continue our struggle and work" (212). This can be seen as a background and precursor to Lorde's "erotic."[29] And in October 1977, Barbara Smith's "Toward a Black Feminist Criticism" was published, which was the first "writing about Black women writers from a feminist perspective and about Black lesbian writers from any perspective at all" (25).[30] While Smith writes of the "overwhelming" task of breaking "such a massive silence" (25) in the field of criticism, she does note work being done in literature, including Audre Lorde's first three volumes of poetry.[31] The essay concludes with a call that Audre Lorde would soon answer:

> I finally want to express how much easier both my waking and my sleeping hours would be if there were one book in existence that would tell me something specific about my life. One book based in Black feminist and Black lesbian experience, fiction or non-fiction. Just one work to reflect the reality that I and the Black women whom I love are trying to create. When such a book exists then each of us will not only know better how to live, but *how to dream* (42, italics mine).

Lorde's entire life's work can be read as an attempt to learn and to teach how to dream. How do we learn to dream, how do we learn to envision, to imagine a better future? The answer lies in learning how to remember the pasts that we would rather forget, to remember the dreams that haunt us, and to speak of the dreams that scare us silent. Lorde teaches us that learning to dream the future is only possible by learning to speak through the silence of the past. Lorde's concern with silence shows us that paradoxically it is only through the very act of speech that there is any hope for the survivor. Lorde writes in *The Cancer Journals,*

> We can learn to work and speak when we are afraid in the same way we have learned to work and speak when we are tired. For we have been socialized to respect fear more than our own needs for language and definition, and while we wait in silence for that final luxury of fearlessness, the weight of that silence will choke us.
>
> The fact that we are here and that I speak now these words is an attempt to break that silence and bridge some of those differences between us, for it is not difference which immobilizes us, but silence. And these are so many silences to be broken.[32]

We should note several things about Lorde's remarks. First, as we have seen, silence can only be overcome by speaking, and furthermore, such speech must come even in the face of fear. Second, we have seen how "there are so many silences": the silence that results from a history of collective, institutionalized sexual violence enforced upon black women, as well as the silence that results from a history of individual, traumatic sexual violence survived by black women. These silences are both external and internal, both collective and individual, and the speech that overcomes it must occur at both levels. To this end, Lorde addresses her speech to others. This is the third important point in Lorde's remarks: speech must be addressed to someone, and together, the speaker and the listener may change, may heal. Her essays, like this one, are often given first as speeches that she writes for a specific audience; her poems, likewise, are like letters, written to specific people or to her selves, to other parts of her self. Thus, Lorde shows us that even in the face of fear, silence can be overcome by speaking to someone, and that this act of speaking can lead to a regeneration on both the individual and collective levels.[33]

In the poem, "Chain," Lorde moves from assessing the effects of a violent, collective history coupled with a traumatic, individual history to suggesting a way to heal from these histories.[34] In this poem, Lorde witnesses to the true story of three girls who petitioned the court to be returned to their home after having been sexually assaulted by their father, which resulted in pregnancies and births of children for two of the daughters. The courts allowed them to return to their home.[35]

Some of the figures of trauma that we traced in Sexton's "Kind Sir: These Woods" are evident here as well. As in Sexton's poem, these children are from a time and space different from our own, and they intrude upon the present, "advancing against us," from where we are not, our own past. This is our collective past, which, "advancing," demands a response from us as in war.[36] These children have "no smell or color no time"; they exist as traumatic memories, as images one might see in a dream. And like a traumatic dream, they return and repeat: "repeating themselves over and over"; "repeat themselves"; "over and over."

However, this poem differs from Sexton's in that it not only serves as a reminder of unresolved, unacknowledged trauma, but it also shows how to testify. As Lorde writes in the essay, "Sisterhood and Survival," "All of our children are prey. How do we raise them not to prey upon themselves and each other? This is why we cannot be silent, because our silences will come to testify against us in the mouths of our children." (7). In this poem, Lorde shows how silence testifies to destruction while speech may testify to survival. The form of the poem, a ballad, gives a clue to how such testifying speech takes place. Like a ballad, the testifying occurs orally, through dialogue, in plain language, with frequent repetition that has the effect of discharging emotions that might otherwise overwhelm the speaker or listener.[37] Through these ways—dialogue, plain language, and repetition—Lorde attempts to reach the community, to speak to the collective, to the group, about matters that concern their very own survival.

The speaker not only addresses the daughter/children, but also the readers, as she asks us, commands us, twice in the first section, to "[l]ook at the skeleton children / advancing against us." The command is repeated by the children who ask their mother to "write me a poem" that can provide them with the language they need to speak—"tell them the lies"—of what happened. The children of this poem look to the mother for language, just as children of survivors of trauma need their parents to tell the story of the trauma. Before this happens, the silence of the trauma is like an elephant in the living room, large and obtrusive, which family members walk around but never discuss. As Nadine Fresco writes of the children of the survivors of the Holocaust: "Putting a name on what the silence of others had made strictly unnameable generally remained impossible for the child. . . . It was a silence that swallowed up the past, all the past, the past before death, before destruction" (419). Speaking of this past would not only help the children of survivors but would provide healing for the generations after—"for our children."

Speaking in this poem is presented not as an option but as an imperative, as the children ask the mother, "what other secrets / do you have to tell me." Speaking is an imperative in that it is necessary to bring about the possibility of healing for the next generation. In order to heal, the children *have to* know the "secrets," the traumas in the past that the previous generations have survived. Speaking is also an imperative that comes from within the survivors themselves. Parents also feel that they *have to,* must tell, what happened in order to heal themselves. If this does not happen, the pattern will be repeated in subsequent generations, as the children will pass on the effects of trauma to their children. Lorde's work shows the ways in which individual and collective trauma are connected, as each generation passes on their silence to the next. As Fresco writes, "suffering takes the place of inheritance" (421) as parents "transmitted only the wound to their children" (419). The wound of a traumatic history that this silence represents then becomes a substitute for love. Lorde's work testifies that silence is indeed not love, and then Lorde goes on to pose the question: is it possible for a mother in our generation to be able to love her daughter differently, or will she continue "to love her / as you have loved me?"

Chapter 3

"Una Herida Abierta": The Border as Wound in Gloria Anzaldúa's *Borderlands/La Frontera*

Gloria Anzaldúa's *Borderlands/La Frontera: The New Mestiza* has been praised as a visionary, ground-breaking work by many.[1] Literary critics, Sonia Saldívar-Hull, Ramón Saldívar and Paula Gunn Allen, have all referred to Anzaldúa's work as a seminal text in both contemporary Chicano/a literary studies and "border studies."[2] The work has likewise been hailed by scholars in other disciplines, such as Carl Gutiérrez-Jones in critical legal studies, Oscar J. Martínez in sociology, Ruth Behar in anthropology, and Ronald Takaki in history; most conclude their works with a reference to her work.[3] Why is it that scholars in the humanities and social sciences alike claim her work as exemplary? The answer lies primarily in the figure of the "border" that she uses, a figure that parallels Freud's figure of trauma as a wound.[4] As Anzaldúa shows and as I will explore, the border functions as a marker of an open wound—the marker of a collective traumatic history. Anzaldúa's work explores the literal U.S.–Mexico border as a wound, as a site of historical trauma that continues to affect the present experiences of individuals and communities. Further, Anzaldúa's work presents a vision of the figural Borderlands, sites where there arise positive possibilities for healing from the effects of traumatic events, both individual and collective, both separate and shared.

What scholars such as the ones mentioned above recognize in Anzaldúa's work is a treatment of the connections between the individual and collective aspects of experience, identity, and history. Despite the many collective catastrophes in history, scholars tend to study these events by focusing on the individuals affected by them. We do not have the language that we need to talk about how we are not only connected to each other but are, indeed, together. Maria P. P. Root criticizes theorists of trauma for continuing to view trauma theory as "a theory of individual distress."[5] Before moving to Anzaldúa's work, then, we will take the time in the next section to examine the possibilities for defining trauma as a collective phenomenon. As Root concludes, "a feminist conceptualization of trauma moves the problem beyond an individual perspective to a larger sociopolitical, systemic framework of conceptualization."[6]

This parallel between the individual and the collective views of trauma has been repeated in our explorations thus far. In the first chapter on Sexton, we viewed trauma primarily as an individual phenomenon, when we saw how Sexton's individual trauma is connected to the collective in that it is shared by other girls and women. In chapter two, we moved between two different ways of looking at trauma; we saw how Lorde's individual trauma stemmed in part from her own individual experiences and in part from her collective identification as an African American woman with the effects of a silent history of sexual assaults upon black women in the United States. In this chapter, we move toward an exploration of the collective aspects of trauma: in what ways can trauma be said to be purely collective, bound up in the relations between us, stemming from a source beyond us as individuals both temporally and spatially, and hence out of our own individual control?

Toward a definition of collective trauma

Before we explore Anzaldúa's figure of the border as wound for what it can teach us about collective, traumatic history, we should review Freud's definition of trauma as departure and return.[7] As was mentioned earlier, trauma can be said to be constituted by a delay which is both spatial and temporal. The individual survivor survives precisely because she leaves the experience of the trauma behind. As Caruth writes, "[T]he paradoxically *indirect* structure of psychic trauma means that the traumatism is felt and suffered in the psyche due to the fact that it is precisely *not* accessible to experience."[8] Thus what characterizes a trauma is not so much its referent, or what happened, but its procedure, how it is survived. As Kai T. Erikson writes, ". . . it is *how people react to them rather than what they are* that gives events whatever traumatic quality they can be said to have."[9]

Thus, what makes an experience traumatic is the fact of survival through departure: survival by leaving, by living on, by going on after loss, by leaving behind the experience. And this comes back, returns to claim the survivor through flashbacks, nightmares, and repetitions, as we have seen with regard to Sexton and Lorde. We might call this the autobiographical level of departure and return. This autobiographical level carries within it the paradoxical structure characteristic of traumatic experience. It is, as we have seen, necessary to leave the past behind in order to survive, but it is also impossible to leave the past if this past is traumatic. The return of traumatic past comes in dreams and nightmares, which must be dealt with in order to survive. But this "dealing" with the past is characterized by its difficulty: dealing is not simply a matter of returning, but of reconstructing.

Throughout his career, Freud himself vacillated between studying collective trauma as a collection of individual experiences and studying all trauma, including individual experiences, as aspects of a larger, collective trauma. In his earliest writings on hysteria, he attempts to grapple with the implications of the dreams and repetitions of individual women with early childhood sexual trauma.[10] Then in *Beyond the Pleasure Principle,* Freud tries to explore the collective experiences of war veterans by focusing on the individual experiences of his patients and of the young boy of the Fort-da game.[11] Thus, during the first half of his career, he tended to view trauma as primarily an individual phenomenon. Near the end of his career and his life, he wrote *Moses and Monotheism,* in which he tries to account for the individual experiences of trauma occasioned by World War II by connecting them to a larger, collective, traumatic history.[12] As Robert M. Paul writes of *Moses and Monotheism,* "Here for the first time the analogy between obsessional neurosis and Western religious history is systematically laid out. The analogous pattern, *repeated on the individual and collective level,* is this sequence: 'early trauma—defense—latency—outbreak of the neurosis—partial return of the repressed material.' "[13] Thus, the same paradoxical structure is found in the historical level of trauma, as well.

Traumatic history at the collective level, then, has a paradoxical structure, which means it is a result of the impossibility and necessity of leaving the past behind, coupled with the impossibility and necessity of returning to it. But, in the case of collective, traumatic histories, the very identity of the group is defined in and through the trauma. This means that, for instance, the birth of a child within that group is already bound up with not only the biological, familial, cultural, and historical determinants of the individual child, but also with the trauma that defines the survival of the group. Moreover, the child's identity is tied to the traumatic history from birth, and these ties are continually reinforced by the practices and institutions of that group, which means that the child grows up and forms her identity through the continuing processes of departure and return.

This structure of departure and return functions, as we shall explore, as an address between members of the group and between groups with different identities. This means that the identity of the group is formed through the "other" of the traumatic history. Thus the relation between one's identity and the other can be characterized as a problem. We see, for example, in Freud's *Moses and Monotheism,* how the Jews are connected to the Christians in their history, just as we will see in this chapter how the border between Mexico and the United States designates not only a geographical limit, but a division which defines the very identities of those in the "pre-colonial" world and the "West." This relation to the other is not simply a problem but, as we will see, is also a possible solution. This connection of "others" through difference makes address possible, and address functions as the possible solution to the literal repetitions of the traumatic history through the processes of witnessing and mourning, which we will explore more fully in Part II.

The border as wound: departures

In Anzaldúa's text, the border functions as a sign of traumatic history. I will explore the significance of the traumatic history through an examination of the literal and figural borders in Anzaldúa's text. As we will see, both the border as literal site and the Borderlands as figure result from the paradoxical structure of the impossibility and necessity of leaving and returning. This is not only a "tradition" that can be traced through history, but it is the condition of the possibility of traumatic history itself. The border-as-wound marks the literal site of trauma, the geographical site of departure and return. Further, the border functions also as a figure of the separation between there and here, as a metaphor for the difference between the past and the present, between the before and the after. That is, the Borderlands is the figure for the spatial gap and the temporal delay that splits our ordinary notions of experience and traumatic experience, which, we might say, is the difference between knowledge and non-knowledge, being and non-being, life and death.

This mixing or multiplicity is mirrored in the structure of *Borderlands/La Frontera,* as well. The book is divided into two main sections: the first, "Atravesando Fronteras / Crossing Borders," includes seven essays; the second, "Un Agitado Viento / Ehécatl, The Wind," contains six sections of poetry. In the essays, Anzaldúa blends the forms of essay, story, history, poetry, and song (lyrics of *corridos* or folk songs), making the essays themselves a form of mestiza writing. The general movement of the chapters goes from the past (through narratives of the history and culture of the borderlands in chapters 1 and 2), to the present/past (through dramatizations of the psychological/spiritual myths that serve as strategies for survival, in chapters 3 and 4), to the present (through essays on language and writing in chapters 5 and 6), and finally, to the future (through a vision of the mestiza consciousness in chapter seven). The poetry sections move back and forth through time as well. The poems in the first section deal with the autobiographical past, while the poems in the second and third sections dramatize the experiences of different characters—a migrant farm worker, an Anglo rancher who rapes and lynches, and an alien among them—who populate the historical past and present of the Borderlands. In sections four and five, we move from the historical to the mythological past and present through encounters with saints, *curanderas,* goddesses and other mythological figures. In the final section, we turn to the future, as we are given examples of how mestiza consciousness provides a vision for future survival. Together, these movements through time in Anzaldúa's text demonstrate how it is necessary to deal with the past in order to advance forward into the future.

First, let us examine the many movements in Anzaldúa's text, departures and returns that are paralleled in the historiography of the "border."[14] As we will see, the pattern of cyclical departures and returns accompanies a traumatic history of catastrophe; as historian Enrique Florescano writes of pre-colonial Mexico, "Instead of a linear progressive time, these societies lived in time that had a beginning, underwent an erosion, and reached its end, generally in catastrophic fashion, in order to reinitiate the cyclical movement" (180).[15] Indeed, the history of the Chicanos (and the Aztecs from whom they descended) is a history of movement, of departures and returns.

The departures that Anzaldúa addresses in *Borderlands/La Frontera* come in the forms of deaths, losses, and leavings. The first loss is the most literal one: the loss of lives through conquest.[16] Anzaldúa cites the numerical figures to attest to the loss: she writes that before conquest, the population of the Yucatan peninsula was 25 million; directly after conquest, it was seven million (5). This parallels the losses throughout the Americas. William Denevan, a University of Wisconsin geographer, estimates that the population of the Americas before Christopher Columbus was 43–65 million. By the 1600s, the Indian population of North and South America had been reduced to less than six million people—down nearly 90 percent from its peak a few centuries earlier.[17]

The loss of lives parallels a loss that cannot be accounted for in numerical terms: the loss of ancient, pre-colonial history. Interestingly, Anzaldúa does not address this loss but leaves it for the reader to fill in. Thus, Anzaldúa does not literally count the cost of this loss but refers to it indirectly by comparing the differences between the knowledge she acquires after leaving her home and the lack of knowledge of the people in her hometown. Further, these losses of knowledge result from literal departures: between 1550 and 1605, Indians were, according to historian Enrique Florescano,

> uprooted from the towns where they had formed traditions that gave them a past and an identity. . . . Seen in historical perspective, this gigantic displacement of the population is one of the most violent acts of social and cultural uprooting of which there is memory in the history of Mexico, especially from the indigenous perspective, because in the pre-Hispanic tradition, the conquest of one people by another was rarely accompanied by the destruction of their gods and traditions (113–4).

Thus, the departures in Anzaldúa's text coincide with the literal departures of a traumatic history.

This traumatic history of departure continues, or rather is repeated, in the nineteenth century, with a difference. This time, the people do not move, but the border moves. In the early nineteenth century, white settlers from the East begin to move into the Southwest. Meanwhile from 1810 to 1825, Mexico, like most of Spain's colonies in the Americas, freed itself from Spanish domination, and soon after, in 1836, Texas came under U.S. rule. And in 1848, with the Treaty of Guadalupe Hidalgo, the border moved again; as Patricia Zavella puts it, "the border literally migrated to them—imposing on them a foreign language and sociolegal system."[18] Anzaldúa writes, "Con el destierro y el exilo fuimos desuñados, destroncodos, destripados—we were jerked out by the roots, truncated, disemboweled, dispossessed, and separated from our identity and our history" (7–8).[19] The violent verbs that Anzaldúa uses to describe the movement of the border stem in part from the move away, or abandonment, of the U.S. government from the promises of the treaty that were never honored, as Anzaldúa reminds us (7).

There are continued losses in twentieth century that Anzaldúa lists: Anglo vigilante groups lynching Chicanos, U.S. governments troops quenching protests, drought, land buy-outs, the move from dry land farming to agribusiness corporations, the economic necessity of sharecropping, *maquiladoras,* the devaluation of the peso, and rising unemployment (8–10). In her own family, both of her grandmothers lost their land when poverty forced them to sell it (8). During World War II, many Mexican women, like women throughout the United States, began to find work in ever-increasing numbers, usually as fieldworkers or factory workers.[20] Anzaldúa's own family—her father and mother, and all of the children—became sharecroppers, living on three different farms during her childhood. She and her sister and brothers worked on the farms every day after school; she continued to do so during college (9). After college, she, too, departs by leaving her family and home-land: "I was the first in six generations to leave the Valley, the only one in my family ever to leave home" (16). In leaving, she separates from her culture, and in so doing develops the ability to critique it, but she also carries it within her: "I am a turtle, wherever I go I carry 'home' on my back" (21).

The simultaneous leaving and carrying is addressed in a poem entitled, "Nopalitos" (112–113).[21] In this poem she describes defanging a cactus during a visit home. The work takes hours, but what keeps her going is the vision of the meal, the end result. We can read this as an allegory of her own process of picking the thorns of history, which is also difficult and arduous, and can also provide food, nourishment for her and her culture. She is able to defang the cactus, perhaps, because of the fact that she has left:

> Though I'm part of their *camaradería*
> am one of them
>
> I left and have been gone a long time.

The space between the women on the other porches and her on hers is the space between the lines, the space delineating her departure. The departures are repeated: "I keep leaving and when I am home / they remember no one but me had ever left." The repeated departures are connected to memory: they, the people she left, remember her, and she, in turn, remembers their history.

The distance enabled by her departure also enables her to be their memory. Thus she becomes like the cactus itself, as, at the end of the poem, there are "thorns embedded in my flesh." She herself becomes the cactus that needs to be dethorned, which she does by picking out the thorns of her autobiographical and collective histories. This connection of a collective history and an individual autobiography is enacted through the body. As we see throughout *Borderlands/La Frontera,* Anzaldúa shows us how history, pulled painfully from the body, can provide food for the nourishment of the people.

The border as wound: returns

One of the marks of a collective, traumatic history is a heightened sense of nostalgia or idealization of the past. This manifests itself in myths of origin that valorize the past, as well as in "commemorative narratives" that stress a people's continuity and renewal.[22] The tendency to provide a heroic narrative for the past, a narrative that can not admit of ambiguity or negative aspects, is itself a mark of a traumatic history that has been left behind but which, inevitably, threatens to return. "According to Mircea Eliade's classic definition, the mythic story is an eternal return to the origins, a concentrated search for the primordial moment of creation, when everything was new, strong, and full" (Florescano 179). Thus, just as we saw how it was necessary to leave the traumatic event behind in order to survive it, we now see that it is also necessary to return to it. The return to the traumatic past happens as the survivor is confronted by the repetitive returns *of* the past as well as by the desire to go back *to* an idealized era before the traumatic event. These many returns of and to a traumatic past are enumerated in Anzaldúa's writing.

In the first chapter of *Borderlands/La Frontera,* Anzaldúa ties the present to the past by describing a border culture as an open wound "where the Third World grates against the first and bleeds. And before a scab forms it hemorrhages again, the lifeblood of two worlds merging to form a third country—a border culture" (3). Then she traces the history of this culture by going back to attempt a narrative of origin, which she begins with, "During the original peopling of the America . . ." (4). The originary narrative continues as she describes the Aztec's originary mythical home-land, Aztlán, in the present-day Southwestern United States: "land of herons, land of whiteness, the Edenic place of the origin of the Azteca" (4). She further reinforces the origin with "evidence": by remarking that archeologists have found 20,000 year old campsites in the area (4), and that in precisely the year 1168 A.D., the Aztecs left the area, guided by the God of War, Huitzilpochtli, to migrate to present-day Mexico City (5).

The concern for origins also manifests itself in a double birth story. Anzaldúa writes that the mestizo was born with the Spanish conquest of Mexico: "*En 1521 nació una nueva raza, el mestizo. . . .* Chicanos, Mexican-Americans, are the offspring of those first matings" (5, her italics). And later, she claims the birth of the Chicano people coincides with the establishment of the present-day border in 1848: "The border fence that divides the Mexican people *was born* on February 2, 1848 with the signing of the Treaty of Guadalupe Hidalgo" (7, italics mine). As a result, Mexicans became U.S. citizens by default when approximately one-third of Mexican territory was ceded to the United States, including California, Nevada, Utah, most of Arizona, New Mexico, and parts of Wyoming and Colorado.[23]

In addition to the concern for a return to origins, there are other returns, as well. Anzaldúa describes the historical return to the North, which began after the Conquest when the Spanish conquistadors left Mexico to look for gold with indigenous and mestizo guides and servants; she writes that the return from Mexico to the United States in the sixteenth century "constituted a return to the place of origin, Aztlán, thus making Chicanos originally and secondarily indigenous to the Southwest" (5). Anzaldúa concludes, "the Southwest became our homeland once more" (7). These returns continue in the twentieth century through migrations. Anzaldúa puts the present-day return of Mexicans to the United States in terms of tradition: "We have a tradition of migration, a tradition of long walks. Today we are witnessing *la migración de los pueblos mexicanos,* the return odyssey to the historical/mythological Aztlán" (11).

These returns parallel her own, literal return home to Texas, which is narrated in the text in a section entitled, "El Retorno" (88–91). The return trip allows her to remember what she has missed by leaving. It allows her to "still feel the old despair" (89). And it allows her to remember her own loss, which was perhaps her greatest, in remembering her father who has died. In remembering her father, she returns to the scene of his death, after a time lag, or departure, of several years. This return is strikingly different from its earlier manifestation in an essay published several years before. In the earlier essay from 1981 Anzaldúa wrote:

> My father dying, his aorta bursting while he was driving, the truck turning over, his body thrown out, the truck falling on his face. Blood on the pavement. His death occurred just as I entered puberty. It irrevocably shattered the myth that there existed a male figure to look after me. How could my strong, good, beautiful god-like father be killed? How stupid and careless of god. What if chance and accident ruled? I lost my father, god, and my innocence all in one bloody blow.[24]

In 1981, Anzaldúa writes of her father's death as a scene in the present tense, with quick, flashing images of "dying . . . bursting . . . turning . . . falling." When she returns to this scene several years later, the return occurs *as a narration,* as a story that she tells while talking to her brother in the field during a return trip home. As she talks to and watches and listens to her brother, she remembers her father who has "been dead for 29 years, having worked himself to death. . . . It shocks me that I am older than he" was when he died (90). This realization also allows her to see the differences between herself and her father. She knows what he did not: the "names" of the rain god and the maize goddess that they both worship. Thus, in returning, she is able not only to remember what is the same but is also able to recognize what is not: "Today I see . . . it will never be as I remember it" (90). This realization comes through not only a literal return home but also through a narrated reconstruction of this return. Thus, this return is different from the earlier, literal repetitions; this return is figural— a narrative that tells a story and attempts to provide integration.[25] The story ends with another narration of a memory from childhood: she and her family planting seeds, caring for them, watching them grow, harvesting and beginning again: "Growth, death, decay, birth" (91). These cycles of death and birth, leaving and returning, continue, she realizes. In her return, she recognizes the inevitability of final departures.

From literal to figural, from past to future

Throughout *Borderlands/La Frontera,* Anzaldúa refers to "bouts with death" (35), encounters that are not narrativized in the text. The lack of narrative calls attention to the effects of a traumatic history. As we have seen with regard to Sexton and Lorde, traumatic history is one in which gaps, forgettings, and competing interpretations all point to a violent past that has been skipped over, and survived, by not having been experienced. Before making a conscious return through reconstruction, a survivor is caught in an unconscious return through negative effects that are literal repetitions. As Caruth writes of trauma survivors, "they become themselves the symptom of a history that they cannot entirely possess" (5).[26]

Thus, the subject as symptom embodies the effects of trauma that we have discussed previously. Anzaldúa shows these symptoms as well. She admits the "agony of inadequacy" and the "defense strategies" that she uses to "escape:"

> I have split from and disowned those parts of myself that others rejected. I have used rage to drive others away and to insulate myself against exposure. I have reciprocated with contempt for those who have roused shame in me. I have internalized rage and contempt, one part of the self (the accusatory, persecutory, judgmental) using defense strategies against another part of the self. (45)

Further, Anzaldúa shows that she is aware that these individual symptoms stem from a collective identity, a collective past, a collective problem, as is shown by the switch of pronouns in the following sentences: "As a person, I, as a people, we, Chicanos, blame ourselves, hate ourselves, terrorize ourselves. Most of this goes on unconsciously; we only know that there is something 'wrong' with us, something fundamentally 'wrong' " (45). While these effects of a traumatic history are evident in the text, what makes *Borderlands/La Frontera* literature and not sociology is the turn from the literal to the figural. The literal description of history or autobiography is, as we have seen, a return to the site of trauma that is doomed to failure and repetition. However, it is not until the return is made consciously through figuration that positive possibilities may arise.

Let us explore this turn from the literal to the figural, as we examine more closely how the border as literal wound becomes the border as figural wound in Anzaldúa's text. Both the border and the Borderlands are wounds defined by *"un choque,* a cultural collision," the collision of past and present, here and there, where

> *lo pasado me estirá pa' 'trás*
> *y lo presente pa' 'delante* (3).

A translation of these lines might read, "the past draws me back/ and the present draws me forward." However, the verb "estirar" means not only to draw but also to stretch and to pull; thus there is ambiguity as to the source of the action: does it come from within or from without the subject? Further, the terms "atrás" and "adelante" connote not only spatiality but also temporality; "atrás" means back in space and also back in time (ago), while "adelante" likewise means both forward or ahead in space and also ahead in time (later).[27] Thus the Borderlands is structured, like a trauma, by a difference that is both inside and outside and both spatial and temporal at once.

In Anzaldúa's text, the border functions not only as a literal site but also as a figural reconstruction. After two quoted excerpts from other sources, the first chapter of *Borderlands/La Frontera* opens with a poem, which includes the following lines:

> mile-long open wound
> > dividing a *pueblo,* a culture,
> > > running down the length of my body,
> > > > staking fence rods in my flesh,

> splits me   splits me
> *me raja   me raja* (2)

The "splitting" here is not the literal survival mechanism associated with trauma, as we saw above. Here the border as wound becomes a figure for the very bodily being of the speaker. The border as wound is not only a literal site of either history or autobiography in these lines, but rather, leaves behind the literal return in order to make way for the figurative. As Cherríe Moraga writes,

> This image holds, speaks to something more profound than the intellectual knowledge of the loss of half our territory to the U.S. with the signing of the Treaty of Guadalupe in 1848. It speaks of a *collective wound* we remember as a people and proffers the possibility of healing. This vision informs the whole book.[28]

The wound, even in these few lines, moves from the literal ("1,950 mile-long") through measurement, to the figural ("of my body," "in my flesh") through embodiment. By taking the wound into her body, the speaker creates the possibility that the body can also heal the wound. The embodied wound can heal in a way that an unrecognized wound can not. The healing, as we will see, lies in the recognition of the positive, creative potential of the border as wound. The wound opens itself to healing precisely because it is acknowledged and recognized as part of the body/being. The border becomes embodied not only in the flesh but in the poem with the lines,

> splits me   splits me
> *me raja   me raja*

In the switch from English to Spanish lies the border as wound, as pain, *and* as conscious acknowledgement, as positive difference. As linguist Susan Gal points out, code-switching is often a form of "subversive reworking of dominant linguistic forms by subordinate groups: in short, the forging of new forms, and identities, out of the already symbolically weighted linguistic material at hand."[29]

The switch from Spanish to English, and the positive potential they hold in their difference, occurs again in the poems, "No se raje, Chicanita," in Spanish, and "Don't give in, Chicanita," in English, which are the last two poems in the book (200–203). In these poems, the speaker addresses her niece and gives her advice on how to survive in the Borderlands. Survival comes, the speaker tells the young woman, not in literal returns but in figural ones: through the metaphors that provide a source of origins and nurturance for the future. Throughout the two poems, the speaker uses similes that show not only what the figural origins are but how they may be used for survival. At the beginning of the poems, she compares the young woman to the surroundings: "sus raíces como las de los mesquites" / "Your roots are like those of the mesquite," and, like the mesquite, are "bien plantadas . . . a esa corrente . . . tu origen" / "firmly planted . . . toward that current . . . your origin."

But then, as in the poem discussed above that began the book, the poem switches from the literal, the surroundings of the border landscape, to the figural. This switch is, as we have seen, designated by the difference between languages. While for the most part, the translation between the two is parallel, in the middle of the poem two different terms are used, which I have emphasized in the following lines:

> Tiempos duros como *pastura* los cargamos
> Hard times like *fodder* we carry

In both versions, "pastura" and "fodder" are used to represent the "tiempos duros/hard times" of the continued effects of traumatic history. While the two terms do not have significantly different semantic meanings—"pastura" refers to "grass or other growing plants used as food by grazing animals," and "fodder" is "dry coarse food for cattle, horses, and sheep"—the significance of their difference lies in, precisely, their roots or origins.[30] The term in the Spanish version, "pastura," comes from the Late Latin, "pastura," which is the past participle of "pascere," a verb meaning to feed or to graze.[31] The term used in the English version, "fodder," comes from the Middle English word, "fodder," and before that the Anglo-Saxon "fodor," which comes from Middle Dutch and Dutch, and even earlier from Old High German and Middle High German.[32] Thus, the term used in Spanish can be traced back through its Spanish and Latinate origins, while the term used in English can be traced back through its Anglo-Saxon and Germanic roots. The source of food, of nurturance and sustenance, lies not in the present-day meanings of the similes, *but in their very histories.* It is history, then, that provides food for these people who are, like grazing animals, both moving across the earth and finding nurturance from it.

Further, it is through history that the people themselves, the "we," come to be at all. Before the line that we have been examining, "Hard times like fodder we carry," the preposition, "we," has not appeared in the poem. It is through a recognition of this collective experience that the identity of the people moves from a collection of individuals, "you . . . your mom . . . and I," to a collective whole, "we." At the end of both poems, the speaker moves not only to the collective "we" but also to the future tense to show how "we" use this nurturance for the future.

In this poem and throughout the entire text, it is the figural return to history that provides the "pastura" / "fodder" that is necessary to move from the past to the future. Through the figures of the Borderlands, the speaker and the girl survive by becoming "like" the land and its inhabitants: "like the horned toad and the lizard . . . like serpent lightening." These figures enable a move to the future as seen in the use of future verb constructions: "vamos a paracer/we'll be [we're going to seem]"; "caerá/will fall"; "nos moveremos/we'll move"; "¡Ya verás!/You'll see." To move from the past to the future means to move from the position of an individual object of history, one who is caught in the cycles of departures and returns, to the position of a participant in the collective action of history, as the collective subject, "we," comes together to turn history into food, into the energy to propel the group forward into the future.[33] Thus, it is necessary to return to the past both literally and figurally in order to regain the sense of a collective, which itself was destroyed by the traumatic past. And, in returning to the past, a departure from the repetitions of the past is made possible, as, once the collective "we" is reestablished, it is possible to move forward into the future.

This collective move to the future comes through the text of *Borderlands/La Frontera* itself, as Anzaldúa moves from the literal return of history, which is an unconscious repetition of the trauma, to the figural return of metaphor, which opens the possibility for conscious healing. Through the figure of the Borderlands, Anzaldúa leaves behind, finally, the repetitive returns to the past in order to look ahead to the future. She thinks of this reconstruction of the history and myth of the Chicano people as a mutual process that will lead to the understanding of her own culture and others': "we need to know the history of their struggle and they need to know ours" (86).

Anzaldúa's text provides us with not only the necessary reminders of this traumatic history as she returns to the site of trauma, but also with the possibilities to deal with the trauma, paradoxically, by leaving it behind. When the reality of a literal return is given up, there arises the possibility of healing through a figural return, or reconstruction. Anzaldúa's autobiographical essays in *This Bridge Called My Back,* first published in 1981, show a concern about the literal return home: she desires, fears, and rejects it.[34]

Then, as we have seen in *Borderlands/La Frontera,* Anzaldúa realizes that she cannot really, literally, return to the past or go home, and she turns away from the literal to the figural: "And if going home is denied me then I will have to stand and claim my own space, making a new culture—*una cultura mestiza*—with my own lumber, my own bricks and mortar and my own feminist architecture" (22). This "architecture," as we will see in chapter six, is the reconstruction of the trauma in order for healing. What she builds is a mix of theory and art, song and medicine. Thus, the return to history is a return in order to leave, in order to move from the repetitions of the past into a vision for the future.

Anzaldúa's figure of the Borderlands, then, is not only an effect of having survived a traumatic history; it is also intended for the purpose of promoting a collective, future survival. Anzaldúa thus goes beyond "border theorizing," which, as Rosa Linda Fregoso points out, is not alone sufficient to change "the actual social conditions of the vast majority of 'border crossers' [and] border inhabitants."[35] Consequently, Anzaldúa reminds us that survival necessitates collective actions, and it is through collective actions that the group not only regains a sense of the collective but also works toward ensuring its own survival.

PART II

I will never be gone. I am a scar, a report from the frontlines, a tal-
isman, a resurrection. A rough place on the chin of complacency. . . .

So what if I am afraid? Of stepping out in the morning? Of
dying? Of unleashing the damned gall where hatred swims like a tad-
pole waiting to swell into the arms of war? And what does that war
teach when the bruised leavings jump an insurmountable wall where
the glorious Berlin chestnuts and orange poppies hide detection wires
that spray bullets which kill?

My poems are filled with blood these days because the future is so
bloody. When the blood of four-year-old children runs unremarked
through the alleys of Soweto, how can I pretend that sweetness is any-
thing more than armor and ammunition in an on-going war?

I am saving my life by using my life in the service of what must be
done.

—Audre Lorde, in a journal entry
dated June 7, 1984

Chapter 4

"This Kind of Hope": Anne Sexton and the Language of Survival

It might seem strange to begin our examination of the healing process with the example of a writer who was ultimately unsuccessful at healing. Or was she? As we will see, many critics point out that Sexton's life ended in suicide and they take this as evidence to support their own negative assessment of Sexton's life and work. But the distinction between life and work, which we explored in the first chapter, must be attended to again here, as we now turn to Sexton's attempts at healing. We will see how, while her life ended in suicide, her work was filled with creative endeavors to survive. Through her poetry, Sexton not only shows progress in the processes of remembering and reconstructing of trauma, but moreover, she invents a language of survival, a language through which she—still—survives.

One might question the applicability of the term "progress" to Sexton's life and work. In addition to the fact that her suicide in 1974 allows us to read backwards, looking for signs of her eventual "failure," part of this hesitancy to use the term, "progress," may derive from our unwillingness to impose a dialectical pattern to the healing process. We may fear that to emphasize the positive outcomes of the process somehow implies a necessity or destiny to the traumatic event. If, we might ask, all these good things result from healing from trauma, then couldn't we say that trauma itself is the cause, and somehow good? Some might say yes, that in the end it was "for your own good" to survive and to heal from trauma. Some might say no, that in the end there is no complete healing, and the experience of trauma always results in loss. While this is perhaps an impossible question to answer, it is important to attend to it, to keep it in mind, and to realize that it cannot be answered unequivocally either yes or no. This balance of yes and no, the ability to see both sides as both positive and negative, is, as we will see, exactly the strategy for survival that Sexton's poetry teaches us. For Sexton conceived of survival, not as a matter of success or failure, but as a delicate balance between both the positive and the negative in life.

Still many critics agree that progress can be found from Sexton's early to her later work. They call it a "progression" or a "mouvement d'expansion" or a "sequence from sickness to cure."[1] One critic even uses the very term, "progress," albeit with clarification.[2] Another notes that the progress of Sexton's poems follows the psychoanalytic model of working backwards, as many poems begin in the present and work back in time.[3] And another calls Sexton's corpus a story that moves from the psychological to the social to the spiritual.[4]

These movements backward and forward remind us that, when healing from trauma, progress is not linear. As one moves through the healing process, one finds oneself moving forward into witnessing, for example, and then later backward into remembering, as one re-encounters similar patterns at different levels of intensity. To support this, one might note that while many critics point to "Flee on Your Donkey" and *Transformations* as pivotal works in Sexton's career, there are signs of progress evident in the four works before this middle period, as well.[5] There are in the early poems female speakers who decide to use their voice, announcing, commanding, proclaiming and demanding to be heard. There is evidence of a self who is changing the old image of herself as absolutely good or absolutely evil in the poem "Ghosts" (65). And there is a persona in "Mother and Jack and the Rain" who is allied with her literary predecessor, Virginia Woolf, in claiming a room of her own, her own voice and her own self in order "to endure, / somehow to endure" (109–111).[6]

In the first chapter on Sexton, we saw representations of the states of pre-remembering and remembering in the poems, "Kind Sir: These Woods" and "Music Swims Back to Me." Now we will move to another aspect of healing from trauma: the process of reconstruction. Remembering happens, as we have seen, when dreams, images, or flashbacks interrupt a survivor's daily life, forcing her to deal with the "unclaimed experience" of the trauma.[7] Reconstructing the trauma is the next task for the survivor; this happens when she puts the memories into a story through therapy, writing, or other creative work. Sexton's attempts at reconstruction appear throughout her poetry, even as these attempts were made difficult by her own guilt, her family's disapproval, and her illness.[8] As she noted during a lecture in 1972, "When writing . . . it is like lying on the analyst's couch reenacting a private terror, and the creative mind is the analyst who gives pattern and meaning to what the persona sees as only incoherent experience" (Middlebrook 64). Sexton's writing, then, shows her attempts to remember, reconstruct, and heal from her traumatic past.

From reenactment to reconstruction

Even from her first book, *To Bedlam and Part Way Back,* published in 1960, we can see Sexton's attempt to deal with the manifestations of trauma in the present.[9] As we have seen, Sexton was acting out the effects of the trauma in her daily life; in her earliest poetry, throughout *To Bedlam and Part Way Back,* the effects of childhood sexual trauma manifest themselves in similar ways: in images of clinging love, forgetting, dissociating, silencing, and perceiving oneself as a witch—evil, guilty, damned.

As she clung to lovers in life, the persona of her poetry clings to past and present loves. She immortalizes her therapist in "You, Doctor Martin" (3). She is nostalgic for Nana in "Some Foreign Letters" (9–10). She wants to forget the past, or she can't remember it, or she doesn't want to deal with what it means, as we have seen in "Kind Sir: These Woods" (5) and "Music Swims Back to Me" (7). She goes numb, plays dead, and dissociates in "Elizabeth Gone" (8), while in "The Moss of His Skin" she pretends others have not seen what has gone on between her and her father.[10] She is guilty, possessed, an evil witch damned by other witches in both "Her Kind" (15–16) and "Double Image" (36–37).

A decade later, Sexton's fifth book, *Transformations,* shows how these earlier repetitions of a painful past turn into a "kind of hope," as the poems move from scenes of dreams as reenactments of trauma to dreams as reconstructions.[11] As one critic has written of *Transformations,* it shows that the characters' "current condition . . . can be ameliorated by unlocking memories of the stories (and the ensuing bad dreams) of their childhood" (Leventen 137). As character after character in the fairy tales awakens from horrific dreams, Sexton shows us the way to begin to turn our memories into solutions.

The images from dreams, from the unconscious, float up, as many of the speakers in the poems awaken. The act of waking, so prominent in the plots of fairy tales, is important in the healing process as well. To wake from a dream like this one is to wake to the realization of having survived. Further, waking from this type of dream, which is like a reenactment of the trauma, allows the dreamer to feel fear, which helps her begin to integrate the experience into her memory and identity.

As the dreamer wakes to these nightmarish dreams, she is forced to feel the physical panic of the traumatic experience for the first time, as the dreams reveal scenes of women condemned to death or married off without consent, or amputated or bleeding, with limbs reduced to stumps.[12] The last poem of the book, "Briar Rose (Sleeping Beauty)," describes the daughter waking from these dreams to call out for her daddy to protect her, only to discover in him "another kind of prison" (294).

These traumatic memories, then, are experienced as a crippling possession from within, which are experienced as uncontrollable forces invading and controlling the survivor's life.[13] And upon awakening, it is not enough simply to remember; these memories must be voiced. Thus, what seems to be only a negative reenactment of the trauma holds inside itself the possibility for healing. To begin to remember and reconstruct these memories in the presence of another eases the pain of having survived the trauma alone. The voicing of memories takes the trauma (that which had gone inside without mediation) and puts it back outside, into the world, where it can no longer fester into craziness.

The work of dreams, then, is to bring to consciousness these memories, while the work of the dreamer is to reconstruct the dreams in the presence of a listener. From the very first poem, *Transformations* calls attention to itself as an address: "The speaker in this case/is a middle-aged witch, me—" ("The Gold Key" 223). This witch is not the witch of the earlier poetry who, as in "Her Kind," repeats and reenacts the trauma, but an older, wiser witch. As Dawn Skorczewski has written of the witch in *Transformations:* "Building bridges between collective and personal history, the witch becomes a kind of cultural critic who teaches us how to see how folk tales directly influence the individuals in a culture, how 'a' story is also 'our' story."[14] The witch as cultural critic, then, turns the music of traumatic memory from "Music Swims Back to Me" into a question and a command to the audience: "Remember? / Remember music / and beware" ("The Wonderful Musician" 264).

In remembering and voicing the memories, one begins to reconstruct the traumatic event, and in so doing, one makes of the private terror a public story, thus connecting this story with others and with others' stories. This allows the survivor to realize that she is part of a community of survivors. In reconstructing the event, in telling the story, one is also giving back, preparing the way by giving warnings and lessons to those who will come after.

Transformations tells us that "many a girl" has survived and warns us that "many are the deceivers" to come.[15] As Rose Lucas puts it, "the traumas of *Transformations* are common in Western culture."[16] And Carol Leventen concludes that in *Transformations* Sexton transforms her personal memories into stories of social significance.[17] Thus, in Sexton's work we see how an individual experience of trauma holds lessons of significance for the entire culture. These lessons are two-fold: first, the reconstruction of individual trauma allows the culture to reflect upon its role in responding to the needs of the survivor; and second, the culture itself, in acknowledging trauma, is forced to confront the ideological structures that make possible such traumatic events.

Beyond victimization to cultural critique

Such a cultural critique of the ideological structures that reinforce a culture of trauma can be read in Sexton's "Snow White and the Seven Dwarfs" (224–229). In this poem, we are given further lessons about what society does to women: commodifies them, consumes them, and uses other women to keep the system going. The speaker portrays Snow White as a commodity, or as Carol Leventen puts it, "a hodge podge of marketable parts" (140). Conversely, the figure of the step-mother suffers from the loss of her beauty (which determines her worth in society) as a result of aging. Thus, the opposition between Snow White and the step-mother shows how violence to women connects directly to women's "worth," or economic viability.

Snow White runs to the woods, where the dwarves warn her to be on the watch for her step-mother, but Snow White does not heed their advice. Thus, Sexton shows how women themselves fail to avoid the potential dangers waiting for them. Snow White allows in the disguised step-mother, and after biting the poison apple, Snow White "fell down for the final time," which implies that other instances of "falling" have occurred in Snow White's life. The dwarves prepare her body, and in so doing, repeat her commodification; they prepare her body and put her under glass, like food to be sold and consumed.

In Sexton's version, not even the prince has agency; he does not save her by kissing her; instead, he drops the coffin, thereby ensuring that Snow White's repeated "falls" continue, even after death. This time, the fall is redemptive, as it causes the apple to become dislodged and wakes her up. The story does not end, however, happily ever after, for Snow White marries the prince and simply takes the place of her step-mother in society. In portraying Snow White as continuing her step-mother's role, Sexton shows how women themselves repeat the patterns laid out for them by society. In the end, as Sexton shows us, it is clear that women cannot completely escape the repetitions that shape their experience.

Until recently, most critics stop here in their esteem of Sexton's work. *Transformations* is seen as her last good work, and the social significance of her warnings are thought to apply to her own life as well. As Herman and Hirschman conclude in their study in 1977, "The victims who feel like bitches, whores, and witches might feel greatly relieved if they felt less lonely, if their identities as special guardians of a dreadful secret could be shed" (755). But by the time of her suicide in 1974, Sexton did not feel any less lonely; she killed herself alone, divorced, estranged from her children, and having worn out many of her family and friends. Thus, Sexton's life and work are seen as a portrait in victimization; for example, Leventen concludes that in *Transformations,* Sexton shows how women not only remain victims (140) but also how women participate in their victimization (142). And Rose Lucas concludes that "Briar Rose" shows how going into memory does not lead to understanding or healing (83).

The problem with these critical assessments lies in their tendency to take the early and middle work of Sexton's career as the final product without attending to the later work. As we will examine in the next section, in reading Sexton's entire corpus, one begins to notice a pattern of images, motifs, and metaphors, which I call "a language of survival." This language of survival shows how Sexton conceives of survival, unlike many in her own and our time, not as a game of triumph, with winners on one side and losers on the other. Instead, Sexton envisions survival as the ability to balance—and to see the connections between—both the good and the bad, both life and death, and both self and other.

Furthermore, to read Sexton's later work forces one to recognize the ultimate optimism in Sexton's corpus. While *Transformations* shows us the devastating consequences of cultural myth, Sexton's later work opens the way to the possibility of writing new myths. For as one sees oneself as part of something larger, once one's own pain becomes part of the picture of the whole, the way is opened to a meaning larger than oneself. Beyond the personal, beyond the political, the poetry of *Transformations* prepares the way for the spiritual explorations of Sexton's work to come.

Surviving without a witness

In her willingness to write about traumatic violence, Sexton attempts in her poetry to tell the truths about the violence in women's lives. We can only guess how Sexton's life could have been different if she had found a witness to her truths during her lifetime. However, as her poetry shows, Sexton did survive—through language. She survived by writing, and her writing survived. Next we will examine how Sexton's poetry invents a language of survival.

The language of survival is the language of melancholia. Many critics have remarked upon the prevalence of melancholic themes in Sexton's poetry.[18] However, we need to remember that Sexton's melancholia arises from a loss that is traumatic, that is, it arises from an experience that is unexpected and threatens life. According to Freud and Melanie Klein, if there is no witness to help a survivor work through her trauma, the survivor will have to make of melancholia a survival tool.[19] Thus, melancholia arises when there is a failure to recognize the traumatic nature of the wound causing pain. As in Sexton's case, this failure may arise from the refusal of those around her and of society as a whole to recognize the traumatic wound and to allow the survivor to witness to her trauma; in other cases, the refusal may come from the survivor's own denial and refusal to witness. In either case, melancholia is an attempt to deal with a failure to recognize and to witness to having been wounded.[20] As Abraham and Torok write of the connection between traumatic wounding and melancholia, "C'est cette plaie que le mélancholique cherche à dissimuler, à entourer d'un mur, à encrypter. . . . [It is this wound that the melancholic wants to conceal, enclose in a wall, entomb. . . .]."[21]

The primary forces of melancholia are negation and incorporation.[22] When we negate, we push away the pain and sadness of the loss, and lose ourselves in work, school, achievements—all of which allow us to feel successful and triumphant over others and over our emotions. When we incorporate, we give in to the pain of the loss, allow the tears to flow, and express grief through creative activities, such as writing poetry. Throughout her career, Sexton's poetry shows a variety of perspectives on incorporation and negation until, late in her career, the poetry attempts to achieve a balance between them, as both good and evil are recognized as possible in both self and other.[23]

Our culture's valorization of negation can be seen in Sexton's poem, "Courage" (425), which traces a lifetime of courageous acts, first from childhood and later in adulthood: "faced the death of bombs and bullets . . . did not fondle the weakness inside you . . . endured a great despair . . . you did it alone." It is interesting to note that in this poem the characterization of the positive aspects of negation become increasingly male-identified, while later we will see how Sexton characterizes incorporation as female-identified.

There are other positive characterizations of negation, as well, such as refusing to identify with the other who was the source of oppression, and who has become the internalized evil within. Thus, negation succeeds in helping the survivor "To take the you out of the me" ("Begat" 322). This occurs in other poems, such as "Rowing" (417–418) and "The Civil War" (418–419). In addition to dissociating oneself from the oppressive other, negation helps to locate the proper blame and responsibility externally, such as in "The Falling Dolls": "Why is there no mother?. . . . Was there a father?" (486).

Francis Bixler writes that Sexton "saw her greatest problem as being full of personal, internalized evil" ("Journey" 205). This evil has been incorporated through the figures of hunger and eating, and these figures are negative, particularly when they show Sexton's own identification with the abuse committed against her. Sexton also presents incorporation as a form of female-identification with men, which results in complicity, as in "Loving the Killer" (185–188). Together, the incorporation of abuse and identification with the abuser results in the survivor's internalization of evil.

In the later poetry, however, Sexton begins to characterize negation as negative and incorporation as positive. While in the earlier poetry, negation is viewed as positive, male-identified independence and success, now it is characterized as negative, male-identified indifference, as in the poem, "The Children" (419–420). Beyond indifference, Sexton warns us, an imbalance of negation leads to violence, as we will see in the next poem.

Sexton's poem, "The Wifebeater," from *The Book of Folly* (1972) has not been treated by most critics (307–308). Perhaps this is because the poem comes from Sexton's later work, which critics have not yet written about extensively. Or perhaps the absence of critical voices for "The Wifebeater" speaks to our continued reluctance to deal with this problem. Sexton herself was beaten by her husband, as a letter, dated April 7, 1973, and written in an obviously agitated state after her divorce, indicates:

> Still—the first elation of getting HOME and being in a life where i'm not scared every minute of being killed at the most extremem—but very literally true—or depsised or put down or if for a moment a little liking only if I were weak—dependant—quiet-etc. And after all what was the marragie all about—big chief father with little girl wife-child. Sado-masochistic . . . hit me again, big chief for d I am so guilty.[24]

Yet "The Wifebeater," like all of Sexton's poetry, is not purely personal.[25] For as critic Eniko Bobolas asserts, "as soon as the personal experience is given the frame of a poem, the 'I' ceases to refer to the historical poet and the experience cannot be taken as purely autobiographical."[26] This, cou-pled with the estimate that 50 percent of American wives will be battered during the course of their marriages, makes Sexton's poem political as well as personal.[27]

Throughout the poem, Sexton presents images of a man, a family, and a society in which there is such an imbalance of negation that nothing is untouched by the violence. The poem begins, "The will be mud on the carpet tonight/and blood in the gravy as well." The husband drags in the dirt and violence—the "mud" and "blood"—from the outside, from the society that gives him dominion over his wife and child, and brings it inside the house. In locating the wifebeater as outside both the wife and the house—"The wifebeater is out, / the childbeater is out"—Sexton is mark-ing his character as a result of the imbalance of negation over incorpora-tion: "out." This is seen by the positive ways in which negation allows him to be a "success": he is "a man in the world . . . upright . . . conserva-tive . . . evasive."[28] And, as a "man in the world," he is active: "He strides . . . he makes . . . he was walking . . . he built." His success, his triumph is also "contagious," both dangerous and spreading, as the danger is being passed on to others. He so valorizes negation that even his actions of incorpora-tion are violent, as he "eat[s] soil and drink[s] bullets," "chew[s] little red pieces of my heart," and makes his wife and child into "hamburg."

His character is not formed randomly, as the poem shows. All of the institutions of society—nation, church, and family—support his negation and, in so doing, support his violence. The nation supports his violence by valorizing his ability to "buil[d] me a country." The church supports his violence by establishing his dominion over his wife and child: their family structure parallels the Holy Family, and the coffin he makes is "for the madonna and child." The institution of the family also contributes to his violence, as the poem tells us that together, this unholy trinity, "we three will color the stars black/in memory of his mother." This leads the reader to wonder if the husband's mother, too, was a victim of such violence. Or perhaps he is taking out on his family the hatred he feels toward his mother. However, the poem moves from these questions about the man's individual mother to a collective *"women"* in italics, who, as the poem says, become the "enemy" to man, and to the institutions that support him: fam-ily, church, and nation. Thus, Sexton leaves us in the final lines with a pre-diction and a warning of what will happen if this collective violence against women is not recognized, not stopped: "Tonight all the red dogs lie down in fear/and the wife and daughter knit into each other/until they are killed."

Increasingly the later poetry warns of the violence inherent in a society that valorizes negation over incorporation, triumph over emotion. By learning to balance negation with incorporation, Sexton tells us in the later poetry, we might be able to listen, to take in the needs of the other in sympathy, which might lead to unity: to "build a whole nation of God / in me—but united" ("The Civil War" 418). This "whole nation," or "inner world" in Melanie Klein's terms, is, in fact, the condition of possibility of the survival of the self, or the self as surviving through a life of loss. Klein writes:

> This inner world consists of innumerable objects taken into the ego, corresponding partly to the multitude of varying aspects, good and bad, in which the parents (and other people) appeared to the child's unconscious mind throughout various stages of his development. Further, they also represent all the real people who are continually becoming internalized in a variety of situations provided by the multitude of ever-changing external experiences as well as phantasied ones. In addition, all these objects are in the inner world in an infinitely complex *relation both with each other and with the self.*[29]

Sexton's poetry, too, describes these processes as happening throughout our lifetimes and constituting our "selves." As Alicia Ostriker writes, "Her work repeatedly implies that the self is constituted by other(s) or that self and other overlap."[30] Incorporation and negation are always in tension and arise not only at the literal death of someone, but all throughout our lives—when we realize our parents are separate from us around the age of two, after break-ups with lovers, when we graduate, move, lose touch with our friends, divorce, or when someone we love dies. Thus, for Sexton and for all of us, incorporation and negation are the tools of survival. At all of these moments, we have the opportunity to balance the tension between incorporation and negation.[31]

While Sexton's poetry puts forth this vision, we can now see that it is precisely the imbalance of triumph over emotion that made the process of witnessing—of reconstructing the event and feeling the emotion of the past with another—impossible for Sexton during her lifetime. Sexton's continual struggle to balance this tension, and through so doing, to find a language of survival is dramatized in her poem, "Is It True?" (446–454), published in *The Awful Rowing Toward God* in 1975. In this poem the speaker attempts to tell the story of how, "Occasionally the devil has crawled / in and out of me." She goes to a priest, hoping he will be able to hear her story of this evil: "I tell the priest I am evil. . . . What I mean is evil / (not meaning to be, you understand, just something I ate)." Here the speaker attempts to grapple with the difference between agency and oppression: Is the evil—the violence in her life—something that she ate, took in willingly, or is it something that was forced onto her against her will? No matter what the answer to the question, the speaker ultimately looks for forgiveness, for the possibility that there can be goodness after such evil, as she repeatedly asks, "Is it true? Is it true?"

However, the priest refuses to be a witness to her suffering and instead asks what sins she has committed: "The priest shakes his head. / He doesn't comprehend." If the priest were to share in the retelling of the story with the speaker, then, together, they would be able to find an answer to this question of whether good can come after evil: "Is it too late, too late / to open the incision and plant Him there again?" The priest does not understand the metaphor of planting; he only understands the desire for triumph, the desire to kill oneself or another. An early draft of the poem underscores the speaker's frustration with the priest and the discourse of negation and triumph:

> Do not kill in the name of God.
> Do not partition countries in the name of
> some president or dictator
> Deep earth,
> redeem us from our redeemers.[32]

In the end of the final version of the poem, the speaker turns away from the priest and realizes she must answer the question of how to survive for herself, and she allows herself to become "priest," one who has the power to bless. Thus, the speaker turns to the natural world that she names and blesses, praising both female and male:

> the sea without which there is no mother,
> the earth without which there is no father.

In this way both incorporation and negation, which elsewhere in Sexton's poetry have been figured as gendered, are here balanced for survival. Survival is characterized as a passing through of danger, of death, which occurs repeatedly throughout the poem: "Yet I pass through. / I pass through." "I pass through. I pass through." Thus, through the balance of incorporation and negation, the speaker finds her answer, finds her hope, makes of herself a survivor, someone "who lives on, lives on," someone who survives "despite it all, / despite it all." Sexton's poetry shows that not only must the gendered tendencies of incorporation and negation be balanced for survival, but also that such a balance might lead to compassion, and forgiveness, and the end of violent retribution.

Sexton survives through language; she was not, however, able to find an interlocutor—in this priest or elsewhere—with whom she could witness in order for her healing to occur on an intersubjective level. We might conclude that through poetry, Sexton was herself a "triumphant failure." This term, her own, comes from an address on the poet's function. She uses it to refer to Icarus' "desire to reach the sun." She then lists John F. Kennedy, Robert Kennedy, the three civil rights workers who died in Philadelphia, Mississippi, William Sloan Coffin, Benjamin Spock, the three burned space men aboard the Apollo, and Dr. Martin Luther King, Jr., saying of them: "Each of these men dared to take off for the sun. Even though they fail, they are all men of triumph."[33] It is evident that Sexton, like Icarus, was destroyed in her flight, that she did not have the societal support (which, incidentally for both Icarus and Sexton, should have come from "the father") that was necessary in order to throw off the weight of her history.

At a memorial service after Sexton's suicide in 1974, Adrienne Rich urged the women present to take her death as a challenge not to let women die this way anymore:"We have had enough suicidal women poets, enough suicidal women, enough of self-destructiveness. . . ." Rich concludes,

> I think of Anne Sexton as a sister whose work tells us what we have to fight
> in ourselves and in the images patriarchy has held up to us. Her poetry is a
> guide to the ruins, from which we learn what women have lived and what
> we must refuse to live any longer.[34]

This implies that Sexton's life and work are negative examples—examples of what feminists should not be and do. But we cannot and should not stop here in our attention to women's histories. To dismiss her life and writing as a case study in victimization is to write out the history of the millions of women who have lived under oppressive conditions throughout the world. Likewise, such an assessment forecloses the possibilities of reading her work for its import in the present.

Certainly, the contributions of women writers of the 1960s like Anne Sexton paved the way toward an acceptance of women's voices and experiences as legitimate subjects for feminist writing, theorizing, and critique. But as we look more closely at Sexton's work, we will see how she did not only pave the way for those after her, but she did assert agency and did live a life of vision and value. We might want to say her work anticipates the future, but we must not forget the conditions of the past under which she lived. While her life may be a lesson for us, her work is more: it is indeed a "guide to the ruins" through which we must crawl if we are to be able, inch by inch, to come to terms with our painful pasts and to forage from them something of value, "something special / for someone / in this kind of hope."[35]

Chapter 5

"My eyes are always hungry and remembering": Audre Lorde and the Poetry of Witness

I n the previous chapter, we saw how Anne Sexton was unable to wit-
ness because she had no one with whom she could witness.[1] Now we
turn to the work of Audre Lorde, for whom such witnessing and
rebuilding of intersubjective relations were possible. The difference in
social and historical contexts is striking as we turn to Lorde's life and work,
approximately a decade after Sexton's suicide. We will see that in Lorde's
lifetime she had friends, lovers, and a society who were able to be listeners
to her witnessing.[2] In this chapter, we will explore the process of witness-
ing more thoroughly and show how Lorde overcomes the legacy of silence
through witnessing. Lorde deals with the personal and collective effects of
trauma in several ways. As we have seen, her work remembers and recon-
structs her own painful history and, in so doing, recalls and responds to the
history of African Americans. In the first section of this chapter, we will
look at how Lorde's poetry is a call to witness an unrecognized traumatic
history. In the next section, we will examine how her poetry itself wit-
nesses to this history, and in so doing, opens the way to the possibility of
mutual recognition between all the players in this history.

We are measured by the dreams we avoid

Audre Lorde tells us in an interview with Adrienne Rich that she did not
speak in the first years of her life.[3] And when she did begin to speak, often
it was through poetry: she would recite poems she had memorized. Quite
literally, poetry was a language for Lorde: as a child, she used the poetry of
others to express when she didn't know what to say; later, she wrote her
own when she didn't know how to feel. In poetry, then, she found not a

means to run away, but a means to face what was painful. Further, poetry allowed her to face what she did not yet have clear feelings or a complete story for: as she writes in the essay, "Poetry is Not a Luxury," "[T]hrough poetry we give name to these ideas which are—until the poem—nameless and formless, about to be birthed, but already felt."[4] By speaking through poetry, Lorde teaches, one finds what has been buried, and this leads to positive change: "For as we begin to recognize our deepest feelings, we begin to give up, of necessity, being satisfied with suffering and self-negation, and with the numbness which so often seems like their only alternative in our society."[5]

As Michael Simpson notes in an essay on the traumatic effects of racial oppression: "[S]tudies of the children and the survivors of the Nazi Holocaust . . . suggest that psychological effects of such traumatic events may persist so as to affect the next generations . . . even when they have had no direct experience of the horrors."[6] The effects of a traumatic history of slavery continue to persist, as well. One of Lorde's poems that addresses the psychological aftereffects that result from unwitnessed historical trauma is "To My Daughter the Junkie on a Train."[7] Through this poem, as in many of her poems, Lorde speaks to an addressee—a daughter, a friend, a lover, a sister, a reader—who shares in the witnessing process with Lorde. Through such an address, Lorde makes it possible for an "us" to be born. As this poem shows, the effects of the traumatic past manifest themselves in the present through lack—lack of speech, lack of knowledge, lack of compassion, and lack of nurturing. In turn, these are passed on both collectively through institutions and individually through generations.

In this poem from 1972, Lorde addresses not only a girl, "the junkie on a train," but all of the "[c]hildren we have not borne"—children who are connected to us through the effects of intergenerational and collective trauma, children who are not our genetic descendants but our historical ones. They are the children who live in a world where, continually, the "dream explodes." As in Sexton's poem, "Kind Sir: These Woods," which succeeds Thoreau, Lorde's poem succeeds Langston Hughes' "Harlem."[8] However, such succession is here a repetition of failure. Lorde answers the question, "What happens to a dream deferred?" with the answer, "Look around you, at the children." These children remind us of a past that we would rather forget or avoid. As Lorde writes, "Little girl on the nod / if we are measured by the dreams we avoid / then you are the nightmare / of all sleeping mothers." These children, like the memories of trauma that exist before memory only as flashbacks or nightmares, impose themselves upon us without our permission. These children—and the destruction and disaster that they live—are that which comes back, returns, and makes us face the effects of trauma: "[Y]ou are the nightmare," the speaker tells the girl. She is a nightmare, and so are all the children whose pain recalls a history we would rather forget.[9]

In order to forget, or in order not to remember, we look away. As in Sexton's "Kind Sir: These Woods," the speaker is afraid to look at the product of the dream/nightmare. In this poem, however, not only the speaker but all of the mothers on the train, all of the ancestors in history, "avert their eyes." And we avert our eyes in other ways: by reinforcing a sense of individualism that confirms our right to feel separate, disconnected, and not responsible for these children. We deny responsibility for these children like the parents in the poem who are returning from a PTA meeting, indignant about their own children's rights and well-being while ignoring other children. Or we look away from these children by numbing ourselves; even the speaker is "locked in my own addictions"—using the repetition compulsion to comfort ourselves or to push away feelings. Or we separate ourselves from these children by asserting our autonomy, keeping "one eye/ out / for my own station"—a station which provides an escape and fulfills our desire not to stay with the nightmare, to deny the nightmare, the past, and the effects of the past. The paradoxical nature of trauma, though, means that these children are "painfully sharp and unavoidable," even as we avoid them in all these ways. Finally, the poem reminds us that it will take more than "concern" to "replace what you once needed"—generations of individual parenting and historical nurturance.

Becoming dragonfish to survive / the horrors we are living

Another of Lorde's poems, "Afterimages," written in 1981, will allow us to examine more closely how Lorde's poetry presents witnessing as a solution to historical trauma.[10] The poem is a poem of witnessing, as the speaker remembers and witnesses to the death of Emmett Till and the destruction of a white woman's home by a flood of the Pearl River in Mississippi. Before turning to the poem itself, it will be helpful to remind ourselves of the story of Emmett Till.[11]

On August 28, 1955, a fourteen year old black boy from Chicago, Emmett Till, called "Bo," was visiting his relatives in Money, Mississippi. While in a store with his cousin, he whistled at—or smiled or greeted, it is unclear—a white woman. Some stories say that he did it on a dare; others say that he was trying to be bold, showing his timid Southern cousins how different he was since he was from the North; another account points to

the fact that having contracted polio at the age of five left him with a stut-
ter, which his mother taught him to cure by whistling when he felt it com-
ing on. Whatever his actions were, they pale in comparison to the actions
of three white men, who kidnapped him from his uncle's home that night.
Later his body was found in the Pearl River: he had been mutilated, shot
in the head, lynched, and drowned with a 200–pound cotton gin tied
around his neck. The news of his death was heard—and seen, in pho-
tographs—around the world. His mother managed to have his body taken
back to Chicago, where the body was viewed in an open casket for 5 days
by more than 600,000 people. The three men put on trial for his death
were acquitted.

Emmett Till's death held significance for many reasons. It occurred at a
crucial time in the history of the Civil Rights Movement and stood as a
marker of the reality of the injustice and violence that African Americans
were enduring. It thus served as a catalyst for African Americans themselves
who might have been unwilling to join the Movement until that time. It
also served as an awakening for many whites, forcing them to recognize
their own complicity in racism. As Michael Dyson remarked, "The blood
of Emmett Till was on the hands of every person who watched in malig-
nant silence as black men were lynched, black women were raped, and
black children were intimidated and even murdered" (195). Audre Lorde's
poem, then, is an attempt to convey the complexity of this event in Amer-
ican history, as she links several violent events together—lynching, murder,
rape, and flood—to show, through the linkage, that the processes of awak-
ening, remembering, and witnessing—in short, ending the silence—are the
same for all of them.

The title of the poem, "Afterimages," alerts us to its status as a memory
of traumatic violence. As we have seen, traumatic memories are not in nar-
rative form but are flashes, images, or "afterimages," that remain with the
survivor, repeating themselves within her, assaulting her from within.
Lorde's description of "afterimages" in the first section of the poem paral-
lels what we have learned of traumatic memories: "the image enters," and
once inside, "its force remains within." The force of the event, as we know,
is not experienced at the time of the event, but returns, comes back later,
from within, through flashbacks, dreams, or "flickering images of a night-
mare." It is a nightmare that awakens the survivor, shaking her into waking,
remembering, and reconstructing the event's images. It is through these
ever-present, flashing images that the event is remembered and recon-
structed, "within / my eyes." The eyes, which eat the images, are learning
how to use the memories for food, for survival: "my eyes are always hun-

gry / and remembering." Through remembering and reconstructing, through eating "fused images beneath my pain," the survivor becomes a "dragonfish," and learns to survive through watching and guarding.[12] But, as we have seen in Sexton's work, it is not enough to remember and reconstruct; one must witness, must tell the story, if one is to begin to heal, to go beyond surviving to living. Telling the story, witnessing to the history, is what the poem goes on to do in the later sections.

This poem witnesses to many histories, and in so doing, works to overcome the silences of these histories. First, there is the history of white womanhood, the myth of her purity that held in place the necessity of slavery so that she would not dirty herself through menial work. Second, there is the history of white male violence toward African American men, through which white men assert their power and dominance in the society. Third, there is the history of rape—the rape of black women during slavery and after and the possibility of rape for all women. Third, there is the history of female victimization by male dominance, the history of women's silence and relegation to the realms of home and motherhood. Finally, there is Lorde's own personal history, her coming of age, and her aging in the context of these other histories. Let us look more closely at how Lorde's poem witnesses to each of these histories.

The poem witnesses to the false image of white womanhood, in the name of whose honor white men kill, as Emmett Till was killed "in the name of white womanhood." This image of the white woman, Lorde tells us, is illusory, as the "white woman stands bereft and empty." The illusion is shattered for the white woman whose home is destroyed by the flood, as Lorde records her saying, "'I never knew / it could be so hard.'" This woman "never knew," lived in ignorance of pain and loss, until this flood, which leveled her home and her illusion of immunity to destruction. Once destruction comes, she looks for a savior, a white knight, "her pale eyes scanning the camera for help." She finds none.

The poem also witnesses to the history of white male violence, through which white men, his "teachers," teach others to give them power, as they taught Emmett Till, whom they "hacked into a murderous lesson." Lorde conveys the guilt of white men, as she shows the "master's houses" covered with guilt: "Trapped houses kneel like sinners in the rain." Despite their acquittal, the poem attests that the white men are guilty for Till's death, for destroying "his 15 years puffed out like bruises," for having "ripped his eyes out his sex his tongue / and flung him to the Pearl weighted with stone."

White men not only murder, as the poem shows: they also destroy through rape. Lorde thus uses the poem to witness to rape, as she links the two actions of murder and rape. Lorde compares the pictures of Emmett Till's mutilated body to that of a rape victim, using images of garbage to convey the waste of life in both murder and rape. The media show images of Till's mutilated body:

> used, crumpled, and discarded
> lying amid the sidewalk refuse
> like a raped woman's face.

Lorde further develops the analogy between murder and rape as she testifies that the killers "took their aroused honor / back to Jackson / and celebrated in a whorehouse / the double ritual of white manhood." The comparison is repeated a third time in the final section of the poem, as Lorde writes that Till's "ghost lay like the shade of a raped woman."

The poem also witnesses to female victimization, as Lorde shows that the white woman in the flood is judged by her looks—she is "no longer young"—and is ignored—and her questions to the reporters go "unanswered." Her most important use is as a mother, which Lorde conveys by presenting her children "hurl[ing] themselves against her / hanging upon her coat like mirrors." Finally, she is dominated by her husband; she speaks only, as Lorde writes,

> until a man with ham-like hands pulls her aside
> snarling "She ain't got nothing more to say!"
> and that lie hangs in his mouth
> like a shred of rotted meat.

Lorde also extends her critique of male dominance by insinuating that Emmett Till himself was not immune to the culture of male dominance and female objectification, as he was "testing what he'd been taught was a manly thing to do." Lorde even shows sympathy for the "white girl besmirched by Emmett's whistle," who, Lorde testifies, was dominated and silenced, as well: "never allowed her own tongue / without power or conclusion / unvoiced." Lorde thus connects the woman who "caused" Emmett Till's death with the powerlessness of the white woman whose home has been flooded, and with *all* women who are dominated by men, forced to live in a culture of male violence.

Finally, the poem testifies to Lorde's own personal history, as she writes, "I inherited Jackson, Mississippi. / For my majority it gave me Emmett Till." Emmett Till is her inheritance from the past, as well as her legacy for the future: "he was baptized my son forever / in the midnight waters of the Pearl." Emmett Till, past and future, thus signifies the chain of history, of which Lorde herself is a link. As such, Lorde has to choose: she can either witness to this past, as she does in the poem, or she can fail to witness, as she did in the past, during that summer when she walked with "eyes averted," looking away from the newsstands plastered with pictures of Emmett Till. Lorde was not the only one to fail to witness, though. The media showed, Lorde writes,

> the length of gash across the dead boy's loins
> his grieving mother's lamentation
> the severed lips, how many burns
> his gouged out eyes
> sewed shut upon the screaming covers
> louder than life
> all over

The media were thus engaged in "false witnessing," by detailing the gore of the murder in order to sell the story, in order to make money, in order to "live off" Till's death.[13] In addition to the past failure of witnessing by the media and by Lorde herself, the poem also alludes the failure of witnessing by whites, who, Lorde surmises, take pleasure in the images of violence:

> the veiled warning, the secret relish
> of a black child's mutilated body
> fingered by street-corner eyes
> bruise upon livid bruise

In the poem, then, all of these failures of witnessing finally come to an end. Now, years after, Lorde witnesses to all of these histories, which together cluster around violence and women: women who have survived violence, and who now, through Lorde's poem, "speak / remembering / we were never meant to survive." These women come together in the poem in the lines, "a woman wrings her hands / beneath the weight of agonies remembered." This woman is Lorde herself, who remembers and witnesses to these histories. This woman is also the figure of white womanhood, worrying over the violence perpetrated in her name. This woman is Emmett Till's mother, still alive, still remembering her lost son. This woman is the raped woman whose face Lorde compares to Emmett's bloodied one. This woman is the woman who has lost her home to the flood, who is being dragged away in silence by her husband. As they come together in

Lorde's poem, all these women remember and witness to the many violent histories of our nation. By witnessing, the separate individuals become a *we,* as together these women, each with different "visions," are forced by memory into "becoming dragonfish to survive/ the horrors we are living." To witness, then, is the way to survive "the horrors we are living," horrors that result from histories that affect the present and will continue to affect the future until they are acknowledged. Witnessing opens the way to survival by creating the possibility of a collective "we" that was destroyed by the history of traumatic violence.[14]

What makes Lorde's poetry of witness so compelling is not only that she brings together these different women and shows that despite their differences they "were never meant to survive." In linking her own story with Emmett Till's and with the white woman's in Mississippi, Lorde demonstrates that witnessing to these histories is a process that is at the same time both political and personal, both collective and individual. She shows that our individual, personal link to a political, collective history necessitates a decision: we must choose to witness or not, we must choose to pass guilt or not, we must choose to take responsibility or not. To refuse these choices is, as we have seen, to be a "false witness," to contribute to the continuation, to the perpetuation of violent destruction. To choose to witness, on the other hand, is our only way to open the possibility of hope for an end to such violence in the future. As Robert Jay Lifton asserts,

> [C]arrying through the witness is a way of transmuting pain and guilt into responsibility, and carrying through that responsibility has enormous therapeutic value. It's profoundly valuable *to society and . . . to the individual.* (138, my italics)

While witnessing thus creates hope for the future, it also, as we will see more clearly in Gloria Anzaldúa's writing, gives rise to the necessity for mourning. Mourning is inevitable because of the pain, loss, and heartache that arise when the full recognition of the "horrors we are living" comes to the surface. At the end of "Afterimages," we see that the women—Lorde, white women, Emmett's mother, the raped woman, the woman in the flood—come together as one woman who "soundlessly . . . begins to weep."

Chapter 6

Healing from Awakened Dreams: Anzaldúa as Individual and Collective Witness

Healing from the effects of traumatic history begins with reconstructing and witnessing, as we have seen with regard to Sexton's and Lorde's writing. Now we will examine Anzaldúa's writing, which shows how witnessing is necessary on both individual and collective levels. As we saw in chapter 3, Anzaldúa's writing demonstrates the ways in which traumatic history continues to affect the inheritors of that history both individually and collectively. In this chapter we will first examine the individual level of witnessing through a close reading of Anzaldúa's poem, "that dark shining thing," in which memories are turned from problems into solutions in the presence of a witness who mutually experiences these reconstructions. Then, we will explore Anzaldúa's poem, "Matriz sin tumba o [Womb without tomb]," as an enactment of collective witnessing. In this poem, Anzaldúa serves as a shaman, one who witnesses to the destruction of a culture, in order to bring about healing for the people.

Witnessing to awakened dreams

We saw in chapter three how Anzaldúa returns to these memories both literally and figurally; now in this section we will look at how she heals from these memories through reconstruction and witnessing at the individual, one-to-one level. In *Borderlands/La Frontera,* she describes how she faces the literal return of the traumatic past in trances, which she calls "awakened dreams" (70). Anzaldúa writes that "some of these images are residues of trauma" (70). In an interview, Anzaldúa explains that an awakened dream "always happens with trauma, with a traumatic shock that opens me so brutally—I'm just cracked open by the experience—that for a while things come inside me, other realities, other worlds."[1] Thus, we might say that a person who suffers from a trauma suffers from memories.[2] As Bessel A. van der Kolk and Onno van der Hart write,

> Traumatic memories are the unassimilated scraps of overwhelming experiences, which need to be integrated with existing mental schemes, and be transformed into narrative language. It appears that, for this to occur successfully, the traumatized person has to return to the memory often in order to complete it.[3]

Anzaldúa's writing shows how the pain and the possibility for healing manifest themselves through the body, which, as we have seen in chapter three, is both a source of pain and creation.[4] Traumatic memories are not only images but, as Anzaldúa writes, "tears" and "thrusts" (39); "pain, suffering, and the advent of death" (47). As Roberta Culbertson, a trauma theorist and survivor, writes, "[T]he memory of trauma . . . is . . . also the memory of other levels of reality, sensed not even by the five senses, but by the body itself, or by the spiritual mind, the interior of the body."[5]

Body memories, or somatization, are reminders of a traumatic history that is unacknowledged and unwitnessed. They are caused by, as one physician explains, "the bypassing of mental processes and language and direct expression of danger in the body"; further, somatization may happen when "there is a fear of being overwhelmed by affect."[6] The beginning of turning memories into a solution lies in recognizing them and accepting them as psychological, spiritual, and physical pains that must be attended to. If these pains are ignored, no healing can take place: "The one who speaks without emotion . . . [has] an 'external' memory—socially constructed, skating along the surface of words and engaging the intellect—not the body's reexperience. . . ." (Culbertson 170). It is by attending to the physical manifestations of the trauma, dreams and illnesses, that Anzaldúa begins to turn them into allies for healing. As Maria P. P. Root writes, "Reconstructing one's life following the pain and deep wounds of trauma necessitates an integration of mind, body, and spirit in the healing process."[7]

We can hear echoes of Lorde when Anzaldúa writes of her resistance to the painful feelings that accompany such reconstructions: "I want not to think/that stirs up the pain/opens the wound/starts the healing" (186). The work of healing is achieved, paradoxically, when one "opens the wound," and moves further into the state of illness, which "stirs up the pain." By feeling the feelings of pain that arise upon reopening the wound, one is enabled to move through them and be healed by them. Anzaldúa writes,

> Let the wound caused by the serpent be healed by the serpent. . . . Those
> activities or Coatlicue states which disrupt the smooth flow (complacency)
> of life are exactly what propel the soul to do its work: make soul, increase
> consciousness of itself. Our greatest disappointments and painful experi-
> ences—if we can make meaning out of them—can lead us toward becom-
> ing more of who we are. (46)[8]

Thus, healing stems from paying attention to one's physical, psychological,
and spiritual wounds.

After the recognition of the pain of these wounds, the next step is the
reconstruction of the causes of the wounds. Anzaldúa writes that during
her "awakened dreams" she sees images, which, if not written about
through metaphors, make her ill. As trauma specialists van der Kolk and van
der Hart write, "[T]raumatic memory is inflexible and invariable. Trau-
matic memory has no social component; it is not addressed to anybody, the
patient does not respond to anybody: it is a solitary activity."[9] The key to
healing lies in the flexibility of consciousness to create metaphors for lit-
eral and painful returns of the trauma: "Memory is everything. Once flex-
ibility is introduced, the traumatic memory starts losing its power over
current experience."[10] Anzaldúa echoes their statements when she writes,
"Rigidity means death. Only by remaining flexible is she able to stretch the
psyche horizontally and vertically" (79). This flexibility enables her to
engage in the process of reconstruction: "in reconstructing the traumas
behind the images, I make 'sense' of them. . . . It is then that writing heals
me, brings me great joy" (70).

We have seen with regard to Anne Sexton that the reconstruction of
trauma alone is not enough. In order to turn trauma into survival, one needs
a witness for the reconstruction.[11] Culbertson writes, "To return fully to the
self as socially defined, to establish a relationship again with the world, the
survivor must tell what happened" (179). The witness is so vitally important
because trauma, which cuts connections between people, also cuts off the
survivor's access to an internal witness. Dori Laub puts it in this way:
"[W]hen one cannot turn to a 'you' one cannot say 'thou' even to oneself."[12]

Thus, witnessing produces healing both within and between selves:
"The testimony is, therefore, the process by which the narrator (the sur-
vivor) reclaims his position as a witness: reconstitutes the internal 'thou,' and
thus the possibility of a witness or a listener inside himself" (Laub 70).
Through witnessing, one rebuilds relations between selves as well as within
selves, allowing one to go on to be a witness to oneself, a guardian who
cares for and keeps promises to oneself and to others. In the reconstruction

and witnessing of trauma, one realizes that "Some buried part of you prevailed" (171), as Anzaldúa writes in the poem we will examine next, "that dark shining thing" (171–172).[13]

The poem begins with the word "You've," which alerts us to its status as an address. The "You" is the survivor, the one who needs to witness, but who has "shut the door," refused to feel or to tell of the "darkness" both inside and out. If the survivor opens this door to the listener, the speaker promises that, together, they will find that what has been buried is the internal witness who needs to be brought from the underground, who needs to be reawakened, who needs to be brought back to life.

It is this internal but buried "part" that asks for the speaker to serve as a witness: "elected me to pry open a crack / hear the unvoiced plea." Although unvoiced, the emotions—"hatred, anger / unaware of its source"—alert one to the pain of an unwitnessed trauma. Witnessing is a process of discovering the unknown, which is the source of pain. Until they witness, survivors are "crazed with not knowing / who they are." Thus witnessing is not only a process of discovering the source of pain but also a process of discovering a new identity.

This identity needs to be discovered through relationship; thus the survivor must find a witness, must "choose me" to serve as the witness. The speaker lists several factors in the survivor's choice: the witness must look like someone who can identify, who looks "alike." This identification is important, for it is through the identification with the other that the survivor can rebuild an internal witness. Hence, during the witnessing process, the "I" and the "you" will be confused: "I am the flesh you dig your fingernails into / mine the hand you chop off while still clinging to it." The process of witnessing shows us quite dramatically how the self is indeed constructed through the other.

The witnessing process is filled with pain, fear, and the risk of craziness for both participants not only because of the painful *content* of the witnessing process but also because of the *process* of identity-confusion itself: "I risk your sanity / and mine." We see how the two people become confused during the process: "I remember hating him/me/they who pushed me / as I'm pushing you." In order not to be submerged by the weight of the content and the process, the listener approaches and retreats, thereby maintaining an equilibrium: "I want to turn my back on you / wash my hands of you / but my hands remember each seam."

Yet, despite her desire to turn away once and for all, the witness is effective *precisely because* she feels and relives the experience through the reconstruction with the speaker: "as you stumble I falter too / and I remember."

Moreover, the witness is often someone who has survived a trauma herself, as shown in the lines that imply that the listener has done her own witnessing: "he/me/they who shouted / push Gloria breathe Gloria." This memory is relived in the present, as we see in the switch of tenses: "until I'm facing that pulsing bloodied blackness / trying to scream / from between your legs." The use of the present tense shows how the listener relives in the present, during the process of witnessing, her own previous traumatic experiences and witnessing processes. Thus, in its intimacy and mutuality, and in its pain and labor, witnessing is giving birth: to the experience as story, to the relationship between survivor and witness, and to the new self that is born within.

However, the end of a successful witnessing process often coincides with feelings of "guilt" at having survived: "It was then that I saw the numinous thing / it was black and it had my name." This guilt arises after witnessing is completed, just at the moment when it seems that the survivor has a chance to leave the trauma behind. Perhaps it is this chance to go on with life that makes the survivor feel guilty for leaving the dead behind.[14] The immensity of the survivor's guilt often keeps one locked in denial, in a premature celebration of healing: "I don't know how long I can keep naming / that dark animal / coaxing it out of you, out of me / keep calling it good or woman-god / while everyone says no no no." The denial also manifests itself as blame: "I know I am that beast / . . . But I know you are the Beast." In blaming others for our guilt, we try to make others our "prey" in order to avoid mourning. Yet, despite all attempts to ignore the "dark animal" or "the Beast," guilt remains after witnessing and must be dealt with through mourning—mourning all that one had to do in order to survive, all that one failed to do in order to have survived. As Henry Krystal, a psychiatrist who has worked with Holocaust survivors in the United States, writes, "to accept the negative aspects of one's self . . . requires a capacity for effective grieving."[15]

Thus, even as witnessing gives birth to a new self and a new way of seeing, of "opening my eyes one day," it also opens one's eyes to a new sense of loss, of "sensing that something was missing." Successful witnessing gives rise to the necessity for mourning all the losses associated with trauma: the loss of the experience itself, the loss of the life that would have been free of trauma, the literal lives of those who did not survive the trauma, and the loss of a life without the necessary and arduous processes of dealing with and healing from the trauma. In the poem, the speaker says, "Missing was the pain, gone the fear / that all my life had walked beside me." We do not want to be too quick to read this as positive, for these lines also carry a deep sadness. We can understand this if we try to imagine how these emotions—pain and fear—were the survivor's companions on her long life journey, and often were the only companions who stayed with her over the years. The end of witnessing marks the beginning of mourning this sadness, this loss.

While witnessing helps to rebuild the relations between and within selves, it also makes us face what cannot be rebuilt. As Dori Laub writes, "the act of bearing witness at the same time *makes* and *breaks* a promise" (Laub 73). The promise that it breaks, writes Laub, is this:

> That there is no healing reunion with those who are, and continue to be, missing, no recapture or restoration of what has been lost, no resumption of an abruptly innocent childhood. . . .The testimony is inherently a process of *facing loss*—of going through the pain of the act of witnessing, and the ending of the act of witnessing—which entails yet another repetition of the experience of separation and loss. (73–74)

It is mourning that will ultimately complete the healing process. The poem concludes with the lines, "I know it's come down to this: / *vida o muerte,* life or death." This is the border between life and death, the border upon which the process of witnessing comes to an end. The end of witnessing gives rise to the process of mourning, as we will see in chapter 9.

But first, let us move from this examination of individual witnessing to an exploration of the process of collective witnessing in Anzaldúa's writing. In doing so, we move from the one-to-one reconstruction and reexperiencing of "awakened dreams" to a reading of these "dreams" at the level of collective myth. Anzaldúa writes:

> My "awakened dreams" are about shifts. Thought shifts, reality shifts, gender shifts: one person metamorphoses into another in a world where people fly through the air, heal from mortal wounds. I am playing with my Self, I am playing with the world's soul, I am the dialogue between my Self and *el espíritu del mundo.* I change myself, I change the world. (70)

In the next section, we will examine how these "shifts" bring change, bring healing, not only for Anzaldúa herself as an individual but for the community, for the people, for the collective.

In the Tradition of the Shaman

In an essay written eight months after the publication of *Borderlands/La Frontera,* Anzaldúa writes, "I realize that I was trying to practice the oldest 'calling' in the world—shamanism. And that I was practicing it in a new way."[16] The practice of shamanism has several elements that can be traced in Anzaldúa's text. First, the shaman is a traveler, one who goes from one side to another and then back again in order to bring back wisdom. As Roberta Culbertson writes, shamanic experiences are about transcending or breaking boundaries just as traumatic experiences are.[17] Second, the shaman's objective is the healing of the body and spirit of an individual or a community.[18] We have seen in chapter three that Anzaldúa uses the image of picking a cactus needle out of the flesh to convey the pain of trauma that is lodged in the flesh; she calls this "an endless cycle of making it worse, making it better, but always making meaning out of the experience, whatever it may be" (73). Third, the shaman works through art, such as painting, music, dance, and poetry. As Anzaldúa writes, "In the ethno-poetics and performance of the shaman, my people, the Indians, did not split the artistic from the functional, the sacred from the secular, art from everyday life. The religious, social, and aesthetic purposes of art were all intertwined" (66). In the Mesoamerican tradition, the literary, like the artistic, is seen as an act that connected the individual with the community and the latter with the gods.[19] Inseparable from the sacramental and the communal, then, both literary and artistic activities were manifestations of the sacred and the collective.[20] In these three ways, then, Anzaldúa's writing follows in the tradition of the shaman: first, she makes a crossing from life through death and back; second, she shares her new understanding of how the splitting of mind and body—good and bad, and life and death—contribute to the blockage of healing; and finally, she connects that which has been split in order to provide a vision of healing for the individual and the community.

We have seen how Anzaldúa's writing shows a life filled with the effects of trauma, with the effects of having survived a threat of death. This threat, as we explored in chapter three, stems from her identity as a Chicana, from her identity as a person belonging to a group that has suffered historical, collective trauma. Her own, individual story has traumatic woundings, as well. In the autobiographical essay, "La Prieta," from, 1981, Anzaldúa writes of suffering from menstrual bleeding from the age of three months; she writes of the pain of it, both physical—"raging fevers . . . cramps"—and spiritual—"there was something wrong with me. . . . I was not of this planet" (199–200).[21] As a young woman, Anzaldúa underwent a full hysterectomy—"My bowels fucked with a surgeon's knife, uterus and ovaries pitched into the trash" (208).[22] Together, these experiences lead her to see herself as having passed through death, and this leads her to ask, "But for what purpose?" (199)

The answer to this question can be found, in part, by reading Anzaldúa's poem, "Matriz sin tumba o [Womb without tomb]" (136–138). Through a reading of the poem, we can examine the ways in which Anzaldúa's writing follows in the tradition of the shaman, as she begins to connect the peculiarity of her "wound" with a collective history of traumatic violence. The poem is one of the few in *Borderlands/La Frontera* that appears only in Spanish; in contrast to those like "No se raje, Chicanita / Don't give in, Chicanita," which we discussed in chapter three, the poem is not focused on an optimistic vision of the future but instead presents a vivid scene of pain. This pain, Anzaldúa reminds us by writing in Spanish, is a particular pain that arises out of her specific identity as a Chicana.[23]

While the poem could indeed be read biographically, as a dramatization of Anzaldúa's experience of a hysterectomy, it is also something more: a rendering of a shamanistic encounter with death. The form of the stanzas parallels the crossing between life and death, as each goes back and forth between the life-world and the death-world. As the first-person speaker, "I," undergoes a near-death encounter in the life-world, the third-person persona, "she," experiences a shamanistic vision in "dream space." The connection between the life and death worlds is made in the first stanza where the speaker, "I," is sick in both body and spirit. She is bleeding and vomiting, as are the figures in a picture that represents the Land of the Dead from an Aztec codex.[24] And she suffers emotionally, feels she is "nothing," "Degenerate." Her sickness, then, may be a result of a trauma, which, unacknowledged, manifests itself in repetitions and a lack of understanding: "revolving and repeating words without meaning." Paradoxically, she must move from being "on the edge / of a cloudy night" to going further into the night, further into the death experience in order to pass through it.

Crossing into death is what happens in the next stanza as "she" goes to the other side when the thorn pricks her. The thorn, which we explored in our earlier reading of the poem, "Nopalitos," is a symbol of the further pain, the further wounding that is necessary in order for healing to begin. In "Nopalitos," we saw how Anzaldúa picks her way through history in order to heal; here she picks her way through death, as she "surrenders" to it. The final two lines of this stanza begin with "Sueña," which means she sleeps and she dreams. This word is repeated in subsequent stanzas. Here I translate it as "She sleeps," since the line reads, "Sueña *con*," "She sleeps *with* a woman who urinates pus / and eats her own excrement" (italics mine). This horrible image recalls the figure of Tlazolteotl, the goddess whose name means garbage, and who represents the earth and all things carnal, including sex and death.[25] Erich Neumann writes that Tlazolteotl is "the goddess of pleasure and death . . . voluptuousness and sin, but also the great generatrix and renewer of vegetation through the sexual act; as moon and earth goddess, she is the goddess of the west, of death, and of the under-world."[26] The term "sueña" then, brings together both the sexual and the spiritual connotations of the encounter with this figure.

The next stanza turns from the shamanistic experience of "she" who encounters the goddess, and returns to the "I" who continues to show the signs of having survived an unacknowledged trauma: she is repeating the same words as in the first stanza. She is "[l]ike trash," blown by the wind that pushes her along, as she goes further into death, further into the "beastly night." Death is eating at her like a "vulture in my belly" that enters her, cuts her, and takes out parts of her. Death then disposes of her womb, her life force, her creative force. It gets no burial, but is simply dropped "in the trash." Like a traumatic loss that is traumatic by virtue of its not being witnessed, this loss is not witnessed, is not acknowledged as a death, is not given the ritual of a burial or a "tomb."

The poem crosses again back into the underworld as, in the next stanza, "Sueña / she dreams" of the goddess of garbage, Tlazolteotl, who is now named. This is a goddess who would transform humanity's mistakes, their garbage, and with yellow and green water, cleanse them, make them anew.[27] Thus, she dreams that Tlazolteotl will bathe what has been disposed of as garbage, will bless her womb. This stanza also connects her own death crossing with history, as the sun is pierced and swallowed, is destroyed "four times, five." This is the number of suns in Mesoamerican mythology; *Borderlands / La Frontera* was written during the time of the Fifth Sun. Thus, she wants to know if she is dead, like the myths, like the earlier worlds destroyed. If so, she asks to have her womb, her life-giving, creative force buried with her. She asks for the death to be acknowledged; she wants a ritual for it.

In the next stanza, the body of the first-person speaker shows signs of being dead; she has the "marks of death" that we will see in Sexton's poetry of crossing. Indeed, her body is dead, as "Someone pushes me into the light," a common image for entering death. As she sees these images of light and fire—"lightning" and "[s]parks"—she takes these as signs of a final death, and she prepares to leave "this murderous life." Someone starts to mourn and cry for her.

We cross again for the final time in the following stanza as "she" sees the shamanistic vision that she will bring back from this place of spirit. She sees the cruelty of a "blackened soul," one that destroys and causes bloodshed and then heartlessly goes on to eat rich food. This figure has "made the west a scar." The significance of the west for Aztec mythology is conveyed by Neumann when he writes,

> The sun sinks down in the west, where it dies and enters the womb of the underworld that devours it. For this reason the west is the place of death. . . . The west is also the place of women, the primeval home, where mankind once crawled from the primordial hole in the earth.[28]

Thus, in her shamanistic vision, Anzaldúa sees that the place of both birth and death, the womb of the world, has been scarred, has been wounded; we might read this as the wounding of the Western part of the United States, and of the globe, through traumatic violence. The traumatic violence that has produced this "scar," or border, has occurred repeatedly ("two times, three"), and will continue to do so as long as we stay in this period of traumatic violence, as is designated by the number, "seven," the number that is a symbol of "a complete period or cycle," as well as a "symbol of pain."[29]

In the end she returns to life; however, it would have been easier, perhaps, if she died. She returns with the knowledge that to live is to survive, and to survive is to suffer, as if with an illness: "a recurring infirmity / that purges me of death." Even after coming back from death, she continues to bleed, to suffer from the destruction she saw in her vision. She is left at the end continuing the turning, the repetitions without meaning. She is left, as well, without an acknowledgment that her womb, her life-force is missing. Further, she is left without a ritual that commemorates the loss.[30] All of this destruction will continue as long as there is no acknowledgment of it, as long as it is unwitnessed. Unless this happens, the "pieces" shattered in the destruction are pushed by the wind. These pieces are the remains of what was broken by the destruction.

Thus we see how Anzaldúa's writing follows in the tradition of a shaman, as she witnesses to the collective destruction of the West. In so doing, Anzaldúa follows in the footsteps of a tradition that dates back to the peoples who crossed the Bering Straights to come to America.[31] And by crossing through the spirit world, Anzaldúa brings back the capacity to diagnose the symptoms of a history of traumatic violence, symptoms that manifest themselves as splits between life and death, body and spirit, good and bad. She then uses this wisdom to enact the healing of these splits for the future survival of the people. Her work, she now knows after this shamanistic journey, is to gather the pieces together, and to make something new from the remains. She does this through a revision of the female figures of mythology, La Malinche, the Virgin of Guadalupe, and Coatlicue, as we will see in the next chapter on Anzaldúa. For all three, Sexton, Lorde, and Anzaldúa, healing from trauma means turning from autobiography to mythology, recognizing the spiritual promise of facing horror, and finding in myth the symbols that might lead to the construction of a new history.

PART III

There's a component that is very much part of the unconscious—part of the spirit world—that's also part of us, but we've been told it's not there so we don't perceive it. . . . According to the Olmacs, the Toltecs, the Mayans, the Aztecs, and others, this physical reality is just one facet or facade of the spirit world. This is a mask for the spirit world, so that you and I are just masks for the spirit. We're just the costume; we're just the clothes. And if you can take the mask off or go behind the mask, you are let into a connection with this other reality, of the spirit.

I think with me it always happens with trauma, with a traumatic shock of some kind that opens me so brutally—I'm just cracked open by the experience—that for a while things come inside me, other realities, other worlds. Like when I was mugged I became aware of things that had to do with the landscape and the trees and this particular ravine where it happened. I could almost hear their vibrations because every living thing has vibrations, has a speed of vibrating. And somewhere really, really, really far back in our history I think someone got really scared of this connection with the spirit and the spiritual world, put down the wall, and concentrated on using our hands rather than our imaginations to achieve certain things.

—Gloria Anzaldúa, in an interview
dated October 25, 1991

Chapter 7

"I wish to enter her like a dream": Anne Sexton and the Prophecy of Healing

As we have seen, it is only now, after twenty years of developments in feminism and psychoanalysis, that the significance of Sexton's life and work can be recognized. Likewise, Sexton's spiritual poetry can be read, only now, for its important and visionary qualities. I will show how Sexton not only struggled alone to make sense of her pain, but also how she managed, alone, to create a vision of healing from her pain. Recent critics, given the benefit of twenty years of change in society, have begun to reassess Sexton's work for its innovative ideas about sexuality and spirituality. Some focus on Sexton's ability to celebrate the body and its erotic life in her poetry.[1] Others link the prophetic quality of her later work to recent developments in feminist spirituality.[2] Still others, and I locate myself in this category, make explicit connections between the attempt to celebrate the sexual and the spiritual.[3] Given the argument I have made earlier concerning childhood sexual trauma, I will argue, Sexton's vision of healing from that trauma consists of a connection between the body and spirit. Trauma injures both the body and the spirit; a vision of healing from trauma must address both the body and the spirit together. As Maria P. P. Root writes, "The [spiritual] characteristic of feminism is important to trauma, because one of the prominent wounds of trauma is the crushing of the human spirit . . . which may be the hardest wound to heal."[4]

Yet such a vision of healing is not wholly disconnected from history, either. As I will show, Sexton's particular vision for a future where women are healed from their trauma comes from her growing understanding of history. We will see how Sexton crosses through history in order to arrive at a vision for the future. Thus, Sexton's vision is not utopian in a strict sense but rather is historical, as Simone de Beauvoir's description of the split between sexuality and spirituality in Christianity shows:

> The Christian is divided within himself; the separation of body and soul, life and spirit, is complete; original sin makes of the body the enemy of the soul; all ties of the flesh seem evil. . . . Evil is an absolute reality; and the flesh is sin. And, of course, since woman remains always the Other, it is not held that reciprocally male and female are both flesh: the flesh that is for the Christian the hostile Other is precisely woman. In her the Christian finds incarnated the temptations of the world, the flesh, and the devil.[5]

Sexton's attempt to rewrite this history of "female sexuality . . . as the agent by means of which sin came into the world" is, then, not only an attempt to heal herself from a history of a personally traumatic past.[6] Sexton's vision is also an attempt to provide a vision for all women of new possibilities for imagining sex and spirit as sources of goodness and not only sites of woundings.[7]

What makes Sexton's attempt particularly remarkable is that she manages to bring sexuality and spirituality together. She does not, as many white feminists of the nineteenth century did, focus only on the higher spiritual nature of women in order to argue for women's worth. Nor does she only celebrate sexuality without an understanding of how body and spirit are connected, as many second-wave white feminists have done. Instead, she shows, as de Beauvoir did, how women's bodies, women's spirits, and women's oppression exist together, and through her poetry, Sexton presents a vision of the possibility for healing at all levels. Sexton's experience as a survivor of sexual trauma allows her to gain a personal as well as philosophical understanding of how women's bodies have been marked by the violent opposition between self and other. To claim her body as her own, Sexton's poetry teaches us, a woman must learn to acknowledge her own feelings, desires, and pains as her own. This means turning from the other as arbiter of needs and desires toward the self, toward a sense of self within. To develop this sense of a spirit internal to the self is, as we will see in Sexton's poetry, parallel to claiming one's body as one's own. And, by showing how both women's bodies and women's spirits have been split and co-opted by violence, Sexton opens the way toward showing how they must be reconnected and reclaimed for a vision of healing.

This vision, as we will examine, while it predates the development of "feminist spirituality" in our country, also uncannily foretells its most essential insights.[8] Feminist spirituality is attentive to the wounding of women and seeks to help to repair these wounds. As Cynthia Eller writes, "concerns that are generally labeled therapeutic—recovering from childhood trauma, for example—are a common focus of spiritual feminist thought and ritual action" (66). Thus, a woman who, like Sexton, has been sexually traumatized, would find in feminist spirituality an avenue for addressing the spiritual, and not only the psychological, pain of surviving the trauma.

The way to heal the spiritual wound of sexual trauma is to reclaim sexuality itself as good. Eller writes that spiritual feminists believe that "Sexuality can be abused—usually by men—but in itself it is not only acceptable, but sacred" (138). To help women see sexuality as sacred, feminist spirituality valorizes all aspects of women's experience, including women's sexuality. Thus, feminist spirituality attempts to attain the goal of "restoring to women the right to be sexual" (17).

Likewise, feminist spirituality valorizes nature, personifying it as a woman or a mother, and interpreting its actions as lessons or guides for human action. Nature often provides, then, the imagery for a re-imagination of the goddess. As Eller writes, "she is in nature, she affirms life and sexuality, she is in each woman" (132). Further, the cycles of nature are said to coincide with the character of the goddess: a figure that is both negative and positive together, and associated with "birth and death (and rebirth)" (139).

Finally, spiritual feminists look to a reconstruction of history for validation of their faith in such a "mother goddess" (143). Many feminist anthropologists, historians, and theologians attempt to reconstruct the matriarchal religions of the past, or reinterpret ancient archaeological remains, or rewrite mythologies in order to lend support to evidence of a cover up of the goddess by patriarchal religion.[9] Sexton's poetry anticipates all of these aspects of contemporary feminist spirituality: an emphasis on healing, a valorization of women and nature, and a revision of history. These elements can be found not only in her later poetry, but, as I will argue, throughout her poetry. Interestingly, Marija Gimbutas, one of the first women to do archeological research on "goddess cultures" in ancient Europe, was, with Sexton, one of the original group of 24 women to receive fellowships from Radcliffe, very early in Sexton's career, in 1961.[10] As a member of the generation of women to develop feminist spirituality, then, Sexton presents a prophecy of healing for the future.

Sexton's prophecy comes through crossings. First, her poetry enacts a crossing through history, as she returns to and revises women's history in order to trace the genealogy of women's oppression. Sexton also presents a striking revision of the possibilities for the character of Mary in women's lives, as Sexton shows how Mary can help women cross through the past, cross over their own pain, and cross out their own death. Sexton also crosses through gender, as, in the middle period of her career, her poetry briefly tries to envision the dissolution of gender categories in the hope that women's oppression might be dissolved with them. Finally, when this attempt at the destruction of gender is unsuccessful, Sexton's poetry crosses through touch. Her later poetry shows how she herself crosses over from death to life, as, through touch, she begins to heal from having been marked by death. Together these crossings enable her to envision the possibility of healing both sex and spirit, a vision of healing for herself and for all women for whom life is marked by violence.

Crossing through history

A reading of "Jesus Suckles" from *The Book of Folly,* Sexton's first book after *Transformations,* shows Sexton's attempt to sketch an outline for her growing understanding of the history of women's oppression (337–338).[11] In this poem, Sexton presents this history as precisely a crossing through, as a negation of earlier periods in history, by which the importance of women's roles is drastically reduced.

The poem is divided into three parts that are different in form as well as content. The whole poem shows three views of the mother: as goddess, as mother, and as woman. These three views correspond to the three stanzas, and these are the three views of the mother that Sexton presents in her poetry, as well.

The first stanza is the longest and contains disparate metaphors, as the speaker attempts to find an image that would convey the relation between the two figures, "You" and "I." At times, the analogies are of a mother and infant: the mother is summed up through her most vital parts, "white apples" and a "heart," while the breastfeeding infant is "glad" as he dozes, coughs, and sucks. In other ways the relationship is more sexual, as the woman becomes a "wife," a "lily," while the male figure calls himself "the bee that gets inside." But the relationship is something more than these common relationships between female and male—wife and husband, mother and son—in our culture; it is something larger, more akin to nature. The woman is the "rock," the foundation for life: "You're a rock and I the fringy algae." And finally, in an image that will reappear throughout Sexton's later poetry, the woman is "the sea": "I'm a kid in a rowboat and you're the sea." As the sea, she is not only the water of Sexton's earlier "Music Swims Back to Me," but she is also the "salt" and "every fish of importance." Thus, the first stanza shows Sexton's attempt to portray the great mother, the ancient goddess, as a great expanse, a source of life, a life-world.

The second stanza moves from an image of woman as goddess and source of life and nurturance to woman as mother, as the former is reduced to "lies." The destruction of the former relationship is communicated through negation: "No. No." Now the relation between the two is not conveyed through images of nature, nor is it in any way sexual. Both of these elements drop out as the female figure becomes a human mother whose only functions are to hold and give milk (which does not necessarily come from her breast anymore) to the infant. Because of the female image's great reduction in importance, and perhaps as a result of their new equal status— "we are the same"—the male figure is "glad."

In the final stanza, which is even shorter than the other two, the female figure is not a goddess, not a mother, not even human. The earlier images are destroyed, as the male figure becomes "a truck," an instrument of the market economy, which "run[s] everything." The male figure thus takes complete power as the female becomes an object owned by him.[12] As the final line, "I own you," shows, she now holds the place of the object "you" to be acted upon rather than the subject "you" who acts. In the move from subject to object, this first poem of "The Jesus Papers" presents a vision of the fall of the female image from nature, goddess, and mother to an owned object.

The poem that ends "The Jesus Papers," entitled "The Author of the Jesus Papers Speaks," prefigures the speaker's attempt in her later poetry to return to the goddess (344–345). However, in this last poem in the series, the "lily" is no longer the succulent flower that the bee crawls into; instead it is "rubber." And the result of the search for a "white mother" is not milk but "blood," which stands for the violence that pervades the society and "cover[s] me with shame."

Hence, the final poem of "The Jesus Papers" parallels the beginning, as Sexton shows how the sacrifice of the mother/goddess has been made to produce a patriarchal religion based on sacrifice, how the milk has been replaced with blood. Through her poetry, Sexton presents a reading of history in which images of women fall through the centuries from powerful agents and sources of life to powerless objects owned and destroyed by men. The move in this series of poems, from the most ancient to the most recent, will be reversed, as we will see; Sexton's subsequent poems show her rowing backwards from the present to the past to search for a vision of healing for women.

Crossing through Mary

Long before *The Awful Rowing Toward God,* which is considered by many critics to be Sexton's first spiritual book, Sexton's poetry is concerned with spiritual questions. One such poem is "Letter Written on a Ferry While Crossing Long Island Sound," from *All My Pretty Ones* (1962), Sexton's second book (81–84).[13] In this poem, Sexton presents three of the elements of her spiritual quest: the sea, Mary, and crossing. The poem begins with the lines, "I am surprised to see / that the ocean is still going on," which marks the ocean, like the speaker who has "made it this far," as a survivor. The speaker survives, as many critics suppose, after the end of an affair, from which she is "going back." But this line, "Now I am going back," can be read in the light of Sexton's larger quest: to go back to the goddess. This search begins with images of Mary:

> The sea is very old.
> The sea is the face of Mary,
> without miracles or rage
> or unusual hope,
> grown rough and wrinkled
> with incurable age. (81)

Here, as throughout the early poetry, Sexton's use of Mary corresponds with the search for a divine female figure in the midst of patriarchal religion.[14] In this poem, Sexton portrays the sea, her figure for the ancient goddess, with Mary's face, the synchretic symbol of the survival of the ancient figure. Thus all three—the sea, which "is very old," Mary, "with incurable age," and the speaker, who says, "Oh, all right . . . I'll save myself"—are all survivors.

Moreover, here, as well as in other early poems, Mary is characterized as a conduit to a crossing. In "For the Year of the Insane" (131–133) from her third book, *Live or Die* (1966), Sexton writes,[15]

> O Mary, fragile mother,
> hear me, hear me now. . . .
> Mary, permit me this grace,
> this crossing over (131).

Thus, through Mary, Sexton prays for survival, and beyond mere survival, a wisdom that comes from surviving the crossings between life and death. As we saw in Anzaldúa's work, there is wisdom to be gained through crossing the border between life and death. This wisdom gives meaning to the experience of survival. For Sexton, the survival of the crossing is made possible by Mary, who hears in ways that those around her do not. As the speaker tries to pray, "Word for word, I stumble. / A beginner, I feel your mouth touch mine" (131). Thus, here, as elsewhere, Sexton equates prayer with touch. The prayer, the touch, is what allows her to survive, to move through death.

The survival of death is made possible by Mary, who hears and guides the crossing, and by water, by the unconscious remembrances of "Music Swims Back to Me." As we will see in the later poetry, Sexton combines the qualities of both Mary and water, and these come together in the figure of the sea. But before we get to that point, we are left at the end of this poem with the speaker still searching:

> O Mary, open your eyelids . . .
> O mother of the womb,
> did I come for blood alone? (133)

We are left with the voice of a woman searching in the age of patriarchal religion, the age of blood. She looks to Mary, the shadow of the earlier mother-goddess, and asks if there is another possibility, another world than the one of sacrificing women, of bloodshed.

Crossing through gender and race

Sexton's increasing dissatisfaction with the possibilities for women in patriarchal religion leads her to envision a disintegration of gender categories. As she writes in "Consorting with Angels" (111–112) also from *Live or Die* (1966): "I was tired of being a woman." The speaker goes on to list the typical women's objects that she is tired of: "the spoons and the pots . . . my mouth and my breasts . . . the cosmetics and the silks" (111). Then, as Middlebrook puts it, Sexton moves from a concern with oppression to the creation of a vision.[16] The first stanza ends, "I was tired of the gender of things" (111). In the rest of the poem, the speaker presents her vision of a world without "my common gender" (112):

> Adam was on the left of me
> and Eve was on the right of me. . . .
> We wove our arms together

and rode under the sun.
I was not a woman anymore,
not one thing or another.
I am black and I am beautiful. . . .
I'm no more woman
than Christ was a man. (112)

Interestingly, Sexton's vision of a genderless world, a world where she can link arms with Adam and Eve and fly under the sun, a world where she is as divine as Christ, is also a world where she is "black and beautiful."[17] Perhaps imagining the destruction of gender enables Sexton to identify with other types of difference, such as race. Or perhaps once gender is not the primary category of analysis, then it becomes necessary to deal with race and racial oppression. In an interview with Barbara Kevles taped on August 15, 1968 and published in *The Paris Review,* Sexton remarked:

> As for the civil right issue . . . I think it's a major issue. I think many of my poems—about the individual who is dispossessed, must play slave, who cries freedom now, power now—are about the human experience of being Black in this world. A black emotion can be a white emotion. It is a crisis for the individual as well as for the nation. I think I've been writing black poems all along—wearing my white mask. I'm always the victim—but no longer.[18]

These remarks show that Sexton did, indeed, identify with the struggles of African Americans at the time—albeit clumsily, and with racist undertones. The linking of gender and race appears in another poem from *Live or Die,* as well. In "Somewhere in Africa," there are two deities: a god of men and of institutions and a goddess of women and of poetry, as Middlebrook points out.[19] This goddess is black:

> Let God be some tribal female who is known but forbidden.
>
> Let there be this god who is a woman who will place you
> upon her shallow boat, who is a woman naked to the waist,
> moist with palm oil and sweat, a woman of some virtue
> and wild breasts, her limbs excellent, unbruised and chaste.
>
> Let her take you. (107)

Sexton foresees a goddess who is a black, "tribal female," and who is unashamedly sexual: "naked to the waist . . . moist . . . wild . . . excellent" while at the same time "of some virtue . . . unbruised and chaste." In this poem, Sexton uses a racially sexualized mythological figure to convey the hope of a healing goddess. One critic, Francis Bixler, names the female figure of this poem a "goddess," who—"beautiful, erotic, unspoiled, virtuous, even wild—suggests hidden fountains of creativity hitherto undiscovered by the human race."[20] As we will see when we examine Lorde's and Anzaldúa's work, this goddess is not undiscovered, but rather, has been covered.

Crossing through touch

In chapter 1, we saw that many critics were sidetracked by debates over whether Sexton's work is feminine or feminist; this allowed them to avoid discussion of the painful ambiguities of her life and work. The same avoidance can be found in the critical debates over Sexton's spiritual poetry. Beginning with *The Awful Rowing Back to God,* critics begin to recognize Sexton as a spiritual poet.[21] In this volume she attempts to envision a deity that is formed through a marriage or coming together of both male and female. One critic calls the book a search for both a mythic mother and father.[22] However, many critics focus more on the father-god images of the volume, and in so doing, are led to conclude that Sexton abandoned her search for a mother-god. After having traveled to Squirrel Island, Sexton's grandfather's home, Diana Hume George remarks that Sexton looks for the source of her god in the family patriarchs: "Collapsing the identities of mother and daughter, this daughter seeks both erotic and spiritual union with the father."[23] Another critic argues that beginning with *The Awful Rowing Toward God,* Sexton "unfortunately seeks connections with a masculine god."[24] And finally, Alicia Ostriker goes so far as to say that Sexton's "religion is determinedly patriarchal."[25] In short, these critics focus on the male image of God in this book in order to avoid dealing with the issue of sexuality that informs Sexton's spirituality. If, as I have argued, the significance of Sexton's life and work stems from her individual attempts at survival and healing in a society that did not recognize her trauma, then it follows that her visions of healing from trauma would not have been recognized either. By recognizing that Sexton was a survivor of childhood sexual trauma, we are enabled also to recognize the ingenuity of her vision of healing from trauma.

Thus, as we turn to examining Sexton's vision of healing from childhood sexual trauma, we should keep in mind the particularity of her wound. In the last poem of *The Awful Rowing Toward God,* "The Rowing

Endeth," (473–474), the speaker has rowed to the island to talk with God the father, and arrives:

> with blisters that broke and healed
> and broke and healed—
> saving themselves over and over. (473)

These wounds that have "broke[n] and healed" repeatedly are the signs of having survived trauma. The effects of sexual trauma, as we have seen in Sexton's life, are both physical and spiritual; the wound is felt as a physical and a spiritual pain. Healing from trauma, then, must take place both physically and spiritually. As we saw in the poem, "For the Year of the Insane," such healing takes place through touch. This touch is difficult to achieve, however, in a world where relationships are characterized more often by violent than mutual touch. As Sexton writes in the first poem of *The Awful Rowing Toward God*,

> Then there was life
> with its cruel houses
> and people who seldom touched—
> though touch is all. (417)

Thus, in order to examine the full significance of Sexton's vision of healing, we must not only look at her images of god but also her images of touch. To do so, we will turn from *Live or Die,* from which we examined the poems, "Consorting with Angels," "For the Year of the Insane," and "Somewhere in Africa," to Sexton's next book, *Love Poems,* from 1969.[26] As one critic writes, "In *Love Poems,* the Cartesian split between mind and body is tentatively bridged by liberation of Eros, the uniting force of love."[27]

The first poem in Love Poems is entitled, "The Touch" (173–174). In this poem, Sexton puts forth her vision of healing through touch. At the beginning of the poem, the speaker says, "For months my hand had been sealed off / in a tin box." She wonders why, and guesses that "it is bruised." Once again, the wound that needs healing is characterized as a physical wound. The way to heal the wound is physical as well; it is, quite simply, the need "for something to touch / that touches back." This mutual touch happens in the last stanza:

> Then all this became history.
> Your hand found mine.
> Life rushed to my fingers. . . . (174)

When healing comes through touch, then the past, the time before healing, becomes "history," becomes a story that can be told, a story of a time that is no more. Lack of touch is death; touch brings back life. Touch not only brings back life, but it prevents death, as the last lines of the poem show:

> My hand is alive all over America
> Not even death will stop it,
> death shedding her blood.
> Nothing will stop it, for this is the kingdom
> and the kingdom come. (173–174)

Thus, we begin to see how Sexton's poetry moves from a critique of patriarchal religion, the religion of blood that we examined earlier, to a vision of healing ("the kingdom come") that includes the connection between sexuality and spirituality.

The spiritual power of sexual touch is developed further in Sexton's 1974 volume of poetry, *The Death Notebooks*.[28] The volume opens with a poem entitled, "Gods," which narrates the attempt by "Mrs. Sexton" to look for the gods (349). After searching various places such as in the sky, in books, and in churches and pyramids, the search ends when

> . . . she journeyed back to her own house
> and the gods were shut in the lavatory. (349).

Thus, the first poem sets the tone for the very physical, raw material characteristic of the entire volume. One such poem that, in lavatory language, shows Sexton's literally crude attempt to link sexuality and spirituality can be found in the following lines from the poem, "The Fury of Cocks" from this volume (369):

> She is the house.
> He is the steeple.
> When they fuck they are God.
> When they break away they are God.
> When they snore they are God. (369)

Even though this is seemingly a celebration of both genders and of heterosexual sex, the language is harsh, revealing an anger consistent with another poem from this volume, "God's Backside":

for God, it seems,
has turned his backside to us,
giving us the dark negative,
the death wing,
until such time
as a flower breaks down the front door
and we cry, "Father! Mother!"
and plan their wedding. (383)

Here we see another example of Sexton's attempt to deal with the "gender of things." God is figured as masculine, while "we" are left with "the dark negative, / the death wing." We could read this as the attempt to explain women's place—the place of "us"—under patriarchal religion. The image that Sexton uses to characterize a revolution of this order is "a flower," an image typically used to represent women's sexuality, which "breaks down the front door." Here Sexton envisions change in religion as effected by the inclusion of women—through the "front door." Moreover, it is not simply women's presence that will make a change, but women's reclamation of their sexuality, a sexuality brought to bear in the context of a blessed union—a "wedding."

In another poem, "When Man Enters Woman," from the same volume, Sexton again equates heterosexual love with reaching God (428). In this poem Sexton narrates how, during sex, man and woman "with their double hunger, / have tried to reach through / the curtain of God / and briefly they have" (428). Heterosexual love is celebrated again in "Two Hands," also from *The Death Notebooks* (421). In this poem, man and woman are figured as two hands that come from the sea. In the first stanza, God creates the hands and together they "applauded. / This was no sin. / It was as it was meant to be" (421). The second stanza takes place after the advent of Christianity, which is marked by the names of the men and women: Levi, Sarah, and Mandrake become Sally and John. These individuals go about their activities separately, in "the prison of their bodies / as Christ was prisoned in His body / until the triumph came" (421). In this stanza, Sexton posits Christianity as the fall from an earlier time of grace, when sexuality was not sinful and when bodies were not prisons keeping individuals separate. The third stanza is a call for the hands to be released from their prisons as they "applaud, world, / applaud" (421). In this poem, then, Sexton retells the story of the fall and redemption as a story in which Christianity itself is the fall from grace, a fall from a state of being where sexuality was good. In the retelling, Sexton is enabled to imagine a time when embodiment and sexuality may again be full of grace.[29]

However, if the move back to grace is to be successful, as we will see, Sexton must move away from images of heterosexual love to make way for her own desire. From *The Death Notebooks* to *45 Mercy Street,* Sexton moves from an attempt to celebrate heterosexuality to the ability to revel in her own, female sexuality. In order to achieve this, Sexton must first return to the "crossing" of the early spiritual poetry, a crossing that allows her to face her own trauma in order to envision a healing. This crossing occurs in the final poems of *The Death Notebooks.*

Crossing through death

As Sexton moves from an attempt to celebrate heterosexual love to an attempt to claim her own desire, she changes her earlier characterization of death as female to death as male. As we saw in "The Touch" from *Love Poems,* Sexton envisions death as a female who sheds her blood:

> My hand is alive all over America
> Not even death will stop it,
> death shedding her blood.
> Nothing will stop it, for this is the kingdom
> and the kingdom come. (173–174)

Later, in *The Death Notebooks,* death becomes a male:

> I died seven times
> in seven ways
> letting death give me a sign,
> letting death place his mark on my forehead,
> *crossed over, crossed over.* (356)

This transfer makes sense if we read it in terms of the survival of sexual trauma. Kai Erikson remarks that many survivors of trauma see themselves as "marked, maybe cursed, maybe even dead."[30] In the transference of "death," which stands for the traumatic experience that was the threat of death, from female to male, Sexton shows how she has moved from locating the source of "death" in herself, in the female, to locating it outside of herself, in the male, in the male-dominated familial and societal structures. This movement allows her to open the door toward accepting her sexuality as good: not as forever tainted by the mark of death, but as having been temporarily crossed by it. And the death experience, once it is seen as having been crossed rather than dwelling within, can then be seen as "over."

Once Sexton claims herself as marked by death, as having "crossed over," then she is free to be "born again." One critic puts it this way:

> The last poems see the self as passing through death, whether symbolic or literal, into a more spacious, freer mode of existence within which the personal and poetic self can be defined and *affirmed through connections,* made at one end of the poetic process with a divine Muse, and at the other with the reader.[31]

Thus, crossing through death enables her to reclaim her sexuality, and this, in turn, will lead her to a vision of a goddess.[32] As Jennifer Manlowe concludes from her study of incest survivors' relationships to religion, "when women become conscious of their incest trauma they feel compelled to let go of their traditional patriarchal understandings of God."[33]

With Mercy for the Woman

By the time of *45 Mercy Street,* published posthumously in 1976, Sexton's poetry shows how far she has come in being able to have mercy for the woman, in being able to re-imagine female sexuality positively.[34] She does so by moving from understanding desire as desire for another to desire in oneself. Thus Sexton's vision of healing ultimately comes through a reclamation of *her own* sexual and spiritual desire, a desire that she reclaims for herself. Elizabeth Waites conveys the need for women to claim their own desire when she writes:

> As a girl grows up, . . . her body—its desires, feelings, impulses—is often gradually eclipsed by appraisals of her body—evaluations of how it should and does look, interpretations of its drives and motives, whether these should be enacted or not, and, sometimes, accusations about the female body as a disturbing factor in the lives of other people.[35]

Two poems from *45 Mercy Street,* "The Fierceness of Female" (546–547) and "The Consecrating Mother" (554–555), dramatize this process of claiming one's desire. "The Fierceness of Female" begins:

> I am spinning,
> I am spinning on the lips (546)

The word "spinning" recalls the first poem we examined by Sexton, "Music Swims Back to Me," in which the speaker goes from "dancing in a circle" to "dancing a circle" (6–7). Here the speaker is spinning, which is not only dancing with the body but creating from the body, as a spider spins a web from her body, and as women have spun throughout history.[36] She is "spinning on the lips," which implies not only the lips that speak but also the lips of female genitalia.

This connection between language and the body is echoed by Luce Irigaray one year after the publication of Sexton's poem, in her essay, "When Our Lips Speak Together," from 1977: "If we keep on speaking the same language together, we're going to reproduce the same history. . . . If we don't invent a language, if we don't find our body's language, it will have too few gestures to accompany our story."[37] Irigaray's well-known and radical reinterpretation of women's lips as sources of language, sources of stories, rather than sites of woundings, opened the way toward advances in feminist understandings of how language—particularly the discourses of medicine and psychoanalysis—has functioned in silencing women and, further, how a development of "women's language" is different from the dominant, male discourse. Given this reading of Sexton's work, then, debates over Sexton's status as a feminist are indeed put in a new light.

The parallels between Sexton and Irigaray continue in the next lines of Sexton's poem:

> they remove my shadow,
> my phantom from the past,
> they invented a timetable of tongues (546)

The "they" here can be read as men, as it is in Irigaray's essay: "They can speak to each other, and about us. But what about us?" (205). In this reading, they/men have erased women from history as they "remove my shadow / my phantom from the past," and made their history, their "timetable," which speaks in their "tongues." For both Sexton and Irigaray, the way out of this story/ history is through a language of women's body. The poem continues:

> and where all was absent,
> all is two,
> touching like a choir of butterflies,
> and like the ocean,
> pushing toward land
> and receding
> and pushing (546)

Thus, through her body the woman may find new words, new images, through which to tell her story, through which to write her way out of being "absent."

Far from being absent, and instead of being unified, the woman's body is "two." As Irigaray writes, "I love you: our two lips cannot separate to let just *one* word pass" (208). And she is more than two: "like a choir of butterflies," she is multiple. Irigaray writes, "We are luminous. Neither one nor two" (207). This multiplicity, this diversity, is, as we have seen in Sexton's earlier poetry, characterized by the figure of the ocean, which "pushing . . . and receding / and pushing," is in constant movement. As Irigaray writes, "Our whole body is moved. No surface holds. No figure, line, or point remains. No ground subsists. But no abyss, either. Depth, for us, is not a chasm" (212–213). In moving from understanding desire as an opposition between self and other to understanding desire as a force internal to the self, both Sexton and Irigaray open the way toward a reclamation of women's desire. The woman herself has all that she needs for desire; no matter with whom she chooses to share herself, the source of her desire comes from within and not from the other.

In the second stanza of this poem, Sexton gives images of female lovemaking. In her celebration of the female body as "drink," as "melon," and as "flower," Sexton presents her vision of the female body as that which nourishes and sustains a new language, a language that "unknit[s]" the old, a language of utopia, "out of place." This language, as in Irigaray, is spoken between women, through their bodies. Finally, this new language, this language of the woman's body, the language of women's bodies speaking together, is a language of survival. Women, by reclaiming their bodies' goodness together, may learn how to survive:

> I raise my pelvis to God
> so that it may know the truth of how
> flowers smash through the long winter. (547)

Thus, Sexton presents a lesson of survival in which the "pelvis" is raised to "God" so that her body and spirit together "may know the truth." The truth of survival, the truth of surviving through the winter until the coming of spring is not merely a matter of waiting for the next season but of coming toward it oneself, bodily, raising oneself, spiritually, sexually, in order to blossom. In this poem, Sexton's first, full vision of how woman's love of her self and her body can lead to survival, we see how such love can lead to spiritual healing. We will see such spiritual and sexual healing occurring again on this "border" time of winter turning into spring in the final poem to be examined in this chapter, "In Excelsis."

Before turning to that final poem, let us first examine the last poem from this same volume, "The Consecrating Mother," in which we see the idea of the goddess developed more fully (554–555). Several critics have remarked on the vision of sexual / spiritual healing that this poem presents.[38] The poem begins, as the last one did, with the speaker, "I," who "stand[s] before the sea" (554). At first, the ocean is an "it," with "green blood." Reminiscent of the earlier images of death, the ocean "made a cross of salt / and hung up its drowned" (554), but the speaker does not retreat: "I simply stood . . . I wanted to share this" (554).

Then in the second stanza, the ocean becomes a "she":

The ocean steamed in and out,
the ocean gasped upon the shore
but I could not define her,
I could not name her mood. . . .
and I thought of those who had crossed her,
in antiquity, in nautical trade, in slavery, in war.
I wondered how she had borne those bulwarks. (555)

Sexton lists the collective traumas of history—colonization, capitalism, slavery, war—traumas, like Sexton's own, that necessitate a "crossing." The crossing brings them through death to survival. The ocean, then, is both the threat of death and the possibility for safe passage, for survival. Through all these traumatic experiences, the ocean "bears" them.

The bearing is a kind of baptism, a kind of resurrection, as the poem goes on to relate:

She should be entered skin on skin. . . .
entered like kneeling your way into church,
descending into that ascension. . . . (555)

Thus, both physically and spiritually, the ocean is the figure for having survived death, having descended into ascension. Survival, and savior, will come not from an external deity but from woman's own sex and spirit:

. . . in the moon light she comes in her nudity
flashing breasts made of milk-water,

flashing buttocks of incurable lust,
and at night when you enter her
you shine like a neon soprano. (555)

Sexton here incorporates images of the earlier phases of spiritual poetry, as the mother, music, milk, and the reclamation of women's bodies come together in a ritual ceremony of blessing, of healing. This ritual takes place at night, with the moon to light the way, the significance of which will become clearer as we see this ritual of healing sex and spirit paralleled in the work of Audre Lorde and Gloria Anzaldúa. And, once again, the "neon soprano" simile connects the music of memory and the unconscious of the earlier poetry to, finally, the ocean goddess as healer of memories. The final stanza reads:

I am that clumsy human
on the shore
loving you, coming, coming
going,
and wish to put my thumb on you
like The Song of Solomon. (555)

The "clumsy human" experience of being on the shore, on the border between life and death, is repeated in the writings of Lorde and Anzaldúa. For all three, Sexton, Lorde, and Anzaldúa, the healing power of the goddess comes through love—through the connection of sex and spirit, through the blessing of women's bodies—that heals the wounds of history. As Sexton writes of love in one of her last poems written on March 24, 1974:

Love? Be it man. Be it woman.
It must be a wave you want to glide in on,
give your body to it, give your laugh to it,
give, when the gravely sand takes you,
your tears to the land. To love another is something
like prayer and it can't be planned, you just fall
into its arms because your belief undoes your disbelief. (607–608)

One final poem from Sexton's late poetry, "In Excelsis," from April 1, 1974, will help further illuminate the vision of feminist spirituality that Sexton puts forth (608–610). The poem begins on the border between winter and spring, between death and life, as we saw in an earlier poem.

However, unlike in the earlier poems, the speaker is not alone; she stands with Barbara, her lover. They are at the border, not only of winter and spring, but of the ocean and the land, where they have "come to worship," to make a "vow"—a vow which, between women, is "unspeakable." Their love for each other, although it is unspeakable, is nevertheless possible. It is made possible by the goddess, by the connection between spiritual love and sexual love, as she "enter[s] her like a dream" (609). In entering "her"— both lover and goddess—the speaker enters a ritual that is both sexual and spiritual, as it, the love from the other, "explode[s] over . . . and outward." Thus the wound itself and the vision of healing from the wound are linked. Rituals are celebrated in cycles, and this ritual serves to address each wound, "blow by blow," repeatedly, "over and over." Thus the ritual serves to heal the wound by repeatedly providing "the great mother arms / I never had." Further, this healing takes place, like the wounding itself, on the border, "here where the abyss / throws itself on the sand." This healing ritual, like the experience of wounding itself, takes place out of time: "since it all began / and will continue into oblivion." Out of time, on the border between life and death, both the wounding and the healing, then, are "past our knowing."

The ritual comes to closure where, at the end of the poem, the opening lines are repeated with a difference: by the end, the goddess "enters us" briefly, "for a small time / in half winter, half spring." In this, one of her very last poems written before her death, Sexton leaves us with a vision of how healing may, indeed, be possible, although not willed through "our knowing." Healing may come, Sexton tells us, through love—through love's healing power, through love's power to enter us, through her power to undo our disbelief.

In the end, Sexton's poetry leaves us with this hope: that sexual / spiritual love, "Be it man. / Be it woman," may be the key to healing from traumatic personal history. In her search for the love that would provide such healing, Sexton seems to have begun to turn toward a vision of the goddess. As Diana Hume George writes, "The quest for the father-god often appears to overwhelm *the matriarchal deity whom Sexton searched out with equal diligence* but could not as clearly name."[39] Now as we move toward an examination of the visions of individual and collective healing in Audre Lorde's and Gloria Anzaldúa's writing, we will see how the search for the name of the goddess is part of the process of healing for women in a society where "the name" is coextensive with "the father."

Chapter 8

Drawing Strength from Our Mothers: Tapping the Roots of Black Women's History

In an essay from 1984, Lorde asks Afro-German women to ask themselves, "How can I draw strength from my roots when these roots are entwined in such a terrible history?"[1] Lorde's own writings can be read as an answer to this very question. In this chapter, I will continue to analyze the historical and conceptual splits between spirituality and sexuality in Western culture that we saw addressed in Sexton's poetry. I will show how Lorde's writing responds to and attempts to heal this split through the "erotic as power," which she treats in theory and narrative form, as well as throughout her poetry. By comparing the non-fiction writings of black women on spirituality and sexuality with Lorde's treatment of these themes in her essay, "The Uses of the Erotic: The Erotic as Power," and in her narrative, *Zami: A New Spelling of My Name,* we will see how Lorde both arises from and reacts to the tradition of black women's thought. Further, by healing this split between sexuality and spirituality, Lorde shows how history may be turned from a problem into a solution.

Tracing the split between sexuality and spirituality

Images of American black women have historically been presented as stereotypes that allow the dominant culture to perceive black women in ways that reinforce their socially and economically lower status. In particular, the stereotypes of Mammy and Jezebel work to split black women's subjectivity into two parts: the spiritual and the sexual. As Patricia Hill Collins writes, the mammy is "asexual, a surrogate mother in blackface"; further, "mammy represents the clearest example of the split between sexuality and motherhood present in Eurocentric masculinist thought."[2] While

Mammy represents the mothering, caring, nurturing, spiritual side of the self, Jezebel represents the sexual side, with her "excessive sexual appetites" and "animal nature."[3] As we will see, the either/or thinking of the dominant culture has operated within the history of black women's writing as well. The themes of spirituality and sexuality have been treated separately in the writing of black women since the nineteenth century.

Black feminists in the nineteenth century used religious and spiritual metaphors in their arguments for black women's equality. Maria Stewart (1803–1879) was born free in Connecticut and was orphaned at age five; she became a domestic servant who worked in the home of a white family in Boston until age fifteen.[4] After an informal education, mostly gained through reading the Bible with the religious family, she became an abolitionist and was the first American-born woman to speak before a mixed gender audience in 1832. In her speeches, she spoke against colonization and for literacy, abolition, economic empowerment, and racial unity. In her 1833 Farewell Address to Her Friends in the City of Boston, she uses historical and religious precedents to show that women are capable of leadership roles.[5] In this speech, she highlights the spiritual nature of women, arguing that "the Deity more readily communicates himself to women" (68–69). As a result, she argues, the "religious spirit" of women has made them "martyrs, apostles, warriors, and . . . divines and scholars" (69).

Sojourner Truth (1799–1883), perhaps the most famous of the early black feminists, was born a slave in New York and eventually gained her freedom. She was a mother to five children (not the fabled thirteen) and, despite illiteracy, became famous for her May 29, 1851, Address to the Ohio Women's Rights Convention in Akron, Ohio, which has become known for its refrain, "And ain't I a woman?"[6] During this speech, she argued for universal suffrage; she believed black men should not get the vote before black women. In another address entitled, "When Woman Gets Her Rights Man Will Be Right," Truth uses faith in God to encourage black women to continue fighting for the vote: "I have faith in God and there is truth in humanity. Be strong women! Blush not! Tremble not! I want you to keep a good faith and good courage."[7] In doing so she connects faith to justice, a theme that continues in black feminism. As Joanne M. Braxton writes, Sojourner Truth and other nineteenth century black women "radicalize the form of spiritual autobiography and recreate it as a tool for temporal liberation."[8]

Fannie Barrier Williams (1855–1944) was born free in Brockport, New York, and became a black suffragist, emphasizing the different experiences of black men and women under slavery as well as the differences between white women and black women. To encourage the understanding of the particularity of black women's experience, Williams called for a black women's history and for the inclusion of this history as an integral part of American history. As part of this project, she addressed the World's Congress of Representative Women, a group of mostly white, progressive women in Chicago in 1893. Her speech, "The Intellectual Progress of the Colored Women of the United States Since the Emancipation Proclamation," documents the monumental progress of black women from 1865 to 1893.[9] In the address she stresses the "benevolence" that is the "essence of most of the colored women's organizations" and the "humane side" of black women's "natures" (699). She does so because "the morality of our home life has been commented upon so disparagingly and meanly that we are placed in the unfortunate position of being defenders of our name" (700). Williams is alluding to the mythical Jezebels who are sexually promiscuous and supposedly cause the instability of marriages, both white and black. Thus, the focus on black women's "moral ability" (700) reinforces the split between Mammy and Jezebel by repressing the sexual and by emphasizing the maternal and spiritual aspects of black women's selves.

Anna Julia Cooper (1859?–1964), daughter of a slave mother and her master, was "one of the first black feminists to urge black women to articulate their own experiences and to make the public aware of the way racism and sexism together affected their social status."[10] In an essay entitled, "The Higher Education of Women" from *A Voice from the South,* first published in 1892, Cooper writes of the particular care that women bring into the world and argues that this "'mothering' influence from some source is leavening the nation."[11] When these women's values are suppressed, Cooper argues, there is capitalism, violence, and imperialism in a culture: "[T]he civilized world has been like a child brought up by his father. It has needed *the great mother* heart to teach it to be pitiful, to love mercy, to succor the weak and care for the lowly" (51, italics mine). In so arguing, Cooper prefigures the contemporary feminists who value women's care and connection and argue that women should bring these into public life for the good of all. To accomplish this, Cooper writes that women should be educated in order to bring the world into balance between masculine and feminine principles: "All I claim is that there is a feminine side as well as a masculine side to truth; that these are related not as inferior and superior, not as better and worse, not as weaker and stronger, but as complements—complements in one necessary and symmetric whole" (60).

Like Maria Stewart and Sojourner Truth, Lorde understands the connection between spirituality and social justice. Like Fannie Barrier Williams and Anna Julia Cooper, Lorde emphasizes the value of what is female for ending violence in the world. Further, as we explored in chapter two, Lorde follows Ida Wells-Barnett, Angela Davis, and Darlene Clark Hine in underlining the need for attention to the pain and silence surrounding sexuality in black women's history. But unlike these sisters before her, Lorde brings spirituality and sexuality together through her theory of the erotic.

Healing the split through the erotic

On August 25, 1978, one year after Barbara Smith's call for black women to break the silences surrounding their sexuality, Lorde delivered a paper at the Fourth Berkshire Conference on the History of Women at Mount Holyoke College, entitled, "Uses of the Erotic: The Erotic as Power."[12] In this piece Lorde brings together the powers of sexuality and spirituality through the erotic: "The erotic is a resource within each of us that lies in a deeply *female* and *spiritual* plane" (53, italics mine). In connecting the spiritual with the sexual, Lorde works against the dominant culture's dichotomy of mind and body: "it has become fashionable to separate the spiritual (psychic and emotional) from the political. . . . In the same way, we have attempted to separate the spiritual and the erotic" (56).[13]

In her essay, Lorde defines the erotic as the production of joy in work and in love: "an assertion of the lifeforce of women; of that creative energy empowered" (55). It is the desire for excellence, the "internal requirement . . . [that we] demand the most from ourselves, from our lives, from our work" (54). It asserts itself in work that we love, in love that we work at. "How often do we truly love our work even at its most difficult?" she asks (55). We need to see love as our work: love of ourselves, love of others, love between us: the erotic "forms a bridge . . . which can be the basis for understanding much of what is not shared . . . and lessens the threat of difference" (56).

Lorde's erotic is not only an implicit critique of this conceptual split between sexuality and spirituality in Western thought, but it also shows how what is commonly accepted as a conceptual split is produced through a specific history of violence.[14] Thus, the coming together of sexuality and spirituality can be seen in the light of black women's history as a necessary attempt to begin the healing process of the sexual trauma of generations. As Lorde writes of the erotic, "[W]omen have been made to suffer and to feel both contemptible and suspect by virtue of its existence" (53). Theorizing the erotic arises out of Lorde's own experience as a multiple subject: "As a black, lesbian feminist, I have a particular feeling, knowledge, and understanding" (59). She brings this particular experience to bear in her critique of the "european-american tradition" that often numbs our feelings even as we experience the erotic, thereby reducing the use of the erotic to abuse: "To refuse to be conscious of what we are feeling . . . is to deny a large part of the experience" (59).[15]

Feeling deep pain is also part of Lorde's experience, which is demonstrated by Lorde's writings on cancer, sexual abuse, violence, and hate.[16] Feeling such pain is necessary for healing, as we have seen, and until such feeling takes place, one's life is not one's own. In order to allow the erotic to empower us, Lorde attests, in order to love ourselves, love each other, and accept difference, women must first overcome their deeply rooted fear of feeling: "We have been raised to fear the yes within ourselves, our deepest cravings" (57). And particularly for black women, given a collective history of sexual trauma, this fear of feeling is compounded by the threats and events of further violence.

These threats of violence and death cannot be destroyed by either silence or fear, however. As she writes in *The Cancer Journals,* "Your silence will not protect you" (20); so we must learn to speak even when we are afraid "in the same way that we have learned to work and speak when we are tired" (23). And as she said in an interview with Adrienne Rich one year after the publication of *The Cancer Journals,* "I'm not going to be made more vulnerable by putting weapons of silence in my enemies' hands."[17]

For black women, given the historical silence surrounding sexuality, and given the historical split between sexuality and spirituality, to speak means to work against history. For as we illuminate our differences in history, we come to see that we are not who we thought we were—as black women, as black Americans, as women, as Americans.[18] Lives lived in fear and silence and repression are lives that are not fully lived. Lorde's call to the erotic is a call for the coming together of sexuality and spirituality in black women's history, but it is also a call to all of us to recognize our shared histories, to "share the feelings of those who participate in the experience with us" (58). Thus, the erotic is a change in history and provides the possibility for further change. Lorde teaches us that overcoming the fear of feeling, ending silence, and recognizing the power of the erotic are not only the goals of black women's history but are goals for all of us who wish "to make our lives and the lives of our children richer and more possible" (55).

Turning to the mother for healing

In her biomythography, *Zami,* Lorde turns to the mother as both a literal and a figural image that will provide her with roots from which she demonstrates how "to make our lives and the lives of our children richer and more possible." By turning to the figural image of the mother, she fits her narrative into the traditions of American women's writing, black women's autobiography, and lesbian narratives.[19] Lorde's *Zami* ends with a final scene of reunion with the mythological, sexual/spiritual mother, Afrekete, through whom Lorde regains her connections to her sexual and spiritual motherland, Africa, and in whom Lorde finds the sexual and spiritual ritual that will enable her to heal from her trauma.

Before turning to the mythological mother, Afrekete, I will first discuss the personal and historical mothers Lorde embraces. For while other critics have emphasized the significance of this figural black goddess in Lorde's work, I will show how Lorde not only is left to *imagine the figure* of the mother in her writing, but also is able to take from *her own real mother* both the literal and figural roots that she needs.[20] Her mother provides her with a way of turning to history and also writing her story into history. Lorde's specific history places her in a line of descent that can be traced through her mother, an immigrant in Harlem, to her mother's birthplace, the West Indian island of Carriacou, and back to Africa, from where her mother's ancestors were sold as slaves. Further, her mother also provides the seeds for the "metaphor" of the sexual and spiritual mother-figure, Afrekete, through whom Audre creates a ritual of healing.

Grounding her narrative in matrilineal history and myth allows Lorde to find and take root: to form her identity. In this section, I will examine the ways in which Lorde digs this root through, first, her portrayal of her mother and the particular knowledges about spirituality and sexuality that her mother gives to the young Audre. In the next section, I will look at how Lorde incorporates her research into the culture and myths of Carriacou, her mother's place of birth, into her narrative in ways that give Lorde's own life meaning and context. Ultimately, Lorde's matrilineage will take her back to Africa to the myth of Afrekete, the great mother.[21] As we will see in the final section, these scenes of healing union between sexuality and spirituality, and between Lorde and the mother, are all the more powerful given Lorde's own history of sexual abuse, numbness, and silence. As Lorde comes to union, feeling, and writing, she connects her own healing journey with the historical journeys of women of the global diaspora, women whose histories are laden with personal and collective sexual trauma.[22]

Lorde's narrative in *Zami* begins by focusing on her mother, Linda, and the wisdom that she passes on to Audre from her birth place of Carriacou.[23] Linda Lorde had emigrated to America with Audre's father, a Barbadian, in 1924, when she was 27 and he was 26 (9). Their new home in America never really feels like home to them. To counteract her feelings of loss, Lorde's mother tells her daughters "stories about Carriacou, where she had been born" (13) amid "the hills of Carriacou between L'Esterre and Harvey Vale" (14).

By these stories, Lorde's mother teaches her a form of spirituality that was different from the Catholicism she was learning in school:

> She knew about mixing oils for bruises and rashes, and about disposing of all toenail clippings and hair from the comb. About burning candles before All Souls Day to keep the soucoyants away, lest they suck the blood of her babies. She knew about blessing the food and yourself before eating, and about saying prayers before going to sleep. (10)

Although Audre did not know it at the time, her mother was passing on the particular mix of Catholic and African spirituality of the people of Carriacou, which includes beliefs in witches who suck the blood of babies and the celebration of All Souls Day on November 2 (Hill 330). Similarly, Lorde writes that her mother "taught us one [prayer] to the mother that I never learned in school," a prayer to the Virgin, *"my sweet mother"* (10). In these ways Lorde's earliest spiritual teachings included mixes of Catholicism and African spirituality, held together by the female imagery of a mother who would care for and protect her.

At the same time that she was learning about spirituality from her mother, Lorde also learned an appreciation for the female physical body from her mother, demonstrated through the scene of her mother combing her hair as she sat between her mother's legs: "I remember the warm mother smell caught between her legs, and the intimacy of physical touching nestled inside of the anxiety/pain like a nutmeg nestled inside its covering of mace" (33). Claudine Raynaud writes that this scene "expresses her rapport with her mother, her sense of belonging to the island of Carriacou, and discloses the source of her lesbianism. . . . The rich red color of the mace netting before the nutmeg is dried. . . . is the secret sign of home, the island of Carriacou, of Grenada, one of the main producers of nutmeg" (227). And directly following this scene in the narrative is a tender scene of Saturday morning in bed with mother where "Warm milky smells of morning surround us" (34), a scene that likewise shows the importance of the physical, maternal presence in Lorde's development.

Closely connected to the spiritual and the physical are the sensuous descriptions of her mother's West Indian mortar: "I loved to finger the hard roundness of the carved fruit, and the always surprising termination of the shapes as the carvings stopped at the rim and the bowl sloped abruptly downward, smoothly oval but abruptly businesslike" (71). In her mother's kitchen, Lorde feels the stirrings of sexual desire:

> with one hand firmly pressed around the carved side of the mortar caressing the wooden fruit with my aromatic fingers. I thrust sharply downward, feeling the shifting salt and the hard little pellets of garlic right up through the shaft of the wooden pestle. Up again, down, around, and up. . . . All of these transported me into a world of scent and rhythm and movement and sound that grew more and more exciting as the ingredients liquefied. (74)

Raynaud connects this with African culture and myth since the "stone for oil crushing is a symbol for female genitalia" in a village of Sudan.[24] And on the day of her first menstruation, Audre's mother agrees to cook her favorite dish for supper and leaves to get tea. While she is away, Lorde prepares the spices: "I smelled the delicate breadfruit smell rising up from the front of my print blouse that was my own womansmell, warm, shameful, but secretly utterly delicious" (77). Then the narrator, as a grown woman, relates her fantasy of her mother and herself, "slowly, thoroughly, our touching and caressing each other's most secret places" (78). As she grinds the spices, "There was a heavy fullness at the root of me that was exciting and dangerous" (78). In the narrative to follow, Lorde will trace this root through her matrilineage to arrive at an understanding of the connection between the spiritual and the sexual. At this point, however, this root is "shameful" and "dangerous" because of the pain associated with it, coupled with the prohibitions against speaking of the pain. In breaking these prohibitions, Lorde rewrites history, both personal and collective.

Turning to history for healing

While as a child Audre was learning these sexual and spiritual lessons from her mother, it was not until she was an adult that she was able to connect the teachings of her mother with a larger, historical narrative. Lorde writes that as an immigrant from an island that could not be found on any map, "my mother was different from the other women I knew" (15). Her parents speak in patois (15), using words the meanings of which Lorde can only guess, words that she calls "my mother's secret poetry" (32).[25] Growing up, her mother would tell her of "the Sunday-long boat trips that took her to Aunt Anni's in Carriacou" (11). Carriacou first enters Lorde's consciousness as a legend that provides her with a vision of women together:

> Here Aunt Anni lived among the other women who saw their men off on the sailing vessels, then tended goats and groundnuts, planted grain and poured rum on the earth to strengthen the corn's growing, built their women's houses and the rainwater catchments, harvested the limes, wove their lives and the lives of their children together. Women who survived the absence of their sea-faring men easily, because they came to love each other, past the men's returning.
>   *Madivine. Friending. Zami. How Carriacou women love each other is legend in Grenada, and so is their strength and their beauty.* (13–14)

As she grows older, Lorde begins to think that her mother is crazy or mistaken, that there really is no place called Carriacou, but she still harbors hopes for its existence: "But underneath it all as I was growing up, *home* was still a sweet place somewhere else which they had not managed to capture yet on paper" (14).

When she is 26 years old, Lorde finally locates Carriacou on a map in the *Encyclopedia Britannica,* which underlines the island's history as a colony. Anna Wilson writes that "The reality of Carriacou as a mapped space indicates the inexorable colonization of the world; but it also reinforces the need for Lorde to redescribe it, to give it a voice and a significance that is not the strangled one of the former colony" (83). As an adult, Lorde visits Grenada, the island where her mother lived after her family left Carriacou. There, she writes, "I saw the root of my mother's powers walking through the streets" (9). Although Lorde's visit to Grenada is not ostensibly part of the narrative, she incorporates this visit and her newfound knowledge of Carriacou into the narrative.

What Lorde discovers is that the love between women in Carriacou is not only legend; it is also history. Since in Carriacou men go away for long periods of time on fishing and trade expeditions, the women have a practice of *zami,* or lesbianism, while the men are away.[26] In Carriacou the men say "women are hotter than men" and only women can satisfy other women (Smith 199). Donald Hill writes, "One informant claimed that virtually every wife whose husband had gone away several years or more is a zami" (280). Further, the women very rarely stop lesbianism once they start (Smith 200). When a man returns, it is often difficult for him to regain sexual favors from his wife, so he permits her to remain zami, "hoping she will become bisexual" (Hill 281). Thus, through the history of Carriacou, Lorde finds the context that gives her own life meaning, the context of lesbian desire and practice.

However, this sexual matrilineage is not entirely separate from the spiritual roots that Lorde finds in Carriacou. From Hill and Smith, Lorde would have learned that Carriacou had been a French colony in the West Indies that imported slaves from Africa. The island became a British colony briefly during the American war of Independence in 1763 and then again in 1784. By then, French cultural forms (including Catholicism) had been established. After 1808, when Britain prohibited the importation of slaves to West Indian colonies, the elite left the island, leaving it an island of people of African descent whose inhabitants speak French patois and English dialect and in whom Catholicism is deeply rooted. Thus, the Catholic/African mix of religion that Lorde learned from her mother has its roots in the history of colonization and slavery in Carriacou. Further, the prayer to the "mother" that Lorde learned would be explained by the link between the Virgin and great goddess religions in Africa. Three basic elements of African spirituality that often survive colonization and are integrated into new forms of syncretic religion—mothering, the connection to the earth, and the connection of spirituality and sexuality—are dramatized in the narrative.[27]

In describing her first sexual encounter in high school with her friend, Marie, Lorde writes, "We lay awake far into the night, snuggling under the covers by the light of the votive candle on Our Lady's altar in the corner, kissing and hugging and giggling in low tones so her mother wouldn't hear us" (120). Thus, Audre's first positive sexual experience happens in the presence of mothers—both the physical mother of Marie and the spiritual mother, Mary. This scene also sets up the connection between sexuality and spirituality that Lorde will draw in her subsequent sexual encounters.

In the description of Audre making love with a woman for the first time, Lorde writes, "I surfaced dizzy and blessed with her rich myrrh-taste in my mouth, in my throat, smeared over my face" (139). We might compare this encounter with the incident with the man in the comic store that we explored earlier. In this encounter, however, Audre goes down into blessing rather than up into danger, emphasizing the source of blessing from below, from the earth, rather than from heaven above. Also, the use of myrrh connotes a holy gift in Christianity, which shows Lorde's connection to elements of Christianity. We should note, as well, that Audre's lovemaking with this woman, Ginger, happens with Ginger's mother's knowledge and in the mother's house.

Lorde again connects the syncretic nature of religion with the mother when in Mexico, her lover, Eudora, whom Lorde describes as having the mark of an Amazon from her mastectomy (169), teaches her how "the women in San Christóbal de las Casas give the names of catholic saints to their goddesses" (170). Eudora also teaches her about the connections "between Mexico and Africa and Asia" and about the destruction of Aztec culture by the Europeans, a "genocide [that] rivals the Holocaust" (170). In addition to these lessons about history and mythology, Audre learns another lesson from Eudora, who "knew many things about loving women that I had not learned" (170): it is with Eudora that Audre allows herself to be made love to for the first time.

Finally, the Amazon from Africa and the myrrh from Jerusalem mix with the corn of America when Lorde writes of all her friends and lovers, fellow zamis, "Their names, selves, faces feed me like corn before labor" (256). This corn image again underscores Lorde's connection to goddess mythologies; the corn mother is a common image in many indigenous cultures of the Americas, and holds within it the power of fertility, the nourishment between generations, and the promise of democracy.[28] In all these ways, Lorde receives spiritual sustenance from her historical and cultural mothers in Africa, the Caribbean, and America.

Turning history into myth for healing

The ultimate connection between sexuality and spirituality can be found in the final scenes of the narrative, which show Lorde's connection to her deepest mother root in Africa through the character of Afrekete. Significantly, just before the narrative turns toward Afrekete, there is a scene in which Audre boards a bus at a "corner," or crossroads:

> The bus door opened and I placed my foot upon the step. Quite suddenly, there was music swelling up in my head, as if a choir of angels had boarded the Second Avenue bus directly in front of me. They were singing the last chorus of an old spiritual of hope:
> Gonna die this death
> on Cal—va—ryyyyy
> BUT AIN'T GONNA

die

no more . . . !

. . . I suddenly stood upon a hill in the center of an unknown country, hearing the sky fill with a new spelling of my own name. (238–239)

This scene prefigures Lorde's transformation of her own African, Caribbean, African American, Christian background into the new self in "an unknown country" through syncretic combination. As we will see, the figure of Afrekete functions as the conduit for the healing of all the different aspects of Lorde's history.

Further, the setting of the meeting between Audre and Afrekete shows that this union is not only one between Audre and Africa, but between Audre and all her cultural mothers. At the party where they meet, Afrekete and Audre dance to Frankie Lymon's "Goody, Goody," a Belafonte calypso, and a slow Sinatra (245), a particular mix of singers that parallels the mix of cultures that have combined to form Audre herself. After the party, Audre goes home with Afrekete to "Gennie's old neighborhood" (247), which connects Audre to her younger self and to the memory of her dead friend.

Background to the role of Afrekete in African myth will provide us with greater understanding of her significance for Lorde's "biomythography." According to Lorde herself in a conversation with Judy Grahn, Afrekete comes from the time of the "old thunder god religion," which preceded the Yoruban culture, in present-day Nigeria. According to Lorde, Afrekete is the female precursor to the Yoruban god, Eshu, the trickster, god of the crossroads. Henry Louis Gates characterizes Eshu as masculine: "the divine linguist . . . guardian of the crossroads, master of style and the stylus, phallic god of generation and fecundity, master of the mystical barrier that separates the divine from the profane world" (286–287). Similarly, in *Women Reading / Women Writing,* Ana Louise Keating remarks that, through Afrekete, Lorde "appropriates for herself the linguistic authority generally associated with masculinity" (166). However, in defining Afrekete as *the precursor* to Eshu, Lorde stresses the figure's mixture of both masculine and feminine characteristics. As precursor, Afrekete is, we might say, the mother of Eshu.

In Yoruban mythology, the mother of Eshu is the god/dess of the crossroads, MawuLisa. Some critics do identify Afrekete as MawuLisa. Claudine Raynaud writes that Afrekete is a bisexual personification of Mawu (the moon, female) and Lisa (the sun, male): "Whenever there is an eclipse of the sun or the moon it is said that Mawu and Lisa are making love" (Parrinder, qtd. Raynaud 237). Mary K. DeShazer also identifies Afrekete as MawuLisa, "a mother of both sorrow and magic . . . [who] created the world" (185–186). Likewise, Ana Louise Keating connects Afrekete to MawuLisa by recalling that Lorde calls Eshu a son of MawuLisa in *The Black Unicorn* (164–165).

Rather than identifying Afrekete as either Eshu or MawuLisa, however, I want to stress the figure's syncretic function, as s/he brings together all the mothers—personal, historical, and mythological—in Lorde's narrative. Afrekete, thus, is part recuperation of cultural myth and part invention. Both cross-gendered and bisexual, Afrekete is both mother and master, nurturing and philosophical; s/he shows that the values of "female" mothering and "male" competence with language and meaning are equally necessary in order to survive on these borders between cultures.[29]

The final scenes in *Zami* show the ultimate connection between sexuality and spirituality as they depict lovemaking as a rite, which includes references to mass, ritual, prayer, transubstantiation, and union. Lorde writes that her lovemaking with Afrekete is an act of "making moon honor love . . . sacred as the ocean at high tide" (252). The site of the lovemaking occurs amid a "mass of green plants that Afrekete tended religiously" (250), and their motions imitate those of religious ritual: *"squeezed the pale yellow-green fruit juice in thin ritual lines back and forth over and around your coconut-brown belly . . . massaged it over your thighs and between your breasts until your brownness shone like a light through a veil"* (251). Their coming together is a prayer: *"Afrekete Afrekete ride me to the crossroads where we shall sleep, coated in the woman's power. The sound of our bodies meeting is the prayer of all strangers and sisters, that the discarded evils, abandoned at all crossroads, will not follow us upon our journeys"* (252). It is a prayer to leave behind her own sufferings, like many prayers, but this prayer goes out not to an external deity but to a meeting of bodies, a connection that is both sexual and spiritual.

Most importantly, the lovemaking as religious rite concludes in transubstantiation. Transubstantiation implies change and becoming, mystery and magic, which, as in Christianity, is performed through the body; in this case it occurs through the body of Afrekete. Here Afrekete is identified as the youngest daughter of MawuLisa, who Lorde herself becomes as she incorporates the inheritance of her mothers: *"Mawu-lisa, thunder, sky, the great mother of us all; and Afrekete, her youngest daughter, the mischievous linguist, trickster, best-beloved, whom we must all become"* (255). As biological daughter of her own mother and spiritual daughter of her cultural mothers, Lorde, through her spiritual-sexual union with Afrekete, loves her mother and becomes her. In loving and becoming Afrekete, Lorde bodily inherits the mothers' histories and myths that give her the sustenance, nurturance, and stability to grow strong and tall.

Lorde writes, "Afrekete taught me roots" (250). Indeed, all her mothers—personal, historical, and mythological—provide her with the roots she needs to work through traumatic history. Digging up these roots, entwined with violence, pain and silence, enables Lorde not only to envision healing but to make it possible. This healing comes through a sexual-spiritual reclamation of her personal, historical, and mythological mother roots. In weaving these mothers into her narrative, Lorde links history and myth by showing how myths can change history. The histories of slavery, rape, and sexual abuse, and their consequences of silence, numbness, and pain, may be transformed, Lorde teaches, not when we leave these histories behind but when we return to them, as together we witness to and are touched by the pain of the past. Only after such a process may traumatic history be accompanied by a history of matrilineage, which leads us toward speaking, and loving, and healing. Lorde's biomythography is, finally, the complex history of all these mother roots.

In digging these mother roots, Lorde not only envisions healing but makes it possible. Through theorizing and practicing the "erotic," Lorde begins to heal the split between sexuality and spirituality, a split that keeps women not only from claiming their lives but from living. As we have seen in Sexton's and Lorde's work and as we will continue to explore in Anzaldúa's work, to be caught in the bind that the split between sexuality and spirituality produces is to be rendered unable to take power in both the private and the public spheres. To claim one's being as both sexual and spiritual is to refuse the limited choice of either whore or virgin, either Jezebel or Mammy, either body or spirit. To claim one's being as both sexual and spiritual also means refusing to tie oneself to a traumatic past. In showing how the erotic is both sexual and spiritual power that has been kept from women, Lorde encourages women to heal this split, to reclaim this power, and to move beyond mere surviving to living, and thriving, as whole and healthy, spiritual and sexual, creative and powerful women.

Chapter 9

Grinding the Bones to Create Anew: Gloria Anzaldúa's Mestiza Mythology

I n the previous chapters on Anzaldúa, we examined how her writing shows the effects of living in the era after the shattering, when all around us we see broken pieces, epitomized by the oppositions between spirit and body, good and bad, and life and death. Anzaldúa's vision of healing, as we will see, stems from her status as a survivor of collective, historical trauma, just as Sexton's and Lorde's visions came from their specific histories as survivors. We saw in chapters seven and eight that Sexton and Lorde's visions of healing reconnect the pieces of this traumatic history, and like both Sexton and Lorde, Anzaldúa's vision includes a revision and revalorization of female figures of cultural mythology.[1] Unlike Sexton, however, Anzaldúa does not have to imagine a goddess mythology; instead, she can, as Lorde does, turn to the archeological and historical knowledge of the past for her myths. In this way, her rewriting of these myths serves as a witnessing of the past belief and subsequent erasure of these myths.[2]

As Roberta H. and Peter T. Markman observe in their book, *The Flayed God: The Mesoamerican Mythological Tradition,* the ancient Mesoamerican culture was one that saw bones as seeds.[3] In one of the myths of the origin of the historical period that they call the Fifth Sun, humans were formed from a bone taken from the underworld by the god, Quetzalcoatl. On his way back from the underworld and pursued by demons, Quetzalcoatl dropped and shattered the bone. He gathered the pieces and gave them to the goddess, Cihuacoatl, who ground them up and made dough from the remains, which she baked to create the first humans of the Fifth Sun, a male and a female. Like Cihuacoatl, Anzaldúa takes the shattered bones of cultural myths and makes them into seeds for the future.

In the first section of this chapter, through a reading of the histories of the figures of La Malinche and the Virgin of Guadalupe, we will see how these figures are like shattered pieces, the remnants of traumatic violence that split what was once whole into the oppositions between bad and good, body and spirit, death and life. Then in the next section, we will see how Anzaldúa's writing recombines the figures of La Malinche and the Virgin of Guadalupe, as Cihuacoatl mixed the bones that Quetzalcoatl dropped, and in so doing she reveals an earlier mythological figure, the goddess Coatlicue, a figure comprised of elements of both figures. We will then go on to examine how Anzaldúa does not conclude with a desire for a return to the past through Coatlicue, but instead makes her own dough from these pieces and creates a new myth, the myth of Antigua, which means "ancient one." She uses this new name, Antigua, to convey a "power greater than the conscious I" (50), a power that sentences her to survival, that gives her the will to survive. Anzaldúa continues,

> That power is my inner self, the entity that is the sum total of all my incarnations, the godwoman in me I call Antigua, mi diosa, the divine within, Coatlicue—Cihuacoatl, Tlazolteotl, Tonantzin-Coatlalopeuh-Guadalupe—they are one. (50)

In the final section, we will examine how the myth of Antigua enables Anzaldúa to reconceive the subject as an "entity that is the sum total" of all the memories and histories, all that have been reclaimed from the past, and all that have been healed from.

Revisioning La Malinche and the Virgin

Two of the most important female figures in Chicana history, La Malinche and the Virgin of Guadalupe, can be read as shattered pieces, as what remains after the breakage of the whole image of woman. Like the dichotomy of Mammy and Jezebel that we examined in the preceding chapter, La Malinche (also called La Chingada) and the Virgin represent the split between bad and good, sexuality and spirituality. First, let us examine this split more closely by reading the history of the two figures. Later, we will show how Anzaldúa rewrites this history in order to unify the splintered pieces.

Despite the apparent unity of the *myth* of La Malinche (also called Malintzin and Doña Marina), there are differing historical accounts of her life. According to one account, she was born Malinztin Tenepal around 1505 in the Aztec city of Painula.[4] In an Aztec account, the chiefs told Motecuh-zoma that the Spaniards were accompanied by a "woman from this land, who speaks our nahuatl tongue. She is called la Malinche, and she is from Teticpac."[5] Thus, even her origin, her birthplace, is uncertain.

Accounts also differ on how she became a translator to Cortés. According to one account, she joined the Spaniards of her own free will after "[t]hey found her there on the coast" (*Account* 35). In another account, she was sold into slavery, probably by her mother, after her father's death, and was later given to Cortés.[6] According to another account by the historian, Bernal Diaz del Castillo, who traveled with Cortés on the expedition to "New Spain," La Malinche was "a *cacique,* an Indian chieftain who was given to the Tabascans who gave her to Cortés" when she was fourteen years old because of internal political manipulation within the city-states.[7]

However she arrived at her position, once she was with Cortés, she used her knowledge of the Mayan and Nahuatl languages to serve as a translator; one Aztec account claims that "she served them faithfully as interpreter throughout the conquest" (*Account* 31). She also became Cortés' mistress and had a child by him. When Cortés was ordered to bring his Spanish wife to the New World, La Malinche was married off to one of his soldiers. Later her son was sent to Spain to be educated and she never saw him again.[8]

What is consistent in all historical accounts is her position as Chingada, as a traitor who sided with Cortés in both body and mind rather than resisting. The Mexicans, since their independence, have generally despised La Malinche as an incarnation of the betrayal of indigenous values, and of servile submission to European culture and power. Once Mexico was freed from Spanish rule, the nation needed a way to define itself against the history of conquest: the myth of La Malinche provided a convenient cause for the conquest.[9] Even one contemporary feminist historian, Jean Franco, perceives La Malinche as a traitor: "'La Malinche' or Doña Marina, the indigenous woman who was given to Cortés by a Tabascan tribe and who became his mistress, mother of one of his children, and an interpreter or translator ('translation' being closely related in its Latin root to 'treachery')."[10] La Malinche's status as a traitor by virtue of her body and her sex is conveyed by the other name by which she is known: "la lengua," which means both tongue and language.[11]

By contrast, the figure of the Virgin of Guadalupe is an embodiment of all of the faith, purity, and goodness that La Malinche does not possess. The Virgin Mary, who traditionally appears to the most humble people in a culture, such as the shepherds in Europe, is reported to have appeared to an indigenous man, Juan Diego, in Mexico in 1531.[12] She appeared at the site of the ancient goddess, Tonantzin, and, after Juan Diego's vision, the Christian Virgin's shrine was built at the epicenter of the goddess' cult. This is a common practice in colonization: religious conquest often consists in establishing the colonizing culture's religion in the places of the indigenous people's sacred sites. As this occurred ten years after the imprisonment of the Aztec emperor, we might infer that the civilization did not "fall" overnight. Even ten years later, the Spaniards found it necessary to ground their authority in something deeper than the political: the spiritual. This has also been interpreted as a return by the Aztecs to the feminine principle, the Mother, in the face of the defeat of their male deities, Quetzalcoatl and Huitzilopochtli.[13] Anzaldúa echoes this interpretation when she remarks that the Virgin of Guadalupe was received by the Aztec people as a welcome balance to the lopsided rule of masculine gods (28).

After this initial visitation, the Virgin's image was changed to fit the needs of the new mestizo culture. From 1550 to 1600, the worship of Guadalupe continued on the site of Tonantzin where an Indian, Marcos, had painted an image of Guadalupe. Around 1575 the image was replaced by the current image. And in 1600 her feast day was changed from September 8, as in Spain, to September 10 and then to December 12, making Guadalupe a Creole, New World spiritual movement.[14] Thus, she unites not only the Old World and the New but also Catholics and indigenous, and hence, she is the patron saint of Mexico, the mother of Mexico. The Virgin of Guadalupe mediates in other ways, as well, such as between heaven and earth, as she intercedes on behalf of those who pray to her to obtain help from her son.

Paradoxically, these two figures, La Malinche and the Virgin of Guadalupe, which are so radically different are, at the same time, so fundamentally important to the self-understandings of Mexican and Chicana women. Currently, the figures of La Malinche and the Virgin of Guadalupe present an impossible bind for many Mexican and Chicana women. A woman in the culture typically strives to be like the Virgin of Guadalupe: virginal, wholly pure, untouched, motherly, unselfish, all-giving, and kind. However, if a woman in the culture is not all of these things, then she is condemned like La Malinche: as a whore, dirty, giving in to lust and selfishness and sin, betraying family and nation and faith, using her body, mouth, tongue, and sex in the pursuit of self-fulfillment, pleasure, evil. Anzaldúa works to undo this opposition by revisioning the myths of La Malinche and the Virgin of Guadalupe. She does this in three ways:

first, she encourages women to revise their expectations of themselves and other women; second, she reinterprets the history of the figures of La Malinche and the Virgin; third, she shows how these figures are not polar opposites but are ultimately connected through the earlier goddess, Coatlicue.

Let us look at how Anzaldúa encourages the rewriting of the La Malinche myth. First, Anzaldúa encourages an examination of our relationships with women: friends, mothers, selves. Anzaldúa connects the hatred of La Malinche with the hate for all women that she was taught during her childhood: "I was taught that women were spiteful and competed against each other and it wasn't worth it to make friends with women, that only men could be your friends" (Anzaldúa 1991, 120). Anzaldúa tells us, then, that regaining faith in other women and in oneself is essential to healing. This can begin with an examination and a reaffirmation of one's mother. Anzaldúa writes that she, like all daughters, have mothers who are not virgins: "Sí, soy hija de la Chingada. I've always been her daughter" (Anzaldúa 17).

Another way that Anzaldúa works to break down the dichotomy between La Malinche and the Virgin is through a rereading of La Malinche's role in history. Anzaldúa asserts that "the Aztec nation fell not because [she] interpreted for and slept with Cortes, but because the ruling elite had subverted the solidarity between man and woman and noble and commoner" (34). La Malinche can be seen, furthermore, as a model for Chicanas who must translate between languages and between cultures. She can be seen as a woman who spoke, who did not remain silent in the face of change, just as Anzaldúa herself speaks:

> I will no longer be made to feel ashamed of existing. I will have my voice: Indian, Spanish, white. I will have my serpent's tongue—my woman's voice, my sexual voice, my poet's voice. I will overcome the tradition of silence. (59)

Similarly, Anzaldúa also refigures La Malinche as the mother of the new mestiza culture, like the Virgin. Anzaldúa prepares the way for two other Chicana scholars who write that La Malinche "did not deny language; she used, assimilated language, and through language and her body she accepted the foreigner."[15] By so doing, La Malinche did what all must do to survive: she adapted. Her adaptation consisted of using her body to translate and to give birth, thereby mixing the cultures to envision a new civilization. As Todorov suggests, La Malinche "heralds . . . the present state of us all, since if we are not invariably bilingual, we are inevitably bi- or tri-cultural . . . she adopts the other's ideology and serves it in order to understand her own better" (101).

Anzaldúa connects La Malinche not only to the present and to history but to mythology, as she shows how La Malinche is connected to earlier goddesses: "La india en mí es la sombra: la Chingada, Tlazolteotl, Coatlicue. Son ellas que oyemos lamentando a sus hijas perdidas [The indian in me is the shadow: la Chinagada, Tlazolteotl, Coatlicue. It is they that we hear lamenting their lost daughters]" (22, my translation). In Anzaldúa's revisioning of the myth, La Malinche mourns not only for her son who is taken from her, but also for all the sons and daughters who are lost to their parents through the effects of a traumatic history—violence, drugs, assimilation. In this way, La Malinche is connected to the myths of La Llorona, who wails in the night for her lost children, and Cihuacoatl, an antecedent of La Llorona, who wailed at the impending loss by Conquest (35).[16] In the Aztec accounts of the Conquest, it is written that right before the arrival of the Spaniards, Motecuhzoma heard "the goddess Cihuacoatl, who cried and shouted many nights."[17] Cihuacoatl is thus associated with "The sixth bad omen: The people heard a weeping woman night after night. She passed by in the middle of the night, wailing and crying out in a loud voice: 'My children, we must flee far from this city!' At other times she cried: 'My children, where shall I take you?'" (*Account* 6). Thus, in her connection to Cihuacoatl, a mother goddess who mourns for her lost children, La Malinche is revisioned as a mother, as a caring and visionary figure who uses her voice to tell the people what she knows, what she sees.

In speaking with her "serpent's tongue," which is split at its tip, Anzaldúa goes beyond revisioning the myth of La Malinche to refigure the other side of the split: the Virgin of Guadalupe. As Anzaldúa highlights the caring and maternal aspects of La Malinche, she emphasizes the sexual roots of the Virgin. She does so by showing the connections between Guadalupe and the earlier fertility goddesses who were both sexual and spiritual. Anzaldúa writes, "The first step is to unlearn the puta/virgen dichotomy and to see Coatlalopeuh-Coatlicue in the Mother, Guadalupe" (84). As a mother, Anzaldúa urges us to remember, Guadalupe *used her body* to bring forth new life. Thus, Anzaldúa urges women to view their bodies as both sexual and good. By linking the Virgin to her capacity as birth mother, Anzaldúa not only refocuses attention upon the Virgin's status as a mother; she also reminds us that the Virgin is a mediator between worlds.

In addition to mediating between the life and death worlds, the Virgin also mediates politically between differing groups. Norma Alarcón calls her the figure of "political compromise between conquerors and the conquered."[18] Anzaldúa echoes this belief in these characteristics of the Virgin when she writes that Guadalupe has functioned historically in Chicano/a culture as a figure that "unites" and "mediates" between opposing groups (30). As an example, Anzaldúa reminds us that the Virgin was heralded on banners during the grape strike of 1965 (29), and goes on to claim that she is the symbol for "the tolerance of ambiguity" that people of cross-cultures possess (30).

Finally, just as she does for La Malinche, Anzaldúa traces the origins of the myth of the Virgin of Guadalupe. Anzaldúa writes that after the Conquest, the Spaniards "desexed Guadalupe, taking Coatlalopeuh, the serpent/sexuality, out of her. They completed the split begun by the Nahuas by making la Virgen de Guadalupe/Virgen María into chaste virgins and Tlazolteotl/Coatlicue/la Chingada into putas" (28). Anzaldúa's genealogy thus connects the Virgin to the characteristics of sexuality and fertility of earlier goddesses: "La Virgen de Guadalupe's Indian name is Coatlalopeuh . . . descended from, or is an aspect of, earlier Mesoamerican fertility and earth goddesses. The earliest is Coatlicue" (27). Coatlicue, who represented creation and destruction together, was split by the Azteca/Mexica culture, as Anzaldúa reminds us, into two goddesses: Tonantzin and Tlazolteotl. These were, as we saw in chapter six, the two goddesses Anzaldúa encountered in her shamanistic journey in the poem, "Matriz sin tumba o [Womb without tomb]." Tonantzin was connected with life, mother-love, and creation; Tlazolteotl with death, sin, and destruction.[19] We usually associate the Virgin with Tonantzin, since she appeared in the place of Tonantzin (Florescano 143–144), and since Tonantzin means "Our Mother."[20] However, there are aspects of the Virgin that parallel those of Tlazolteotl, as well. Tlazolteotl is a mother like Guadalupe; she is also known as a weaver of life to whom people confessed their mistakes, errors, and sins to her in order to be "woven anew"; she also forgave sins with yellow and green waters.[21] By returning to the united manifestation of both Tonantzin and Tlazolteotl through Coatlicue, Anzaldúa revisions the Virgin as a mediator between life and death.

Thus, through Coatlicue, Anzaldúa brings together La Malinche and the Virgin of Guadalupe, as she shows how both La Malinche and the Virgin of Guadalupe share similar characteristics in their desires for creation, care, and mediation. As Anzaldúa writes, "La gente Chicana tiene tres madres. [The Chicano people have three mothers.] All three are *mediators:* Guadalupe, the Virgin Mother who has not abandoned us, la Chingada (Malinche), the raped mother whom we have abandoned, and La Llorona, the mother who seeks her lost children and is a combination of the other two" (30, italics mine). Together, these three mothers are embodied in the figure of Coatlicue, the goddess of wholeness, of sex and spirit, life and death, good and bad. As Anzaldúa writes, Coatlicue "contained and balanced the dualities of male and female, light and dark, life and death" (32). One critic characterizes her as both "goddess and monster, beneficent and threatening" and asserts that she is used by Anzaldúa to represent the need to accept all our aspects, positive and negative.[22] In their roles as both sexual and spiritual mothers, as well as in their roles as spiritual and political mediators, then, the Virgin and La Malinche can be seen as descendants of the goddesses, Tonantzin and Tlazolteotl, who together descend from Coatlicue.

Putting the pieces together again through Coatlicue

Anzaldúa writes that Coatlicue is "something more than mere duality or the synthesis of duality" (46); she "depicts the contradictory" (47). She is a symbol of the paradoxical nature of all traumatic experience, we might say, and as such "is a prelude to a crossing" (48)—from death to life, from life to death, from all states that we consider to be mutually exclusive but in fact exist simultaneously, both together and apart.

First, we see that for Anzaldúa, the Coatlicue state is an encounter with the body. As Anzaldúa tells us, Coatl means "serpent," and Lopeuh means "the one who has dominion over the serpents. . . . I interpret this as 'the one who is at one with the beasts' " (29). Anzaldúa explains that "to enter into the serpent," to give oneself to Coatlicue, is "to acknowledge that I have a body, that I am a body and to assimilate the animal body, the animal soul" (Anzaldúa 26). As the serpent, Coatlicue is "She, the symbol of the dark sexual drive, the chthonic (underworld), the feminine, the serpentine movement of sexuality, of creativity, the basis of all energy and life" (35). As such, "Coatlicue da luz a todo y a todo devora [Coatlicue gives light to all and devours all]" (46, my translation). Through the acknowledgment of the body, Coatlicue teaches Anzaldúa how to "be at one with the beasts," how to see the body not only as a site of wounding but a source for healing.[23] Further, she claims,

> For only through the body, through the pulling of flesh, can the human soul be transformed. And for images, words, stories to have this transformative power, they must arise from the human body—flesh and bone—and from the Earth's body—stone, sky, liquid, soil. (75)

Second, the figure of Coatlicue teaches Anzaldúa to connect the material and the spiritual meanings of her crossings between life and death. The figure of the goddess, Coatlicue, is sometimes represented with the head of a bird, which can be read as a symbol of the duality of sky and earth, upper and lower realms.[24] But a figure with a bird's head also represents the ability to travel between these upper and lower realms, between life and death.[25] Like Coatlicue, who had to be rediscovered, Anzaldúa, too, must rediscover how life and death, body and spirit are connected. Anzaldúa writes, "We're supposed to forget that every cell in our bodies, every bone and bird and worm has spirit in it" (36).

Thus, through the figure of Coatlicue, Anzaldúa learns to remember the spirit in the body, to remember the beliefs of ancient Mesoamerica, in which every "bone and bird and worm has spirit in it." Every bone has spirit: every death brings a birth—indeed, death is necessary for life.[26] Every bird has spirit: every being has the ability to travel, to bring healing from the journey. Every worm has spirit: even the decay, the underground has movement, holds the potential for regeneration. Anzaldúa learns to remember these lessons by taking on the journey to "miktlán, the underworld" (48), as we examined in chapter 6. Her descent is a return that she resists but eventually takes:

> . . . resistance to knowing, to letting go, to that deep ocean where once I
> dived into death. I am afraid of drowning. Resistance to sex, intimate touch-
> ing, opening myself to the alien other where I am out of control, not on
> patrol. (48)

The figure of Coatlicue thus functions as a model for staying conscious during such experiences, for acknowledging both physical and emotional feelings, for overcoming resistance to such feelings, and in so doing, learning from the wounding: "It is this learning to be with Coatlicue that transforms living in the Borderlands from a nightmare into a numinous experience" (73). The third function of Coatlicue, then, is to allow Anzaldúa to explore the grief, pain, depression, and feelings of loss that are the accompaniments to bearing a traumatic history. Coatlicue functions, we might say, as a goddess of mourning.

Let us focus more closely on the figure of Coatlicue as a goddess of mourning through a reading of Anzaldúa's writing that starts the chapter entitled, "La Herencia de Coatlicue" (41–42). The writing, set off from the prose text of the chapter of *Borderlands / La Frontera* as a poem, does not itself

have a title and is not included in the poetry section of the book, all fac-
tors that call attention to its status on the border and as a border between
genres, signifying other borders between death and life, past and future,
traumatic history and future survival.

Visually, the text looks like the statue of Coatlicue from the fifteenth
century, just before the arrival of the Spaniards. To examine the text in the
context of traumatic history, I will focus on intersection of the statue and
its historical symbolism with the text and its images. In order to understand
more fully the implications of Anzaldúa's use of the figure of Coatlicue,
we need to trace the historical roots of the myth of Coatlicue. I do this
not only because other critics have not done so, but because in so doing,
we will see not only how turning to history can help in the healing from
trauma, but also how simply turning to history is not in itself a solution.
We will see how there are four themes that can be drawn from this analy-
sis of the writing. These themes have to do with the present state of being
on the border, the reconstruction of the past events that led to this state,
the impossibility of return to the past, and finally, the future implications
for the subject on this border.

The present state of being on the border is conveyed by the chapter
title, "La herencia de Coatlicue/ The Coatlicue State," and the first three
lines of the text:

> protean being
>
> dark   dumb   windowless   no moon glides
>
> across the stone   the nightsky   alone   alone

There are several ways to interpret Anzaldúa's chapter title, "La herencia de
Coatlicue / The Coatlicue State." Significantly, there are no Spanish words
in the poem, and only one in the title: "herencia," which could be read
politically as the Chicano nation state or philosophically as the "state" of
being on the border. It is this latter meaning that we will explore. The
Spanish word, "herencia," means inheritance, which implies a legacy from
the past to the present continuing into the future, while the English word,
"state" implies a period, but more than that, a condition, an attitude out-
side of linear time, a period of constancy. The first line of the poem is
"protean being," through which the text asks the question, what does it
mean to "be" on the border where "being" is defined by its protean,
changeable, fluid, temporary nature? In the second line, through the words
"dark" and "dumb" we get more of a description of what it means to be
on this border. One is "dark," literally dark-skinned, and also invisible to

others. One is "dumb," without intelligence and without the ability to speak. Without vision or voice, then, the inhabitants of the border are the invisible and silent survivors of a traumatic history.

These inhabitants live in a setting that is "windowless." A window is a division between one and another and also the possibility for seeing through from one state to another, from inside to outside or from outside to inside. Here the window is the division between being and non-being, between life and death. Thus, to be "windowless" is to experience oneself as the border between being and non-being, between what is known and unknown, between life and death. In the transition between the second and third lines, we learn that, on this border "no moon glides"; there is no reflection, no light "across the stone." If there were light from the sun onto the moon, this "moon light" would form a reflection on the stone. But here there is no reflection, only "the nightsky" in which there is no possibility for gaining distance (reflecting) on the experience during the experience itself. In this nightsky the silent and invisible subject of traumatic history is "alone alone." In the fourth line, we see there are "no lights just mirror-walls," no vision, only repetitions of an unacknowledged and unwitnessed traumatic history. Through the reconstruction and witnessing of this history, as we have seen, healing may begin. Healing will mean, then, the end of silence, invisibility and aloneness.

In order to begin this process, as we have seen, it is necessary to attempt a reconstruction of the past events that led to this state. In the poem, it is through "obsidian" that the speaker gains a "window" and a "light" to see through the present to the past. Obsidian, the black rock of ancient Aztec culture, represented, according to Neumann:

> the magical weapon descended from heaven, the life-and-death bringing central symbol of the bloody primeval great Mother. . . . In America, obsidian as a spear point, hunting knife, sacrificial knife, and sword is an instrument of death.[27]

Through the figure of obsidian, the poem refers to the lost civilization of the Aztecs. Other aspects of the poem participate in this attempt to recall the past, such as the lines, "she sees a woman with four heads." There are four, the number of seasons and cycles of ancient civilizations, not three, the number of the dialectic and synthesis of the West. This image also represents the circular conception of time and history of Aztec civilization, "the heads / turning round and round spokes of a wheel her neck / is an axle."[28] These lines recall the myth that Coatlicue was decapitated and two serpents sprang from her severed neck.[29] In the statue of Coatlicue from the fifteenth century, which was found in the eighteenth century, Coatlicue is depicted as headless, with two snakes where her head should be. This has been interpreted as symbolizing the cosmic principle of duality that she represents: she is both masculine and feminine, both creation and destruction, both life and death.[30]

However, the necessity for reconstructing the significance of these symbols associated with Coatlicue also marks the significance of the loss of this civilization, in pointing to the impossibility of full knowledge of what has been lost. Even as the obsidian allows this reconstruction, it also reminds us of the obscurity of the reconstruction: "smoky in the / mirror she sees." The smoky obsidian implies fire, burning, the ignition of mourning brought about by loss.[31] Thus, the "smoky" nature of the scene marks the inevitability of dealing with the loss that the reconstruction of trauma makes impossible to ignore. While the attempt at reconstruction is necessary for witnessing a traumatic past, it is also impossible to complete this reconstruction. True witnessing means the recognition of the loss associated with a traumatic past, and this recognition leads to the necessity for mourning.

The next few lines of the poem remind us that the negation of this loss and the negation of the past are often part of the mourning process.[32] The poem alludes to the desire to negate the lost other: "she stares at each face each wishes the / other not there." Similarly, the desire for negation may give rise to the potential for violence: "the obsidian knife in the air" of ritual sacrifice, human killing for the god. Also, as we have seen in Sexton's poetry, there is the temptation for the negation of self in mourning, as the refusal of survival and the possibility of suicide arise for the subject: "the / building   so high *should she jump.*"

Regardless of whether or not suicide is chosen, in the end nothing will return the lost past to the survivor.[33] What, then, can be a possible next step for the survivor who is starting to recognize the immensity of the loss in traumatic history? Often the next step is a focus on the *cause* of the loss. This impossible desire to know the cause is dramatized in the following lines:

> would she feel
> the breeze   fanning her face

Given the line break, the following questions arise: is the subject here the "she" who wonders about the possibility of feeling in suicide, of feeling the touch of the breeze on her face during the fall? Or is the subject of these lines, "the breeze," which could be read as the agent that is both fanning her face and the cause of her tumbling down the steps:

the breeze   fanning her face   tumbling down the steps
    of the temple

Thus, the impossibility of knowing the agent of "the fall" is precisely what is being dramatized in these lines.

The same question concerning the cause of death is conveyed again later in the poem. As a reading of the following lines shows, the cause of death is precisely what is being put into question here:

she bends to catch a
feather of herself   as she falls

These phrases can be read in three ways: Does she fall because she bent to catch a feather of herself? Does she bend to catch a feather of herself because she fell? Or, as is implied by the use of the present tense, is it impossible to draw a conclusion about the cause? This third possibility, while calling attention to the other possibilities, presents itself as the ultimate possibility. The reconstruction of traumatic history, while calling attention to the desire for cause, also refuses causality. The impossibility of fulfilling the desire for cause parallels the impossibility of fulfilling the desire for the referent in traumatic history.[34] The fulfillment of both desires is impossible, and this, in short, is what makes mourning necessary.

Traumatic history thus recalls the fairy tale lesson of Cinderella in which the coach turns into a pumpkin; it is the end of the ball, the end of the dance with the prince, which is here designated by "turning   turning / at midnight   turning into a wild pig." But in this story, the prince will not send his servants to match the glass slipper so they can live happily ever after. The "return" is refused even as it is put into question:

how to get back
   all the feathers   put them in a jar   the rattling
full circle and back

Thus, the question is put forth: is it possible to gather the lost parts, to encase them where they might be saved and safe? This question goes to the heart of the problem of traumatic history. It is the question of how to recapture what has been lost. It is the question of whether or not it is even possible to recuperate the loss. It is the question of whether or not the recuperation and recapture is not also a return to the jar of snakes. The answer to these questions leads us back to the only place it is possible to go "back" to: "full circle and back" to the beginning of the poem.

> full circle and back   dark windowless   no moon
>   glides across the nightsky   nightsky   night

Thus, the experience of the border turns into the necessity of mourning the "nightsky nightsky night." The repetition of the night reaches us from the border of the ruins where, in the rubble, we must face the decision to re-create ourselves or to refuse survival. It is through identification with the lost other, through time, that the border experience can be said to hold both promises of re-creation and the seeds of further destruction. These promises occur exactly at the point of loss—at the point of recognition of not knowing the past, of not knowing the other. As Edward Casey writes, "we cannot fully commemorate something unless it has come to an end in some significant sense."[35] It is through the recognition of the impossibility of recovering the past of traumatic history, paradoxically, that the possibility of future survival may arise.

Mourning and witnessing, then, are the necessary processes for healing from trauma because, together, they allow for the healing of the self both intrapsychically and intersubjectively, both internally and externally. As Edward Casey writes of memories of the dead, "The commemoration [memories] effect from within, instead of keeping us within, expresses the fact that mind is fashioned from without—known from without via identifications with others. *The intrapsychic is ineluctably interpsychic.*"[36] These processes are continual and must be attended to again and again; as Anzaldúa writes, "It's not enough / opening once" (164). The opening of the self to the other outside and the other within are processes that do not follow a linear progression of beginning, middle, and end, but must continue throughout our lifetimes and, fortunately, can begin at any time.

Bessel A. van der Kolk notes the importance of grieving and communal memorialization for "survivor groups who have no memorial and no common symbol around which they can gather to mourn and express their shame about their own vulnerability."[37] As we begin to come to the close of this chapter and this book, we might ask ourselves, where are the memorials for sexually abused children, for those who were lost in the Middle Passage, for the lives of men and women under slavery, for the loss of lives and entire civilizations due to colonization? Our reluctance to mourn such losses could be due to the vastness of the destruction.

We may feel that even to begin this process of mourning would lead to such overwhelming feelings of guilt that we resist such mourning at all costs. Perhaps it is the fear of guilt that keeps us, as a society, from witnessing. If in some way we know that to witness means, in the end, to have to feel guilt, to feel responsibility, and to act on those feelings, then perhaps this is what keeps us from witnessing. While guilt may indeed not be pleasant, it is, in my view, less painful than continuing to live in the kind of society, comprised of "others," wounded, alone, and torn apart by violence, that we live in now.

Thus, the mourning that the figure of Coatlicue represents applies not only to the specific, historical conditions of Chicana women, but to all of us who survive any border experience between life and death. In a remark reminiscent of Heidegger's distinction between being and Being, Anzaldúa states, "The little 'b' is the actual Southwest borderlands or any borderlands between two cultures, but when I use the capital B it's like a mestiza with a capital M. It's a metaphor, not an actuality" (Anzaldúa 1991, 129). Anzaldúa tells us that the survival of these Borderlands is not only literal but is also "spiritual, psychic, supernatural" (Anzaldúa 1991, 129). Thus the Borderlands represent the ontological difference between being and non-being that must be attended to, ultimately, through mourning.

However, Anzaldúa does not stop here with her revisioning of the connection between La Malinche and the Virgin of Guadalupe through Coatlicue. To do so would be to wish for an impossible return to the past, to the time before the whole was broken into pieces. Instead, by working through the rereadings of the histories of the two figures of La Malinche and the Virgin, Anzaldúa is enabled to create her own myth, the myth of Antigua. Through the myth of Antigua, a new goddess, Anzaldúa moves from an understanding of the past to a vision for the future. This vision of the future, as we will examine in the next section, is not a vision of a utopian end to suffering but is a call to begin the process of healing, a process that continues without end.

Antigua, goddess of survival

Antigua is the name that Anzaldúa uses to refer to the goddess of her new mythology, a mythology of survival. As Anzaldúa writes, "I write the myths in me, the myths I am, the myths I want to become" (71). Antigua, then, symbolizes the past (through all that has come before), the present (through

Anzaldúa herself), and the future (through the vision of the new mestiza). Antigua, the goddess of this new mestiza, is the goddess of both the mestiza self and the mestiza culture. As such she encompasses the new understandings of both history and mythology that Anzaldúa has gained over her lifetime of shamanistic crossings. In addition to being a composite of the past, Antigua also projects the vision of the future that Anzaldúa proposes: a future in which both individuals and cultures begin the process of coming to acknowledge and care for their multiplicity, their diversity, their differences both within and without.

In the poem, "Antigua, mi diosa," Anzaldúa shows her vision of healing from trauma, a vision in which the past (antigua, the ancient) sentences one to survival in the present and for the future (188–189). As we will see in this poem, the crossings between life and death that we saw in "Matriz sin tumba o [Womb without tomb]" do not end in Anzaldúa's vision of the future. Instead, Antigua encourages us to begin the process of healing and learning from these endless crossings. Interestingly, this poem, like "Matriz sin tumba o [Womb without tomb]," appears only in Spanish in Anzaldúa's text; so that we may all begin to heal and learn from Antigua's wisdom, I will provide an English translation for the reading of the poem.

The opening of the poem calls attention to its similarity to the tradition of Aztec songs of migration, such as in *The Florentine Codex:* "We go, we walk, along a very narrow road on earth. On this side is an abyss. On that side is an abyss. . . . One goes, one walks, only in the middle."[38] Anzaldúa follows in a tradition of migrations that are both repetitions of loss and possibilities for gaining wisdom, as the speaker goes along a road that is fraught with peril and pain: "walking to dead-ends," "under the impudent sky." The speaker travels in a body worn out by the road: "splinters in my knees," "with steps of a turtle," "I have sacrificed / the soles of my feet." All this has been done for the goddess, in order to follow the "tracks" and "lines" of the goddess, in order to be a "witness to this long winter." These travels, then, are what enable the speaker to witness the "winter," which, as we saw in Sexton's and Lorde's poetry as well, is a symbol of the season without growth, the season of destruction, the season of death.

The next stanza moves from an account of the speaker's travels to a visitation by the goddess, as Antigua comes to the "ruins" of civilization, symbolized by Brooklyn, filled with poverty, concrete, and the metal screech of trains. Antigua's arrival is marked by sound, the sound of "rattlesnakes," a marker of the ancient civilization and of other goddesses, Cihuacoatl and

Coatlicue, as well as the sound of "a million wings." The term used in Spanish for "wings" is "alas," which is a homophone for Allas, the plural of the Moslem name for god. The word also sounds like the name for love/god/spirit used in meditation by Sufis.[39] Further, the meaning of the term "wings," connotes flight and the ability to travel back and forth from the spirit world. The goddess is also "[l]ike a squall," a term that can mean three things: an act of nature, such as a storm; an act of humans, such as a scream or cry; as well as an act belonging to either nature or humanity, such as a disturbance.[40] She smells of "burnt almonds and copal," signifying an offering or sacrifice. The almond symbolizes "sweetness and delicacy" that may be destroyed by the winter, by the season of death: "one of the first trees to blossom, late frosts can destroy its flowers."[41] In burning almonds, the goddess keeps the winter's freeze, its destruction, at bay. Copal, unlike the delicacy of the almond, is a resin obtained from trees indigenous to Mexico and because of its strength is used in varnishes.[42] Thus, the goddess symbolizes the sacrifice of both of these qualities—delicacy and strength—by fire.

In the next stanza, we see that the goddess works to wake the speaker, who, we might guess, is slumbering through the winter. She is awakened by the goddess' "ax," which falls "like a tree," and forces the sleeper to open her eyes. The destruction of the winter, teaches the goddess, must not be slept through; instead, the goddess makes the speaker feel in her body the pain of this destructive season. The goddess' fingers work like "swords," a symbol of the mind and the intellect, and these swords cut and slice her, wound her, carving wisdom into her body and spirit: "making patterns in my soul."[43] This goddess, then, is both instructive and destructive, much like the further wounding that is necessary in order to heal from trauma, as one goes into the pain of the memory in order to work through it. This healing "light" then enters her body, as the goddess enters as her "cracks," her "holes."

In so doing, the goddess purges the destruction and plants "seeds" of healing, of "light," where there had once been only wounds, in the "furrows." The result, or "harvest," of planting such seeds is growth, marked by "restlessness," by the inability to slumber through the winter destruction anymore. The speaker now cannot numb herself to pain or destruction but must feel the "agony" within her and around her, even after the goddess leaves or "flee[s]." This is the result of healing, then: not a "cure," but a charge, not an ending to pain, but a beginning to feeling. Like Audre Lorde's "erotic," which forces us to demand the best from ourselves and each other, Anzaldúa's Antigua impels us to change ourselves, to be never satisfied, to work endlessly toward healing, even when there is no cure.

This "endless work" is, like some analysis, interminable, as the term used in Spanish, "inacabable," means both endless and interminable.[44] It is also, like analysis, the work of making and unmaking oneself. Finally, it is work that cannot be "surrender[ed]," given over to either the goddess or the analyst, nor can it be "submit[ted]" to the lap of the mother. Yet, neither is the speaker the "dueña,"—the owner or mistress—of her work, either. Thus, while the mother/goddess/healer may plant the seeds of healing, she does not do the work; conversely, while the one to be healed is ultimately responsible for the work, she cannot do it alone.

What the goddess gives, then, is not a cure but an "affliction," as Antigua, in healing her, "sentence[s]" her to survival. And while the goddess helps to heal, helps to ensure survival, the work of living must be done in her absence. There is no miracle, no ultimate cure, no final reunion. Instead, the goddess leaves the speaker with desire: the desire to keep working, the desire to keep searching, the desire to keep moving. While the daughter "wander[s]" and makes mistakes (the term in Spanish is "errante," which means to wander and to err), she does so with desire, with feeling, with a "burning" that disperses the winter.[45] Her life becomes a journey of attempts to "reach," to "look," to "know." A vision of healing from trauma, Antigua teaches, takes the form of neither apocalypse nor prophecy, but something else, which is both hopeful and never-ending. Survival is, in the end, an endless pilgrimage to the goddess, who leaves her charge for us to live: to continue the healing, the growth, the connection, the love, the flowering of our "bud," the small, fragile manifestation of what she planted, the promise of what may grow large and beautiful and sweet.

The budding of the new mestiza

Kai Erikson has written that collective trauma effects a "blow to the basic tissues of social life that damages the bonds attaching people together and impairs the prevailing sense of community . . . 'I' continue to exist. . . . 'You' continue to exist. . . . But 'we' no longer exist."[46] Healing from trauma, then, entails a redefinition of all subjects, both individual and collective. As we have seen in Audre Lorde's writing, the difference between "you" and "I" can become a source of power: positive, creative, and life-affirming power. This connection between Lorde and Anzaldúa has been articulated by Lourdes Torres; for both Lorde and Anzaldúa, she writes, it is not the differences between women that separate them, but the fear of recognizing difference, naming it, and understanding that we have been programmed to respond to difference with fear and loathing.[47]

Anzaldúa, like Lorde, writes of our need to recognize the differences within us in order to live in peace and without violence caused by the desire to do away with the differences between us.[48] As we have seen, Antigua is the force that encourages Anzaldúa to develop this recognition and acceptance of difference without fear. Antigua is also the wisdom that teaches that the fear of difference and violent opposition are the seeds from which grows a culture of traumatic violence. Thus, as wisdom of the past and vision for the future, Antigua is the goddess of the new mestiza, Anzaldúa's hope and vision of a society where "nothing is thrust out, the good the bad and the ugly, nothing rejected, nothing abandoned" (79).

The wisdom that Antigua gives leads to a new conception of the subject, which Anzaldúa calls "the new mestiza": "like corn, the mestiza is product of crossbreeding" (81) that *"tenia un caracter multiplice"* (44). Also, like the corn sacred to the *indigena,* this subject has power: "My power is my inner self, the entity that is the sum total of all my reincarnations, the godwoman in me . . . they are one" (50). Opening oneself to the literal pain of memory in order to reconstruct it figuratively allows one to learn to accept all of the parts of the self. Anzaldúa writes that "What we are suffering from is an absolute despot duality that says we are only able to be one or the other" (19), and she urges us to accept that "There are many personalities and subpersonalities in *you,* and your identity shifts every time you shift positions" (Anzaldúa 1991, 111).[49] As Sidonie Smith characterizes Anzaldúa's conception of the new mestiza subject, "The new consciousness leads to a state of openness, not self-closure; it is not individual but transindividual, not unitary but multiple."[50]

Thus, it is *through her survival* that Anzaldúa is enabled to present a new conception of the subject, one in which "denying the Anglo inside you/is as bad as having denied the Indian or Black" (194). Sonia Saldívar-Hull writes, "While not rejecting any part of herself, Anzaldúa's new mestiza *becomes a survivor* because of her ability to 'live sin fronteras / be a crossroads.' "[51] It is an individual and a collective subject that is "half and half— both woman and man, neither—/a new gender" (194). Thus, internal to the self, the different parts mutually recognize each other: "my theory of identity: all these people are on the stage, and they take turns taking center" (Anzaldúa 1991, 126). As a result of having achieved this mutual recognition within herself, Anzaldúa is able to assert, "I think we can live separately and we can also connect and be together" (Anzaldúa 1991, 111).

In the dramatization of the processes of mourning and witnessing the traumatic history of her people, Anzaldúa helps all Americans to recognize that we, too, share in this traumatic past. Anzaldúa describes how this "inner work" happens:

> I look inside our conflicts. . . . I identify our needs, voice them. I acknowl-
> edge that the self and the race have been wounded. I recognize the need to
> take care of our personhood, of our racial self. On that day I gather the
> splintered and disowned parts of *la gente mexicana* and hold them in my arms.
> *Todas las partes de nosotros valen.* (88)

And this recognition within us is accompanied by work between us, as we "share our history" (85). It is a singular history that has been split by trauma and needs to be reconciled: "we need to know the history of their strug-gle and they need to know ours" (86). By healing the split within us, we begin to heal the split between us, so that we may live together—in peace, in common. To hold together that which is different: this is the paradox and the promise that Anzaldúa poses in her mestiza mythology, the paradox and promise that may arise when, finally, we heal from memory.

Conclusion

The Emperor Wears No Clothes

As in the story of "The Emperor's New Clothes," it has taken a new generation of "innocent children," removed enough from the experience, to be in a position to ask questions.

—Dori Laub, "Truth and Testimony: The Process and The Struggle"

While indeed this book has demonstrated how the poetry of Sexton, Lorde, and Anzaldúa teaches us to witness and heal from America's traumatic histories, it has also shown that we, as a nation, are often not who we think we are. As Dori Laub so wisely observed, it is often the *next* generation who has the courage—or the audacity—to cry out that the emperor has no clothes. I have found this to be true—for myself, young enough to have had any one of these writers as my mother—and for my students, who could be my daughters.

What Sexton, Lorde, and Anzaldúa's writing opens up is the possibility that we might see through the mirages of our society. War as triumph. Women as victims. Family as holy sanctuary. The present as disconnected from the past. The mind as disconnected from the body. Spirituality as disconnected from our sexuality. To conclude, then, I would like to share some of my insights from teaching to suggest ways that we, as teachers—whether in classrooms or out—might serve our children, as Lorde says, "wherever we may find them."

For many students, Sexton's life is a poignant lesson in motherhood. Many of my students have identified Sexton with their mothers, and this identification has taught them to have compassion and respect for the struggles of women they might, in the thrill of some introductory Women's Studies discussions, dismiss as victims of "false consciousness." Studying Sexton's work in the light of feminist research on childhood sexual abuse allows for the possibility that what might seem at first to be "politically retrograde" often stems from a history of severe violence, silence, and misrecognition.

Further, by our recognizing what those around Sexton at the time could not, we also change our perceptions of ourselves. If we, too, have in the past stood as judges upon those whom we could not recognize, then we, too, begin to see ourselves as the mother, priest, therapist, or peer who failed to witness to a woman's pain. We come to see ourselves as having been a part of the problem. In this change—from the "we" who we thought we were to the "we" who we are becoming—lies the possibility for healing from the past, both individually and collectively.

Lorde's work demonstrates to us and to students how the possibility for healing arises through an understanding that the "I" arises as a result of the "we." Through her writing, she teaches that both individual actions and collective traits stem from specific histories. Discerning the individual's place in this collective history leads to the necessity of taking personal responsibility for the pain of the past and the possibility of the future. Lorde's work thus not only shows how the "I" is connected to the "we" through history, but moreover shows how each of us has the responsibility to witness to this history.

One day I was sitting in my office, waiting for students to come in to discuss their final papers with me. Julie, a small, pale, blonde woman came in and sat down. I asked her how her work was going. "Fine," she said. "I want to talk about Audre Lorde, though."

"Okay."

"Well," she started, slowly. I thought she was going to say that she identified with her, perhaps felt in herself desire for women. . . .

"It's nasty," she blurted, and started crying. "I have never thought about lesbians before. I mean, I don't want to hate, but when we read the poems, the love poems, I saw these pictures in my mind, and I just felt gross, and I thought, I hate this woman, and I hated that hate in my heart. I am a Christian, so it really bothers me to hate in this way. But I really have to admit this hate I feel. I don't want to feel it."

I let her cry for a while. I felt like a priest. And then I said, "Feeling these feelings is exactly the right thing to do. Your honesty, and your feelings—your sadness, your disgust, your hate, your fear—all of these need to be felt. It is so courageous of you to come talk to me like this. And to cry. You are doing exactly what is needed. These feelings, if you did not allow yourself to feel them, would still be there. They won't go away by your ignoring them. It's okay."

Her face, red and blotchy, her pale blue eyes lined with tears, suddenly looked right at me. "Okay then," she said, in that way students have of getting back to business. "My paper's going fine. I guess I'll see you in class."

In witnessing, we participate in the reconstruction and recognition of the violence of the past and of the present that it creates. In turn, we come to see that we each, individually, have the responsibility to witness to our own failure to recognize another's history. Through this participation, we come to see our individual selves as a "we" who together make the choice to recognize and respect each other's differences—or not—and contribute to the future survival of us all—or not.

Reading Anzaldúa's writing shows how the destruction of a sense of a "we" is itself a marker of a history of collective, traumatic violence. The profound sense of alienation that one feels—from the past, from each other, and from oneself—is a sign that the effects of an unrecognized traumatic history are still being repeated in the present. Understanding that this alienation—this sense of *having been left*—is a result of a specific history of traumatic violence opens the way to the possibility of remembering and witnessing to that history. And this, in turn, leads to the possibility of rebuilding a sense of "we" who, having survived the past, can survive for the future.

Often, here in the South, those who "have been left" are members of a student's own family: a grandmother or grandfather who is "Indian but nobody talks about it." Students have told me that after years of seeing what happens to their African American neighbors, what gets burned on their lawn, and burned in the town's memory, families decided to "pass" for white. Of course, no one in their families explained this to them outright. They simply had to be the ones to ask questions, to take notice. Reading Anzaldúa for these students means digging through their memories to put the pieces together. Usually this occurs around memories of "faith healing" or "magic" or an elder family member's feeling of spiritual connection with the land. Students write in papers, and sometimes talk out loud, about the "powers" of a relative, and how these were hidden away, forgotten, not passed down. What Anzaldúa's mestiza mythology helps students realize is that we all, in some way, must stop denying the mix of cultures that have gone into creating who we are as individuals, as families, and as communities.

Optimism must, however, be balanced by a sense of the profound difficulties of being the one who asks the questions, the one who tries to reconstruct the family history, the one who engages in a discussion with a racist roommate, the one who breaks off an engagement with a fiancé "because I realized he will never understand, and I can't live my life with someone like that." While remembering, reconstructing, and working through (by witnessing and mourning) have been presented as the "processes of healing," we must also take care not to regard these processes as having an easy or guaranteed outcome.

Indeed, we have seen how Sexton suffered from a lack of recognition of the patterns of her symptoms. While both her life and her work show evidence of her individual attempt to remember and reconstruct her traumatic past, in the end there was no one who could help her through the witnessing process. In Lorde's poetry, as well, we observed the widespread hesitancy to witness, evidenced by the silence in black women's history and the continued devastation of lives through drugs, incest, rape, murder, and violence. In Anzaldúa's work we came to see the immense difficulty in comprehending the devastation of an entire culture. This difficulty is compounded by a lack of knowledge about the past through which we might be able to measure the loss. This leaves us with a need to mourn the loss, and as we saw through Anzaldúa's writing, it is not clear that this mourning has an ending.

Healing, then, cannot be conceived as either simple or certain. Sexton's strategy was neither; in creating a language of survival through melancholia, she paves the way toward an understanding of healing not as a happy ending but as a continuing attempt to balance the positive and negative aspects of incorporation and negation, through which one might hope to achieve a sense of sympathy for oneself and others. For Lorde, as well, healing is not a product but a process. Healing means the endless efforts to come to speech, to wade through the histories of silence, and to overcome fear so that one might be able to witness to a violent history. Anzaldúa's writing shows that healing comes through the acceptance of pain as a sign. She demonstrates that in order to heal, one needs to recognize the wound and to see what it can teach; one needs to feel the pain of the wound in order not to inflict further violence as a way of denying the pain.

Given all of this, what, then, does it mean to say that "We heal from memory"? Sexton's poetry presents her vision of the fruition of this phrase, as she encourages a reclamation of our bodies and spirits, a reclamation that comes primarily through love of ourselves, as we give ourselves the love of "the great mother . . . / I never had." Sexton's poetry assures us, even as it could not assure her, that it is possible to see ourselves as whole and holy, as embodied and beautiful, and that to love ourselves in this way allows us to love others without objectification or violence.

Lorde, too, encourages us to turn to the mother, through the tracing of cultural "mother roots" from which we can derive strength and hope for the future. Lorde teaches that, especially for a culture of people so violently torn from its roots, it is vital to see the still-surviving connections to that source of nurturance, to see our lives as following in the footsteps of others who continue to sustain us. She warns that if we refuse this recognition of our shared journeys, we only contribute to our continued annihilation.

Anzaldúa, like Lorde, asks us to commit to tracing mother roots, but she also invites us to make our own. Anzaldúa's writing makes us realize that wishing for a happy ending, as the West has taught us to do, is to set ourselves up for failure. Through her creation of the myth of Antigua, she reminds us that we have been sentenced to survival, to the work of tracing our roots, remembering the past, healing from our hurts, sharing our stories, and working toward a future. This work is never-ending, and yet, it is the only way that we have *to live*.

Notes

Introduction

1. Psychoanalytic writers include, of course, Freud, and also, more recently, Judith Lewis Herman, *Trauma and Recovery* (New York: Basic Books, 1992); Lenore Terr, *Unchained Memories* (New York: Basic Books, 1994); and Laura S. Brown, "Not Outside the Range: One Feminist Perspective on Trauma," in *Trauma: Explorations in Memory,* ed. Cathy Caruth (Baltimore, MD: Johns Hopkins Press, 1995): 100–112. I include in the category of the historical writers who study theoretically or narratively the Holocaust, writers such as Dori Laub, "Truth and Testimony: The Process and the Struggle," *American Imago* 48:1 (1991): 75–91, among others. For the connections between philosophy and psychoanalysis with regard to trauma, see Michèle Bertrand, *La pensée et le trauma* (Paris: Harmattan, 1990).

2. In his *Case Studies On Hysteria,* through the case of Katharina, Freud shows how trauma is constituted through departure and return. From Freud and Breuer, *Studies in Hysteria* (New York: Basic Books, ND): 125–134. Also in *Project for a Scientific Psychology,* Freud, in the case of Emma, discusses the impossibility of consciously experiencing the traumatic event and the necessity for screen memories to help the ego cope with the traumatic event (404–416). The traumatic dream is discussed by Freud in his *Introductory Lectures on Psycho-Analysis* (New York: Norton, 1966), especially in "Fixation to Traumas—the Unconscious," where he writes that "patients regularly repeat the traumatic situation in their dreams" (340).

3. The significance of the impossibility of direct referentiality and its connection to the ethical nature of address are discussed in Cathy Caruth's "Unclaimed Experience: Trauma and the Impossibility of History," *Yale French Studies: Literature and the Ethical Question* 79 (1991): 181–192.

4. Indeed, Michael Holquist cites "trauma studies" as the location of the most

important, comparative work being done today, and specifically mentions the work of Cathy Caruth. See "A New Tour of Babel: Recent Trends Linking Comparative Literature Departments, Foreign Language Departments, and Area Studies Programs," *Profession 1996*: 103–114.

5. One example of such an unnecessarily deadlocked debate is found between Joan Wallach Scott and Linda Gordon. See Scott, *Gender and the Politics of History* (New York: Columbia University Press, 1988); and Gordon, Review of Joan Scott, *Gender and the Politics of History, Signs* 15 (1990): 853–858.

6. See Leonard Shengold's chapter, "Did It Really Happen? An Assault on Truth, Historical and Narrative," in his *Soul Murder* for an account of the polarities surrounding the debate over truth in trauma studies.

7. (Princeton: Princeton University Press, 1995.)

8. See Dawn Skorczewski, "What Prison Is This? Literary Critics Cover Incest in Anne Sexton's 'Briar Rose,'" *Signs* 21:2 (Winter 1996): 326–329. In this essay, Skorczewski cites only male critics who ignore the signs of incest in Sexton's "Briar Rose," while many female critics have ignored the signs in all of Sexton's poetry, as well. For example, two women critics deny the incest in essays from 1992 and 1994; see Karen Alkalay-Gut, "'For We Swallow Magic and We Deliver Anne': Anne Sexton's Use of Her Name," *The Anna Book: Searching for Anna in Literary History,* ed. Mickey Pearlman (Westport, CT: Greenwood, 1992): 139–49, p. 142; and Jacqueline Banerjee, "Grief and the Modern Writer," *English: The Journal of the English Association* 43:175 (Spring 1994): 17–36, p. 21. Two other women critics resist confirming it; see Ellen Cronan Rose, "Through the Looking Glass: When Women Tell Fairy Tales," in *The Voyage In: Fictions of Female Development,* ed. Elizabeth Abel, Marianne Hirsch, and Elizabeth Langland (Hanover, NH: University Press of New England for Dartmouth Coll., 1983): 209–227, p. 216; and Alicia Ostriker, "Anne Sexton and the Seduction of the Audience," in *Sexton: Selected Criticism,* ed. Diana Hume George (Urbana, IL: University of Illinois Press, 1988): 3–18, p. 13.

9. Anna Wilson writes of the tokenization of Lorde by white critics in her essay, "Rites/Rights of Canonization: Audre Lourde as Icon," in *Women Poets of the Americas: Toward a Pan-American Gathering,* eds. Jacqueline Vaught Brogan and Candelaria Cordelia Chavez (Notre Dame, IN: University of Notre Dame Press, 1999): 17–33.

10. To date the criticism on Audre Lorde has not usually been done with sufficient attention to the multiple aspects of Lorde's existence. For the most part certain aspects of Lorde's writing are highlighted, and others are left in shadows while the critic focuses on a singular aspect of Lorde's identity, as a woman who is lesbian, feminist, black, or a cancer survivor. Critics who place Lorde in a lesbian tradition include Mary J. Carruthers, "The Re-Vision of the Muse: Adrienne Rich, Audre Lorde, Judy Grahn, Olga

Broumas," *The Hudson Review* 36:2 (Summer 1983): 293–322; Judy Grahn, *The Highest Apple: Sappho and the Lesbian Poetic Tradition* (San Francisco: Spinsters Ink, 1985); Bonnie Zimmerman, *The Safe Sea of Women: Lesbian Fiction 1969–1989* (Boston: Beacon, 1990); and Ruth Ginzberg, "Audre Lorde's (Nonessentialist) Lesbian Eros," *Hypatia* 7:4 (Fall 1992): 73–90. Those who place her in a feminist tradition include: Pamela Annas, "A Poetry of Survival: Unnaming and naming in the Poetry of Audre Lorde, Pat Parker, Sylvia Plath, and Adrienne Rich," *Colby Library Quarterly* 18 (March 1982): 9–25; Mary K. DeShazer, *Inspiring Women: Reimagining the Muse* (New York: Pergamon Press, 1986); and Thomas Foster, "'The Very House of Difference': Gender as 'Embattled' Standpoint," *Genders* 8 (Summer 1990): 17–37. Lorde's race is highlighted to the exclusion of other categories in Stephen Henderson, ed., *Understanding the New Black Poetry: Black Speech and Black Music as Poetic References* (New York: William Morrow, 1973). Lorde's identity as a cancer survivor is the focus in Jeanne Perreault, "'that the pain not be wasted': Audre Lorde and the Written Self," *A/B: Autobiography Studies* 4:1 (Fall 1988): 1–16; and G. Thomas Couser, "Autopathography: Women, Illness, and Lifewriting," *A/B: Autobiography* 6:1 (Spring 1991): 65–75. There are some critics who do engage with the multiple aspects of Lorde's self; however, they do not explicitly connect these elements with their historical contexts; see Amittai F. Avi-ram, "*Apo Koinou* in Audre Lorde and the Moderns: Defining the Differences," *Callaloo* 9:1 (Winter 1986): 193–208; Gloria T. Hull, "Living on the Line: Audre Lorde and *Our Dead Behind Us,*" in *Changing Our Own Words: Essays on Criticism, Theory and Writing by Black Women,* ed. Cheryl A. Wall (New Brunswick: Rutgers, 1989): 150–173; Barbara DiBernard, "*Zami*: A Portrait of an Artist as a Black Lesbian," *The Kenyon Review* 13:4 (Fall 1991): 195–213; and Erin G. Carlston, "*Zami* and the Politics of Plural Identity," in *Sexual Practice, Textual Theory: Lesbian Cultural Criticism,* ed. Susan J. Wolfe and Julian Penelope (Cambridge, MA: Blackwell, 1993): 226–236.

11. Only three critics place Lorde's work in a historical context. Sharon Patricia Holland argues that white feminism's use of Sojourner Truth silences the many voices of black feminism and treats Lorde's work as a necessary corrective to tokenism and silencing. See "'Which Me Will Survive': Audre Lorde and the Development of a Black Feminist Ideology," *Critical Matrix* Special Issue, No. 1 (1988): 1–30. Ekaterini Georgoudaki shows how Lorde works against the stereotypical images of black women as mammy, matriarch, Amazon, and whore; see her "Audre Lorde: Revising Stereoypes of Afro-American Womanhood," *Arbeiten aus Anglistik und Amerikanistik* 16:1 (1991): 47–66. And Sagri Dhairyam shows how Lorde's work poses challenges to literary critical traditions that are exclusively poetic, lesbian, Black, or feminist; see her "'Artifacts for Survival': Remapping the Contours of Poetry with Audre Lorde," *Feminist Studies* 18:2 (Summer 1992): 229–256.

12. The closest any critic of *Zami* comes to treating Lorde's narrative of sexual abuse is Anna Wilson, who writes, "The adult that Audre has become has the power to hear and speak both the good news of family as tradition and the bad news of family as site of abuse" (85). However, this is said in reference to Audre's friend, Gennie's abuse, not Audre's. It is interesting to think about the depth of silence and denial surrounding sexual abuse in the criticism given that *Zami* is read and written about so widely. See "Audre Lorde and the African-American Tradition: When the Family is Not Enough," in *New Lesbian Criticism,* ed. Sally Munt (New York: Harvester Wheatsheaf, 1992): 75–93.

13. Examples of the critical focus on the border as positive can be found in Sonia Saldívar-Hull, "Feminism on the Border: From Gender Politics to Geopolitics," *Criticism in the Borderlands,* ed. Hector Calderon and José David Saldívar (Durham: Duke University Press, 1991): 203–220, p. 211; Ramón Saldívar, *Chicano Narrative: The Dialectics of Difference* (Madison, WI: University of Wisconsin Press, 1990), p. 218; Paula Gunn Allen, "'Border Studies': The Intersection of Gender and Color," *The Ethnic Canon: Histories, Institutions, and Interventions,* ed. David Palumbo-Liu (Minneapolis: University of Minnesota Press, 1995): 31–47, p. 45.

14. Such a sociological approach to Anzaldúa's work can be found in Carl Gutiérrez-Jones, *Rethinking the Borderlands: Between Chicano Culture and Legal Discourse* (Berkeley: University of California Press, 1995), p. 118–119; Oscar J. Martínez, *Border People: Life and Society in the U.S.–Mexico Borderlands* (Tucson: University of Arizona Press, 1994), p. 309–310; Ruth Behar, *Translated Woman: Crossing the Border with Esperanza's Story* (Boston: Beacon Press, 1993), p. 10–11; Ronald Takaki, *A Different Mirror: A History of Multicultural America* (Boston: Little, Brown and Company, 1993), p. 426. Anzaldúa is also cited by three contributors to *The Multiracial Experience: Racial Borders as the New Frontier,* ed. Maria P. P. Root (Thousand Oaks, CA.: Sage, 1996). All three treat her work as sociology, not literature. See Cynthia Nakashima, "Voices from the Movement: Approaches to Multiraciality," 79–97, p. 90; G. Reginald Daniel, "Black and White Identity in the New Millenium: Unsevering the Ties That Bind," 121–139, p. 134; Carolina A. Streeter, "Ambiguous Bodies: Locating Black/White Women in Cultural Representations," 305–320, pp. 308, 310.

15. For discussions of the benefits of an "American literature as comparative" approach, see Owen Aldgridge, *American Literature: A Comparative Approach* (Princeton: Princeton University Press, 1982); Elizabeth Fox-Genovese, "The Claims of Common Culture: Gender, Race, Class and the Canon," *Salmagundi* 72 (1986): 131–143; Hector Calderon and Jose David Saldivar, "Editors' Introduction," *Criticism in the Borderlands* (Durham: Duke University Press, 1991): 1–7; Ramon Saldivar, "Narrative, Ideology, and the Reconstruction of American Literary History," *Criticism in the Borderlands*

(Durham: Duke University Press, 1991): 11–27; Luis Leal, "The Rewriting of American Literary History," *Criticism in the Borderlands* (Durham: Duke University Press, 1991): 21–27; and finally, Paul Lauter, "The Literatures of America: A Comparative Discipline," *Redefining American Literary History* (New York: MLA, 1990): 9–34.

16. Bessel A. van der Kolk and Jose Saporta, "Biological Response to Psychic Trauma," *International Handbook of Traumatic Stress Syndromes,* eds. John P. Wilson and Beverley Raphael (New York: Plenum Press, 1993): 25–33, p. 26.

17. Indeed, recent neurobiological research on memory also suggests that "personal" memories depend on the collective context in which our identity is formed. See Daniel L. Schacter, *Searching for Memory* (New York: Basic Books, 1996), p. 52.

18. This work on witnessing is indebted to Dori Laub's essay cited earlier.

19. Bessel A. van der Kolk and José Saporta, "Biological Response to Psychic Trauma," *International Handbook of Traumatic Stress Syndromes,* eds. John P. Wilson and Beverley Raphael (New York: Plenum Press, 1993): 25–33, p. 30.

20. This can be traced in Freud's "Mourning and Melancholia" and "Negation," both from *General Psychological Theory* (New York: Collier, 1963): 164–179 and 213–217; and in Melanie Klein, "A Contribution to the Psychogenesis of Manic-Depressive States" and "Mourning and Its Relation to Manic-Depressive States" both from *Contributions to Psycho-analysis 1921–1945* (London: Hogarth Press, 1948): 282–310 and 311–338. Jessica Benjamin, as well, contributes to the understanding of intersubjectivity in the light of loss and destruction in "The Shadow of the Other (Subject): Intersubjectivity and Feminist Theory," *Constellations* vol. 1, no. 2 (1994): 231–254.

21. The use of this term, recognition, follows Jessica Benjamin's study, *The Bonds of Love: Psychoanalysis, Feminism and the Problem of Domination* (New York: Pantheon, 1988).

22. *Oedipus Anne: The Poetry of Anne Sexton* (Urbana, IL: University of Illinois Press, 1987), p. xiii.

Chapter One

1. See Diane Wood Middlebrook, "1957: Anne Sexton's Bedlam," *Pequod: A Journal of Contemporary Literature and Literary Criticism* 23:24 (1987): 131–143, p. 137.

2. All biographical information, unless otherwise noted, is from Diane Wood Middlebrook's biography, *Anne Sexton* (New York: Vintage Books, 1991), where Sexton's breakdown is narrated on pages 31–40.

3. His suggestion may have been prompted by the growing literature on poetry and therapy in Sexton's lifetime, such as Smiley Blanton, *The Healing Power of*

Poetry (New York: Thomas Y. Crowell, 1960); Jack J. Leedy, ed. *Poetry Therapy: The Use of Poetry in the Treatment of Emotional Disorders* (Philadelphia: J. B. Lippincott, 1969); and Jack J. Leedy, ed. *Poetry the Healer* (Philadelphia: J. B. Lippincott, 1973). In this last volume, Sexton is mentioned by Ruth Lisa Schechter in "Poetry: A Therapeutic Tool in the Treatment of Drug Abuse," where Schechter writes that Sexton's poems were used in Schechter's workshops when "survival was the theme" (17–23, p. 19).

4. In 1986, Diana Hume George wrote that the incest "may be true." See "How We Danced: Anne Sexton on Fathers and Daughters," *Women's Studies: An Interdisciplinary Journal* 12:2 (1986): 179–202, p. 184. In a recent essay from *Signs,* Dawn Skorczewski cites only male critics who ignore the signs of incest in Sexton's "Briar Rose," while many female critics have ignored them as well. See "What Prison Is This? Literary Critics Cover Incest in Anne Sexton's 'Briar Rose,'" *Signs* 21:2 (Winter 1996): 326–329. For example, two women critics deny the incest in essays from 1992 and 1994; see Karen Alkalay-Gut, "'For We Swallow Magic and We Deliver Anne': Anne Sexton's Use of Her Name," *The Anna Book: Searching for Anna in Literary History,* ed. Mickey Pearlman (Westport, CT : Greenwood, 1992): 139–49, p. 142; and Jacqueline Banerjee, "Grief and the Modern Writer," *English: The Journal of the English Association* 43:175 (Spring 1994): 17–36, p. 21. Finally, two critics resist confirming it; see Ellen Cronan Rose, "Through the Looking Glass: When Women Tell Fairy Tales," in *The Voyage In: Fictions of Female Development,* ed. Elizabeth Abel, Marianne Hirsch, and Elizabeth Langland (Hanover, NH: University Press of New England for Dartmouth Coll., 1983): 209–227, p. 216; and Alicia Ostriker, "Anne Sexton and the Seduction of the Audience," in *Sexton: Selected Criticism,* ed. Diana Hume George (Urbana, IL: University of Illinois Press, 1988): 3–18, p. 13.

5. Middlebrook, "Becoming Anne Sexton," *Denver Quarterly* 18:4 (Winter 1984): 24–34, p. 23.

6. Middlebrook, "1957: Anne Sexton's Bedlam," p. 141.

7. In January 1973, Sexton told her friend, Maryel Locke, that she wanted a divorce, that her husband, Kayo, had beaten her and had recently beaten their daughter, Joy. Locke writes, "From then on I wondered what part Kayo's behavior played in Anne's emotional disorder." See "Anne Sexton Remembered," *Rossetti to Sexton: Six Women Poets at Texas,* ed. Dave Oliphant and Robin Bradford (Austin: Harry Ransom Humanities Research Center, University of Texas at Austin, 1992): 155–63, p. 161.

8. This is evidenced by Sexton's own early influences, John Holmes, William DeWitt Snodgrass, and Robert Lowell, to whom she was often linked by her contemporaries. Soon after enrolling in Lowell's writing seminar, Sexton wrote in a letter to Snodgrass: "I wish I were a man—I would rather write the way a man writes." See Middlebrook, *Anne Sexton: A Biography,* pp. 92–93.

9. For example, both Jane McCabe and Suzanne Juhasz criticize Sexton for not being feminist, either because of her "flirtatious parading, her glamorous posing, her sexual exhibitionism" (McCabe 216), or because she fails to "realize and analyze the political implications of being both female and a poet" (Juhasz qtd. in McCabe 220). See McCabe, "'A Woman Who Writes': A Feminist Approach to the Early Poetry of Anne Sexton," in *Anne Sexton: The Artist and Her Critics,* ed. J. D. McClatchy (Bloomington, IN: Indiana University Press, 1978): 216–243.

10. *Moses and Monotheism,* trans. Katharine Jones. (New York: Knopf, 1949), p. 105.

11. In his essay, "Further Recommendations on the Technique of Psychoanalysis: Recollection, Reconstructing, Working Through" (1914), Freud first used the term "repetition compulsion" to refer to the actions of a survivor of a traumatic event, actions which seemed to him to be attempts to master the traumatic event. See *Therapy and Technique,* ed. Philip Rieff (New York: Macmillan, 1963): 157–166, pp. 160–161.

12. See Freud, *Beyond the Pleasure Principle,* trans. and ed. James Strachey (New York: Norton, 1961): 8–11. Also, in his *Case Studies On Hysteria,* through the case of Katharina, Freud shows how trauma is constituted through departure and return. From Freud and Breuer, *Studies in Hysteria,* trans. and ed. James Strachey (New York: Basic Books, ND): 125–134.

13. Pierre Janet first used the term "traumatic memory" in *Psychological Healing* [1919], vol. 1, trans. E. Paul and C. Paul (New York: Macmillan, 1925): 661–663.

14. Elizabeth Waites, *Trauma and Survival: Post-Traumatic and Dissociative Disorders in Women* (New York, Norton, 1993), p. 14.

15. For a succinct summary of the research on traumatic memory, see Judith Lewis Herman, *Trauma and Recovery* (New York: Basic Books, 1992): 37–38.

16. Caruth, "Traumatic Departures: Survival and History in Freud." Lecture given on 3 February, 1994, Emory University, Atlanta, Georgia.

17. All citations are from *To Bedlam and Part Way Back* (1960), in *Anne Sexton: The Complete Poems* (Boston: Houghton Mifflin, 1981): 1–46.

18. The play of words, "bell buoy's bell," reminds one that the scene takes place near the ocean; a buoy functions to guide a ship through water, and danger ensues if one does not follow the buoy. We will see the echoes of danger in the water in the next poem, "Music Swims Back to Me," as well.

19. Long before Sexton, in both history and literary history, the woods have been characterized as places of sexual and racial danger: in medieval Europe, the woods were associated with pagan peoples and witches; in Puritan America, in a carry-over from the medieval fear of pagans, the woods become the place of the evil savages. See, for example, Ronald Takaki for an account of the demonization of Native Americans, in *A Different Mirror: A History of Multicultural America* (Boston: Little, Brown, 1993), pp. 40–44.

20. From an early draft of "Kind Sir: These Woods," originally entitled "Between Grapes and Thorns," in the Sexton Collection, Box 7, Harry Ransom Humanities Research Center, University of Texas at Austin. Hereafter cited as HRHRC. Quoted with permission.

21. *The Politics of Survivorship: Incest, Women's Literature, and Feminist Theory* (New York: New York University Press, 1996), pp. 24–25.

22. Judith Herman and Lisa Hirschman, "Father-Daughter Incest," *Signs* vol. 2, no. 4 (1977): 735–756.

23. Leonard Shengold, as well, writes of similar patterns in the survivors of child abuse, including guilt, identification with the abuser, and a tendency to pass on the abuse to the next generation. See his *Soul Murder Revisited: Thoughts about Therapy, Hate, Love, and Memory* (New Haven: Yale University Press, 1999).

24. Middlebrook writes of *Mercy Street,* "Drawing the theme of father–daughter incest into the larger arena of Daisy's spiritual questioning, Sexton's play anticipates by several years current debates in both feminist psychoanalysis and feminist theology" (23). See "Seduction in Anne Sexton's Unpublished Play *Mercy Street,*" in *Sexton: Selected Criticism,* ed. Diana Hume George (Urbana, IL: University of Illinois Press, 1988): 19–26. I have also read the unpublished play and agree with Middlebrook that the scene replicates Sexton's own memories of a sexual encounter with her father. It is also interesting that she invented four witnesses as characters in the play, perhaps as an artistic way of providing what in life could not be provided for her. From the Sexton Collection, Box 14, HRHRC.

25. Anne's daughter, Linda, writes of the painful process of remembering these scenes in her memoir, *Searching for Mercy Street: My Journey Back to My Mother, Anne Sexton* (Boston: Little Brown, 1994): 264–282. Unlike her mother's analyst, her analyst believed her memories, responding, "What you know is enough. You don't have to be raped by your father to call it incest. When there's radioactive fallout over Europe you don't need to be told there was a nuclear explosion at Chernobyl" (267–8). When the session was over, however, Linda asked the analyst if her husband would think she was disgusting, and he replied, "'Why would you want to let him know that you fooled around with your mother?' . . . looking appalled that I would even make such a suggestion" (268).

26. See Erikson, *Everything In Its Path* (New York: Simon and Schuster, 1976), p. 184; and Janis, (New York: Harcourt Brace Jovanovich, 1971).

27. In *Trauma and Recovery,* Judith Lewis Herman writes that survivors of complex (repeated) trauma "often feel they have *lost themselves*" (158, italics mine).

28. *Oedipus Anne* (Urbana, IL: University of Illinois Press, 1987), p. 28.

29. From an early draft of the poem in the Sexton Collection, Box 7, HRHRC.

Chapter Two

1. Lorde describes herself in these terms in *The Cancer Journals* (San Francisco: Spinsters/Aunt Lute Press, 1980), p. 21. The quote in the chapter title is from Lorde, "Sisterhood and Survival," *The Black Scholar* (March April 1986): 5–7, p. 7.

2. Steven Krugman, Ph.D., "Trauma in the Family: Perspectives on the Intergenerational Transmission of Violence," *Psychological Trauma*, ed. Bessel A. van der Kolk, M.D. (Washington, D.C.: American Psychiatric Press, 1987): 127–151, p. 138.

3. For arguments supporting treating black women's subjectivity as multiple, see Francis Beale, "Double Jeopardy: To Be Black and Female," *The Black Woman*, ed. Toni Cade Bambara (New York: Penguin, 1970): 90–100; Deborah K. King, "Multiple Jeopardy, Multiple Consciousness: The Context of a Black Feminist Ideology," *Signs* 14:1 (Autumn 1988): 265–295; and Mae Gwendolyn Henderson, "Speaking in Tongues: Dialogics, Dialectics, and the Black Woman Writer's Literary Tradition," originally published in *Changing Our Words: Essays on Criticism, Theory, and Writing by Black Women*, ed. Cheryl A. Wall (New Brunswick, NJ: Rutgers University Press, 1989), reprinted in *Reading Black, Reading Feminist*, ed. Henry Louis Gates (New York: Meridian, 1990): 116–142.

4. Critics who place Lorde in a lesbian tradition include Mary J. Carruthers, "The Re-Vision of the Muse: Adrienne Rich, Audre Lorde, Judy Grahn, Olga Broumas," *The Hudson Review* 36:2 (Summer 1983): 293–322; Judy Grahn, *The Highest Apple: Sappho and the Lesbian Poetic Tradition* (San Francisco: Spinsters Ink, 1985); Bonnie Zimmerman, *The Safe Sea of Women: Lesbian Fiction 1969–1989* (Boston: Beacon, 1990); and Ruth Ginzberg, "Audre Lorde's (Nonessentialist) Lesbian Eros," *Hypatia* 7:4 (Fall 1992): 73–90. Those who place her in a feminist tradition include Pamela Annas, "A Poetry of Survival: Unnaming and naming in the Poetry of Audre Lorde, Pat Parker, Sylvia Plath, and Adrienne Rich," *Colby Library Quarterly* 18 (March 1982): 9–25; Mary K. DeShazer, *Inspiring Women: Reimagining the Muse* (New York: Pergamon Press, 1986); and Thomas Foster, "'The Very House of Difference': Gender as 'Embattled' Standpoint," *Genders* 8 (Summer 1990): 17–37. Lorde's race is highlighted to the exclusion of other categories in Stephen Henderson, ed., *Understanding the New Black Poetry: Black Speech and Black Music as Poetic References* (New York: William Morrow, 1973). Lorde's identity as a cancer survivor is the focus in Jeanne Perreault, "'that the pain not be wasted': Audre Lorde and the Written Self," *A/B: Autobiography Studies* 4:1 (Fall 1988): 1–16; and G. Thomas Couser, "Autopathography: Women, Illness, and Lifewriting," *A/B: Autobiography* 6:1 (Spring 1991): 65–75.

5. See Amittai F. Avi-ram, "*Apo Koinou* in Audre Lorde and the Moderns: Defining the Differences," *Callaloo* 9:1 (Winter 1986): 193–208; Gloria T.

Hull, "Living on the Line: Audre Lorde and Our Dead Behind Us," in *Changing Our Own Words: Essays on Criticism, Theory and Writing by Black Women,* ed. Cheryl A. Wall (New Brunswick, NJ: Rutgers, 1989): 150–173; Barbara DiBernard, "*Zami:* A Portrait of an Artist as a Black Lesbian," *The Kenyon Review* 13:4 (Fall 1991): 195–213; and Erin G. Carlston, "Zami and the Politics of Plural Identity," in *Sexual Practice, Textual Theory: Lesbian Cultural Criticism,* ed. Susan J. Wolfe and Julian Penelope (Cambridge, MA: Blackwell, 1993): 226–236.

6. Sharon Patricia Holland argues that white feminism's use of Sojourner Truth silences the many voices of black feminism and treats Lorde's work as a necessary corrective to tokenism and silencing. See "'Which Me Will Survive': Audre Lorde and the Development of a Black Feminist Ideology," *Critical Matrix* Special Issue, No. 1 (1988): 1–30. Ekaterini Georgoudaki shows how Lorde works against the stereotypical images of black women as mammy, matriarch, Amazon, and whore; see her "Audre Lorde: Revising Stereotypes of Afro-American Womanhood," *Arbeiten aus Anglistik und Amerikanistik* 16:1 (1991): 47–66. And Sagri Dhairyam shows how Lorde's work poses challenges to literary critical traditions that are exclusively poetic, lesbian, black, or feminist; see her "'Artifacts for Survival': Remapping the Contours of Poetry with Audre Lorde," *Feminist Studies* 18:2 (Summer 1992): 229–256.

7. From Afterword to C. Vegh, *I Didn't Say Goodbye,* trans. R. Schwartz (New York: E. P. Dutton, 1984), p. 166.

8. From *The Black Unicorn* (New York: Norton, 1978): 31–32.

9. These aspects of the process of witnessing are addressed in Dori Laub, "Truth and Testimony: The Process and the Struggle," *Trauma: Explorations in Memory,* ed. Cathy Caruth (Baltimore: Johns Hopkins University Press, 1995): 61–75.

10. While black women's sexuality is dramatized in many narratives by black women, it is seldom that black women analyze these scenes in critical ways that "would attempt to discover, layer by layer, the symptoms of culture that engender this order of things" (94). See Hortense Spillers, "Interstices: A Small Drama of Words," in *Pleasure and Danger: Exploring Female Sexuality,* ed. Carol Vance (London: Pandora, 1984): 73–100.

11. Beverly Guy-Sheftall, "The Impact of Slavery On Black Women," Lecture, September 22, 1994, Emory University, Atlanta, Georgia.

12. *The White Man's Burden: Historical Origins of Racism in the United States* (London: Oxford University Press, 1974), pp. 71–72.

13. *Arena* (January 1900): 15–24, reprinted in *Words of Fire: An Anthology of African-American Feminist Thought,* ed. Beverly Guy-Sheftall (New York: The New Press, 1995): 70–76.

14. Freud's reading of "true" and "official" stories of a history of violence appears in *Moses and Monotheism,* trans. Katherine Jones (New York: Vintage Books, 1939).

15. Davis' essay first appeared in *The Black Scholar* (December 1971), reprinted in *Words of Fire,* pp. 200–218. The Moynihan Report, as it has come to be known, was published as *The Negro Family: The Case for National Action,* in Lee Rainwater and William L. Yancey, *The Moynihan Report and the Politics of Controversy* (Cambridge: MIT Press, 1967): 39–124.

16. The belief in the "official" story that black women assented to slavery still persists. In *Vessels of Evil: American Slavery and the Holocaust,* Laurence Mordecai Thomas writes that "The nanny role required genuine cooperation on the part of the slave if ever a role of slavery did," which he qualifies by saying "I do not for a moment mean to suggest that black women . . . gave no thought to the conditions of slavery . . . only that . . . *black slave women accepted* the role of nanny." This is awfully close to saying black women assented to their roles of nanny—and whore. (Philadelphia: Temple University Press, 1993), p. 131, my emphasis.

17. Ten years later bell hooks published *Ain't I A Woman: Black Women and Feminism,* in which she draws from Davis' essay to attempt a further reconstruction of this history. (Boston: South End Press, 1981), pp. 15–49.

18. *Signs* 14:4 (1989), reprinted in *Words of Fire,* pp. 380–387.

19. Beverly Guy-Sheftall, "The Women of Bronzeville," *Sturdy Black Bridges: Visions of Black Women in Literature,* ed. Roseann P. Bell, Bettye J. Parker, and Beverly Guy-Sheftall (Garden City, NY: Anchor/Doubleday, 1979): 157–170, p. 168.

20. Judith Herman and Lisa Hirschman, "Father-Daughter Incest," *Signs* vol. 2, no. 4 (1977): 735–756, p. 749 and 751. Although the term "incest" is used in the title, their findings apply to survivors of rape and other forms of sexual trauma as well. See Judith Lewis Herman's *Trauma and Recovery* (New York: Basic Books, 1992), for a discussion of the commonalities of different traumatic experiences, from domestic abuse to political terror.

21. San Francisco: Crossing Press, 1982.

22. I am following Anna Wilson's lead in referring to the character in the narrative as Audre and the narrative presence as Lorde. See Anna Wilson, "Audre Lorde and the African-American Tradition: When the Family is Not Enough," in *New Lesbian Criticism,* ed. Sally Munt (New York: Harvester Wheatsheaf, 1992): 75–93, p. 91.

23. Elizabeth Fox-Genovese notes that the coming-to-consciousness of race happens around the age of seven in many African American autobiographies. See "My Statue, My Self: Autobiographical Writings of African American Women," in *Reading Black, Reading Feminist,* ed. Henry Louis Gates, Jr. (New York: Meridian, 1990): 176–203, p. 190.

24. Janet R. Brice-Baker, "West Indian Women of Color: The Jamaican Woman," *Women of Color: Integrating Ethnic and Gender Identities in Psychotherapy,* ed. Lillian Comas-Díaz and Beverly Greene (New York: The Guilford Press, 1994): 139–160, p. 147.

25. The closest any critic of *Zami* comes to treating Lorde's narrative of sexual abuse is Anna Wilson, cited above: "The adult that Audre has become has the power to hear and speak both the good news of family as tradition and the bad news of family as site of abuse" (85). However, this is said in reference to Gennie's abuse, not Audre's. It is interesting to think about the depth of silence and denial surrounding sexual abuse in the criticism given that *Zami* is read and written about so widely.

26. Jennifer Gillan notes that Audre's mother "dragged Audre from doctor to doctor in order to discover why she has not started menstruating . . . [and] the visits terrify Audre," but she does not mention how this connects to the earlier incident with the boy. See "Relocating and identity in *Zami: A New Spelling of My Name,*" in *Homemaking: Women Writers and the Politics and Poetics of Home,* ed. Catherine Wiley and Fiona R. Barnes (New York: Garland, 1996): 209–221, p. 209.

27. Anne Louise Keating writes that Audre learns the legacy of silence from her mother, "who used silence to protect herself and her daughters from a reality she was powerless to control." See Keating, "Making 'our shattered faces whole': The Black Goddess and Audre Lorde's Revision of Patriarchal Myth," *Frontiers* 13:1 (1992): 20–33, p. 21.

28. Such intergenerational effects of trauma in the effects of children of the survivors of the Holocaust are discussed in Nadine Fresco, "Remembering the Unknown," trans. Alan Sheridan, *International Review of Psycho-Analysis* 11:417 (1984): 417–426. Originally published in *Nouvelle Revue de Psychanalyse* 24 (1981).

29. Originally published in 1978, "A Black Feminist Statement" is reprinted in *This Bridge Called My Back: Writings by Radical Women of Color,* ed. Cherríe Moraga and Gloria Anzaldúa (New York: Kitchen Table Press, 1981): 210–218.

30. *Conditions Two* 1:2 (October 1977): 25–44.

31. *New York Head Shop and Museum* (Detroit: Broadside Press, 1974); *Coal* (New York: Norton, 1976); *Between Our Selves* (Point Reyes, CA: Eidolon Editions, 1976).

32. (San Francisco: Spinsters/Aunt Lute, 1980), p. 23.

33. Lorde's ending of silence about these histories serves as a model for others, as can be seen in Melba Wilson's *Crossing the Boundary: Black Women Survive Incest,* in which Lorde is credited for breaking silence about anger, lesbianism, and sexual assault (Seattle: Seal Press, 1993), pp. 75, 82, 90, 200.

34. This poem is from Lorde, *The Black Unicorn* (New York: Norton, 1978): 22–24. Lorde describes reading the story of these girls in the newspaper on the tape recording, *Shorelines,* published by The Watershed Foundation, 1985.

35. In Inspiring Women, Mary K. DeShazer writes that the poet is "helpless" in "Chain" as she is "forced to watch this crime of incest and abandonment

assert itself again and again. . . . All the poet can do, what she indeed *must* do, is to hear and give voice to their cries" (191). We will see in the reading of the poem that, far from being "helpless," the speaker proposes the movement from silence to voice as the solution to the repetitions of traumatic history.

36. A description of these characteristics of the ballad can be found in Alfred B. Friedman, "Ballad," *The Princeton Encyclopedia of Poetry and Poetics,* ed. Alex Preminger (Princeton: Princeton University Press, 1965): 62–64.

Chapter Three

1. (San Francisco: Aunt Lute Press, 1987).
2. Sonia Saldívar-Hull, "Feminism on the Border: From Gender Politics to Geopolitics," *Criticism in the Borderlands,* ed. Hector Calderon and José David Saldívar (Durham, NC: Duke University Press, 1991): 203–220, p. 211; Ramón Saldívar, *Chicano Narrative: The Dialectics of Difference* (Madison, WI: University of Wisconsin Press, 1990), p. 218; Paula Gunn Allen, "'Border Studies': The Intersection of Gender and Color," *The Ethnic Canon: Histories, Institutions, and Interventions,* ed. David Palumbo-Liu (Minneapolis: University of Minnesota Press, 1995): 31–47, p. 45.
3. Carl Gutiérrez-Jones, *Rethinking the Borderlands: Between Chicano Culture and Legal Discourse* (Berkeley: University of California Press, 1995), p. 118–119. Oscar J. Martínez, *Border People: Life and Society in the U.S.-Mexico Borderlands* (Tucson: University of Arizona Press, 1994), p. 309–310. Ruth Behar, *Translated Woman: Crossing the Border with Esperanza's Story* (Boston: Beacon Press, 1993), p. 10–11. Ronald Takaki, *A Different Mirror: A History of Multicultural America* (Boston: Little, Brown and Company, 1993), p. 426. Anzaldúa is also cited by three contributors to *The Multiracial Experience: Racial Borders as the New Frontier,* ed. Maria P. P. Root (Thousand Oaks, Ca.: Sage, 1996). All three treat her work as sociology, not literature. See Cynthia Nakashima, "Voices from the Movement: Approaches to Multiraciality," 79–97, p. 90; G. Reginald Daniel, "Black and White Identity in the New Millennium: Unsevering the Ties That Bind," 121–139, p. 134; Carolina A. Streeter, "Ambiguous Bodies: Locating Black/White Women in Cultural Representations," 305–320, pp. 308, 310.
4. This appears in Freud's *Beyond the Pleasure Principle,* trans. James Strachey (New York: Norton, 1961), p. 16.
5. "Reconstructing the Impact of Trauma on Personality," *Personality and Psychopathology: Feminist Reappraisals,* ed. Laura S. Brown and Mary Ballou (New York: The Guilford Press, 1992): 229–265, p. 235.
6. Root, p. 238.
7. In addition to Freud's *Beyond the Pleasure Principle* and *Moses and Monotheism,* cited previously, other theorists develop the implications of Freud's

definition of trauma as departure and return as well. The spatiality of traumatic experience (what we call "the outside gone in without mediation") is put forth by Jean Laplanche in *La sublimation* (Paris: Presses Universitaires de France): p. 195–202. The temporal nature of traumatic departure and return is addressed in Jean Laplanche, "Notes on Afterwardsness," in *Seduction, Translation, and the Drives,* ed. John Fletcher and Martin Stanton, trans. Martin Stanton (London: Institute of Contemporary Arts): 217–23. Most influential of all for me has been Cathy Caruth's work on trauma as departure and return in "Unclaimed Experience: Trauma and the Impossibility of History," *Yale French Studies* 79 (1991): 181–192, (cited as Caruth 1991); "Départs traumatiques: La survie et l'histoire chez Freud," in *Le passage des frontières: Autour du travail de Jacques Derrida,* Colloque de Cerisy (Paris: Editions Galilée, 1994): 435–439, (cited as Caruth 1994); and the lecture at Emory cited in chapter one (cited as Caruth lecture).

8. Caruth 1994, p. 436. The original reads, "la structure paradoxalement *indirecte* du traumatisme psychique [veut dire que] le traumatisme soit subi et souffert dans le psyché du fait qu'il n'est précisement pas accessible à l'expérience." The translation is mine.

9. *A New Species of Trouble: Explorations in Disaster, Trauma, and Community* (New York: Norton, 1994), p. 239, her emphasis.

10. Josef Breuer and Sigmund Freud, *Studies on Hysteria,* trans. James Strachey (New York: Basic Books, n.d.), Reprint of Volume II of the Standard Edition of the Complete Psychological Works of Sigmund Freud (London: Hogarth Press, 1955).

11. This aspect of Freud's writing was discussed at more length in chapter 1, "'My night mind saw such strange happenings': Anne Sexton and Childhood Sexual Trauma."

12. *Moses and Monotheism,* trans. Katherine Jones (New York: Vintage Books, 1939).

13. "Freud's Anthropology: A reading of the 'cultural books,'" in *The Cambridge Companion to Freud,* ed. Jerome Neu (Cambridge: Cambridge University Press, 1991): 267–286, p. 280, italics mine. The quote in Paul's writing is from *Moses and Monotheism,* p. 80.

14. Without attempting to provide a complete bibliography of U.S.–Mexico history, I'll mention some sources that have helped me most in understanding some of the many complexities of this history. Enrique Florescano, *Memory, Myth, and Time in Mexico: From the Aztecs to Independence,* trans. Albert G. Bork and Kathryn G. Bork (Austin: University of Texas, 1994). Miguel León-Portilla, ed. with intro. *The Broken Spears: The Aztec Account of the Conquest of Mexico,* trans. from Nahuatl into Spanish, Angel Maria Garibay K. Eng., trans. Lysander Kemp (Boston: Beacon, 1992). Matt S. Meier and Feliciano Ribera, *Mexican Americans/American Mexicans: From Conquistador to Chicano,* rev. ed. of *Chicanos* (1972), (San Francisco: Harper

Collins, 1993). Maria Montes de Oca Rickes, *Mediating the Past: Continuity and Diversity in the Chicano Literary Tradition,* Ph.D. dissertation (University of South Carolina, 1991). Tey Diana Rebolledo and Eliana S. Rivero, "Introduction," *Infinite Divisions,* ed. Tey Diana Rebolledo and Eliana S. Rivero (Tucson: University of Arizona Press, 1993): 1–33. Ronald Takaki, *A Different Mirror: A History of Multicultural America* (Boston: Little, Brown and Company, 1993). Tzvetan Todorov, *The Conquest of America: The Question of the Other,* trans. Richard Howard (New York: Harper and Row, 1984). Patricia Zavella, "Reflections on Diversity Among Chicanas," *Frontiers,* vol. XII, no. 2 (1991): 73–85.

15. It is also interesting to note that, according to Aztec mythology, the Fifth Sun is called the movement sun. This sun comes after four earlier ones that were destroyed by great catastrophes: the earth sun destroyed by ferocious jaguars; the wind sun destroyed when the sun was knocked down, which raised a wind storm; the fire sun destroyed by fire raining from the sky; finally, the water sun "ended with a great deluge that flooded the earth" (Florescano 3).

16. I realize this is a large topic in history, and I am not going to address the debate surrounding the figures. I mention Anzaldúa's use of the numbers here in order to show how she tries to account, literally, for the loss.

17. Deneven is quoted in Mike Turner, "Relearning Ancient Lessons," *The Atlanta Journal Constitution* (Saturday, March 19, 1994): E1, E8, p. E8.

18. Patricia Zavella, "Reflections on Diversity Among Chicanas," *Frontiers,* vol. XII, no. 2 (1991): 73–85, p. 77.

19. The movement of the border is significant for racial as well as geographical reasons: the nineteenth century in "Aztlán" saw the birth of a pyramid of social domination, with white settlers on top, Native Americans on the bottom, and Mexicans caught in the middle. According to one historian, the racial composition of Mexico in the nineteenth century, during the Mexican-American War, was 60 percent Native American, 22 percent Mestizo, 18 percent European; while in North America, the composition was 18 percent African and 82 percent European. While these numbers are not necessarily true, the reversal of 82/18 shows how race played a role in the United States' othering of Mexican-Americans (Rickes 24). This same historian, in 1913, called Mexican-Americans "an utterly alien race . . . [with] whole ideals and virtues and modes of thought . . . radically different from ours" (Rives vi, cited in Rickes 24).

20. See Tey Diana Rebolledo and Eliana S. Rivero, "Introduction," *Infinite Divisions,* ed. Tey Diana Rebolledo and Eliana S. Rivero (Tucson: University of Arizona Press, 1993): 1–33, p. 19.

21. Kate Adams also notes the "leaving and returning" theme of this poem in "Northamerican Silences: History, Identity and Witness in the Poetry of Gloria Anzaldúa, Cherríe Moraga, and Leslie Marmon Silko" in *Listening to*

Silences: New Essays in Feminist Criticism, ed. Elaine Hedges and Shelley Fisher Fishkin (New York: Oxford, 1994), 130–145, p. 140.

22. My understanding of collective memory and its impact on nationalism has been influenced by Yael Zerubavel's essay, "The Death of Memory and the Memory of Death: Masada and the Holocaust as Historical Metaphors," *Representations* 45 (Winter 1994): 72–100. She discusses commemorative narratives on page 80.

23. See Rebolledo and Rivero, p. 9. See also Meier and Ribera, *Mexican Americans / American Mexicans* for maps that show the changing geography of the border.

24. From the essay, "La Prieta," in *This Bridge Called My Back,* ed. Anzaldúa and Moraga (New York: Kitchen Table Press, 1981, 1983): 198–209, p. 200.

25. For more on the healing effects of narrativization, see Jodie Wigrin, "Narrative Completion in the Treatment of Trauma," *Psychotherapy* 31.3 (Fall 1994): 415–423. In this essay Wigrin writes, "incomplete narrative processing of traumatic experience causes symptoms of posttraumatic stress" (415).

26. See Cathy Caruth, *Introduction to Trauma: Explorations in Memory* (Baltimore: Johns Hopkins University Press, 1995): 3–12, p. 5.

27. *The New World Spanish-English and English-Spanish Dictionary,* ed. Salvatore Ramondino (New York: Signet, 1969), pp. 72, 31.

28. "Algo secretamente amado," from *The Sexuality of Latinas,* ed. Norma Alarcón, Ana Castillo, and Cherríe Moraga (Berkeley: Third Woman Press, 1993): 151–156, p. 152. Italics mine.

29. "Language and Political Economy," *Annual Review of Anthropology* 18 (1989): 345–367, p. 358.

30. *Webster's New Twentieth Century Dictionary Unabridged,* 2nd ed. (USA: William Collins Publishers, 1980); "pasture" is defined on page 1312, and "fodder" is defined on page 710.

31. *The Compact Edition of the Oxford English Dictionary,* vol. II (Oxford: Oxford University Press, 1971), p. 544.

32. *The Compact Edition of the Oxford English Dictionary,* vol. I (Oxford: Oxford University Press, 1971), p. 378.

33. It should be noted that this movement comes through an address—from the aunt to the niece in this poem, and between the sister and the brother in the earlier narrative of Anzaldúa's return home. We will explore the significance of the address more fully in Part II.

34. Anzaldúa expresses her desire for, fear of, and ultimate rejection of returning home on pp. 169, 171, 198.

35. "From Il(l)egal to Legal Subject: Border Construction and Re-construction," *The Bronze Screen: Chicana and Chicano Film Culture* (Minneapolis: University of Minnesota Press, 1993): 65–153, pp. 82–83.

Chapter Four

1. The term "progression" is from Alkalay-Gut; "mouvement d'expansion" is from Cunci; and George calls *Letters to Dr. Y* a "sequence from sickness to cure." See Karen Alkalay-Gut, "'For We Swallow Magic and We Deliver Anne': Anne Sexton's Use of Her Name," *The Anna Book: Searching for Anna in Literary History,* ed. Mickey Pearlman (Westport, CT: Greenwood, 1992): 139–49, p. 140; Marie Christine Cunci, "Anne Sexton (1928–1974), ou comment faire taire Jocaste," *Revue Francaise d'Etudes Americaines* 7:15 (Nov. 1982): 383–394, p. 392; Diana Hume George, "Death Is a Woman, Death Is a Man: Anne Sexton's Green Girls and the Leaves That Talk," *University of Hartford Studies in Literature: A Journal of Interdisciplinary Criticism,* 18:1 (1986): 31–44, p. 32.

2. Jacqueline Banerjee notes that in *The Awful Rowing to God* progress has been made in that there is a sense of promise, yet the rower is still afraid and is not reconciled or released. See "Grief and the Modern Writer," *English: The Journal of the English Association* 43:175 (Spring 1994): 17–36, p. 28.

3. See Suzanne Juhasz, "Seeking the Exit or the Home: Poetry and Salvation in the Career of Anne Sexton," in *Sexton: Selected Criticism,* ed. Diana Hume George (Urbana, IL: University of Illinois Press, 1988): 303–311, p. 304.

4. See Diane Wood Middlebrook, "Poet of Weird Abundance," *Parnassus: Poetry in Review* 12–13:2–1 (Spring–Winter 1985): 293–315, p. 295.

5. Alkalay-Gut, cited above, calls "Flee on Your Donkey" a "pivotal poem" (145), while Middlebrook, cited above, presents it as a transitional poem on the perspective of illness, where the speaker is not a victim but an interrogator of her illness (296, 298). Cunci, also cited above, sees *Transformations* as a turning point where Sexton leaves personal confession behind for something larger (392), and Leventen points out that Sexton focuses on social context, not individual psyche in *Transformations;* see Carol Leventen, "*Transformations*' Silencings," in *Critical Essays on Anne Sexton,* ed. Linda Wagner-Martin (Boston: G. K. Hall, 1989): 136–149, p. 139.

6. The connection between Sexton and Woolf, of course, does not stop here, as both were survivors of childhood sexual abuse as well as brilliant writers and suicides. See Louise DeSalvo's groundbreaking biography, *Virginia Woolf: The Impact of Childhood Sexual Abuse on Her Life and Work* (Boston: Beacon, 1989).

7. The term is from Cathy Caruth's *Unclaimed Experience: Trauma, Narrative, and History* (Baltimore: Johns Hopkins University Press, 1996).

8. Sexton notes on May 15, 1958: "*I realize, with guilt, that I am a woman,* that it should be the children, or my husband, or my home—not writing. But it is not—" (Middlebrook 63, italics mine). The sentiment expressed in italics is an interesting expression of the extent to which Sexton's traumatic guilt is tied up with the self-hate she feels as a woman in our culture.

9. From *To Bedlam and Partway Back* (1960) in *Anne Sexton, The Complete Poems* (Boston: Houghton Mifflin, 1981): 1–46.

10. It is interesting to note that while the final version of this poem reads, "I fall / out of myself and pretend / that Allah will not see / how I hold my daddy / like an old stone tree" (26–27), an early version of the poem concludes with "to pretend the goddesses will not see / how I hold my daddy like an old stone tree." The significance of this will become clearer in chapter seven. Also, a very early draft of the same poem, originally entitled "Where are you going, little girl?," reads, "I think I'm going / to rest with my daddy awhile / I think I'm going / to a very important surprise / in the ground, where I'll shut my eyes / and I wouldn't be afraid and I wouldn't mind / about being a girl there with my big kind / daddy with [*sic*] used to smile / until he lay over / until he stopped everything." From the Sexton Collection, Box 7, HRHRC.

11. All citations in this section are from *Transformations* (1971) in *Anne Sexton, The Complete Poems* (Boston: Houghton Mifflin, 1981): 221–295.

12. See "Snow White and the Seven Dwarfs" (224–229), "The White Snake" (229–232), "Cinderella" (255–258) and "The Maiden without Hands" (273–276).

13. For more on the specific nature of traumatic memories as "frozen images" see Lenore Terr, *Unchained Memories: True Stories of Traumatic Memories Lost and Found* (New York: Basic Books, 1994), especially pages 41–60.

14. "What Prison Is This? Literary Critics Cover Incest in Anne Sexton's 'Briar Rose,'" *Signs* 21: 21 (Winter 1996): 309–342.

15. The lines are from "Rapunzel" (245) and "Red Riding Hood" (267), respectively.

16. See "A Witch's Appetite: Anne Sexton's Transformations," *Southern Review: Literary and Interdisciplinary Essays* 26:1 (March 1993): 73–85, p. 76.

17. Contrary to McCabe, Leventen does see Sexton as feminist in her critique of patriarchal culture (Leventen 143).

18. Among those who address the melancholic themes in Sexton's poetry are Diana Hume George, "How We Danced: Anne Sexton on Fathers and Daughters," *Women's Studies: An Interdisciplinary Journal* 12:2 (1986): 179–202, pp. 184 and 193; Susan Adler Kavaler, "Ann Sexton and the Daemonic Lover," *The American Journal of Psychoanalysis* 49:2 (June 1989): 105–14, p. 113; Caroline King Barnard Hall, who writes of *Bedlam* as about loss: "The speaker, surviving, is diminished, and that survival is not, or is barely, worth the effort"—"a sense of guilt at having survived" in "Transformations: A Magic Mirror," *Original Essays on the Poetry of Anne Sexton*, ed. Frances Bixler (Conway, AR: University of Central Arkansas Press, 1988): 107–129, p.122; and Banerjee, throughout. Hilary Chark, in particular, reads Sexton's poetry as a tool for healing from melancholia, but identifies the "lost object" as the mother, in "Depression, Shame, and Reparation:

The Case of Anne Sexton," in *Scenes of Shame: Psychoanalysis, Shame, and Writing,* eds. Joseph Adamson and Hillary Clark (Albany, NY: State University of New York Press, 1999): 189–206.

19. For more on melancholia, see Freud, "Mourning and Melancholia," and "Negation," in *General Psychological Theory* (New York: Collier, 1963): 164–179; 213–217. See also Melanie Klein, *Contributions to Psycho-analysis 1921–1945* (London: Hogarth Press, 1948): 282–338.

20. It has been found that "depression is the most commonly reported symptom among adults who were molested as children," writes Arthur Green in "Childhood Sexual and Physical Abuse," *International Handbook of Traumatic Stress Syndromes,* ed. John P. Wilson and Beverley Raphael (New York: Plenum Press, 1993): 577–592, p. 581.

21. See Nicolas Abraham and Maria Torok, "Deuil ou mélancholie: Introjecter-incorporer" in *L'Ecorce et Le Noyau* (Paris: Flammarion, 1987): 259–275, p. 272, my translation.

22. Freud himself wavers between the terms, "incorporation" and "introjection," while Klein makes a distinction that Abraham and Torok elaborate on in "Deuil ou mélancholie: Introjecter-incorporer," in which they write that incorporation is a fantasy that belongs to the intrapsychic, melancholic wish to preserve what has been lost by denying that it has been lost. They distinguish this from introjection, which they say is a process by which mourning proceeds and by which intersubjectivity develops. I am using the term "incorporation" in order to focus attention on Sexton's failed attempt to witness.

23. All poems cited in this section are from *Anne Sexton: The Complete Poems* (Boston: Houghton Mifflin, 1981).

24. From the Sexton Collection, letter to Alice Smith, Box 26, HRHRC. Transcribed exactly, with typos and misspellings.

25. See Deborah Nelson, "Penetrating Privacy: Confessional Poetry and the Surveillance Society," in *Homemaking: Women Writers and the Politics and Poetics of Home,* ed. Catherine Wiley and Fiona R. Barnes (New York: Garland, 1996): 87–114, for a discussion of how Sexton's poetry breaks down the barriers between private and public discourse.

26. Eniko Bobolas, "Woman and Poet? Conflicts in the Poetry of Emily Dickinson, Sylvia Plath, and Anne Sexton," in *The Origins an Originality of American Culture,* ed. Tibor Frank (Budapest: Akademiai Kiado, 1984): 375–383, p. 381–382.

27. Lenore Walker, *The Battered Woman* (New York: Harper and Row, 1979), p. ix. Judith Lewis Herman also notes that "Numerous studies have now confirmed the strong association between wife-beating and sexual abuse of children," which leads us to read Sexton's poem as more than personal—perhaps intergenerational. See Herman, "Father-Daughter Incest," *International Handbook of Traumatic Stress Syndromes,* ed. John P. Wilson and Beverley

Raphael (New York: Plenum Press, 1993): 593–600, p. 593. In the same let-
ter quoted previously, Sexton touches on the possible connection between
incest and domestic violence when she writes: "no sex (well maybe twice a
year but it was always when we were away—kind of like taking your
daughter away to have an affair with her)," which indicates that she saw her
marriage as a repetition of a sexual relationship between father and daugh-
ter. From Sexton Collection, Box 26, HRHRC.

28. It is interesting to compare Sexton's description of this man with
Klineberg's 1964 description of the authoritarian from psychoanalytic lit-
erature: He "tends to be a supreme conformist, he sees the world as men-
acing and unfriendly . . . he is rigid . . . he is hard-minded, exalting his own
group and disliking many out-groups." Cited in Michael A. Simpson, "Bit-
ter Waters: Effects on Children of the Stresses of Unrest and Oppression,"
p. 607.

29. Klein, *Contributions to Psycho-analysis 1921–1945* (London: Hogarth Press,
1948), pp. 330–331.

30. See "Anne Sexton and the Seduction of the Audience," *Sexton: Selected Crit-
icism,* ed. Diana Hume George (Urbana, IL: University of Illinois Press,
1988): 3–18, p. 8.

31. Jessica Benjamin addresses the need to balance both identification and nega-
tion in order for recognition to have a chance to succeed, in her essay, "The
Shadow of the Other (Subject): Intersubjectivity and Feminist Theory,"
Constellations 1:2 (1994): 231–255.

32. From Sexton Collection, Box 1, HRHRC.

33. From Sexton Collection, Box 16, HRHRC.

34. From "Anne Sexton: 1928–1974," in *On Lies, Secrets, and Silence* (New York:
Norton, 1979): 121–123, p. 123.

35. From "For John, Who Begs Me Not to Enquire Further" (34–35), p. 35.

Chapter Five

1. The quote in the chapter title is from Audre Lorde's poem, "A Litany for
Survival," in *The Black Unicorn* (New York: Norton, 1978): 31–32, which
we will examine in this chapter. The term, "poetry of witness," is used by
Adrienne Rich in an interview with Matthew Rothschild in which Rich
pays tribute to Lorde. See *The Progressive* (January 1994): 31–35, p. 31.

2. In a conversation between Audre Lorde and James Baldwin published in
Essence, the editors call them both "uncompromising witnesses to a world
in which they struggle to carve out possibility—to create a future that
looks like hope" (73). See "Revolutionary Hope: A Conversation Between
James Baldwin and Audre Lorde," *Essence* (December 1984): 73–74,
129–130, 133.

3. These insights are from the interview with Adrienne Rich in *Sister Outsider* (Freedom, CA: Crossing Press, 1984): 81–109, especially p. 82.

4. From *Sister Outsider,* 36–39, p. 36.

5. From "Uses of the Erotic: The Erotic as Power," from *Sister Outsider,* 53–59, p. 58.

6. Michael A. Simpson, "Bitter Waters: Effects on Children of the Stresses of Unrest and Oppression," *International Handbook of Traumatic Stress Syndromes,* ed. John P. Wilson and Beverley Raphael (New York: Plenum Press, 1993): 601–624, p. 610.

7. The poem is in Lorde, *Chosen Poems: Old and New* (New York: Norton, 1982): 79–80.

8. The frequently anthologized poem, "Harlem," can be found in many places, including *Six American Poets,* ed. Joel Conarroe (New York: Random House, 1991): 257.

9. In a conversation with James Baldwin, Baldwin asked Lorde, "You are saying you do not exist in the American dream except as a nightmare," to which Lorde responded, "That's right" (73). From "Revolutionary Hope: A Conversation Between James Baldwin and Audre Lorde," *Essence* (December 1984): 73–74; 129–130; 134.

10. The poem is from *Chosen Poems: Old and New* (New York: Norton, 1982): 102–105.

11. The following summary has been gathered from these sources: Taylor Branch, *Parting the Waters: America in the King Years, 1954–63* (New York: Simon and Schuster, 1988), pp. 257–258; Lerone Bennett, Jr. *Before the Mayflower: A History of Black America,* 6th ed. (New York, Penguin, 1988), pp. 377, 553; Michael Dyson, "Remembering Emmett Till," *Reflecting Black: African American Cultural Criticism* (Minneapolis: University of Minnesota Press, 1993): 194–198, p. 195.

12. The significance of the term, "dragonfish," becomes clear through its origins: dragon comes from the Greek, "drakon," which means "dragon, serpent, literally, the seeing one." It also refers to a "fierce, violent person; especially a watchful female guardian." From Webster's *New Twentieth Century Dictionary,* unabridged, 2nd ed. (Williams Collins Publishers, 1980), p. 552. According to Caitlin Matthews, the dragon is also a symbol of "The Black Goddess" of ancient, earth-based spiritualities in which "vows were always *witnessed* by the earth, who would hear and remember." See *Sophia: Goddess of Wisdom* (London: Aquarian, 1992), p. 22, my emphasis.

13. The idea of "false witnessing" is put forth by Robert Jay Lifton in an interview with Cathy Caruth, in which Lifton says that false witnessing is a process by which "we reassert our own vitality and symbolic immortality by denying them their right to live and by identifying them with the death taint, by designating them as victims. So we live off them." See *Trauma:*

Explorations in Memory, ed. Cathy Caruth (Baltimore: Johns Hopkins University Press, 1995): 128–147, p. 139.

14. Ana Louise Keating remarks that "Lorde's 'we' is performative" in *Women Reading / Women Writing: Self-Invention in Paula Gunn Allen, Gloria Anzaldúa, and Audre Lorde* (Philadelphia: Temple University Press, 1996), p. 49.

Chapter Six

1. See Anzaldúa's interview with AnnLouise Keating, "Writing, Politics, and las Lesberadas: Platicando con Gloria Anzaldúa," *Frontiers* 14:1 (1993): 105–130, p. 112. Cited in text as Anzaldúa 1991.

2. Sigmund Freud and Josef Breuer, in their "On the Psychical Mechanism of Hysterical Phenomena: Preliminary Communication," write, *"Hysterics suffer mainly from reminiscences"* (7, their italics). *Studies on Hysteria,* trans. and ed. James Strachey (New York: Basic Books, ND).

3. Bessel A. van der Kolk and Onno van der Hart, "The Intrusive Past: The Flexibility of Memory and the Engraving of Trauma," *Trauma: Explorations in Memory,* ed. Cathy Caruth (Baltimore: Johns Hopkins University Press, 1995): 158–182, p. 176.

4. In an interview, Anzaldúa remarks that she has written a poem entitled, "la vulva es una herida abierta," which she doesn't read at poetry readings because the audience "would have gone away real sad" (Anzaldúa 1991, 122–3).

5. See her "Embodied Memory, Transcendence, and Telling: Recounting Trauma, Re-establishing the Self," *New Literary History* 26 (1995): 169–195, p. 176.

6. Ada Burris, M.D. "Somatization as a Response to Trauma," *Victims of Abuse: The Emotional Impact of Child and Adult Trauma,* ed. Alan Sugarman, Ph.D. (Madison, WI: International Universities Press, Inc., 1994): 131–137, pp. 133 and 135.

7. Root, "Reconstructing the Impact of Trauma on Personality," *Personality and Psychopathology: Feminist Reappraisals,* ed. Laura S. Brown and Mary Ballou (New York: The Guilford Press, 1992): 229–265, p. 238.

8. The term "soul" here is used with reference to one of Anzaldúa's influences, James Hillman, particularly in his *Re-visioning Psychology* (New York: Harper and Row, 1975).

9. "The Intrusive Past: The Flexibility of Memory and the Engraving of Trauma," p. 163.

10. Ibid, p. 178.

11. In his seminal work on collective memory, Maurice Halbwachs writes, "One witness we can always call on is ourself" (22). While this is true for ordinary experience, what makes traumatic experience different is precisely the absence of an internal witness during the event itself. See *Collective*

Memory, trans. Francis J. Ditter, Jr. and Vida Yazdi Ditter (New York: Harper and Row, 1980).

12. "Truth and Testimony: The Process and the Struggle," *Trauma: Explorations in Memory,* ed. Cathy Caruth (Baltimore: Johns Hopkins University Press, 1995): 61–75, p. 66.

13. AnaLouise Keating reads this poem as one that "graphically illustrates the highly emotional, terrifying nature of this encounter with the self-become-other(ed)" in her "(De)Centering the Margins?" in *Other Sisterhoods: Literary Theory and U.S. Women of Color,* ed. Sandra Kumamoto Stanley (Urbana, IL: University of Illinois Press, 1998): 23–43, p. 32.

14. Lawrence Langer notes that Holocaust survivors' testimonies tend to carry the most anguish over issues of guilt, what one did and did not do that caused one's survival in the face of others' deaths. See Langer, *Holocaust Testimonies: The Ruins of Memory* (New Haven: Yale University Press, 1991).

15. See "Trauma and Aging: A Thirty-Year Follow-Up," *Trauma: Explorations In Memory,* ed. Cathy Caruth (Baltimore: Johns Hopkins University Press, 1995): 76–99, p. 83.

16. "Metaphors in the Tradition of the Shaman," *Conversant Essays: Contemporary Poets on Poetry,* ed. James McCorkle (Detroit: Wayne State University Press, 1990): 99–100.

17. Culbertson, p. 177. The connection between trauma and shamanism is also made by Joan Halifax in *Shamanic Voices: A Survey of Visionary Narratives* (New York: E. P. Dutton, 1979), p. 5.

18. See Markman and Markman, p. 4–5. Also see Vicki Noble, *Motherpeace: A Way to the Goddess* (San Francisco: Harper Press, 1983), p. 4.

19. Amos Segala, "Literature nahuatl," *Cuadernos Americanos* 6:24 (Nov.–Dec. 1990): 9–29, p. 12.

20. Maria Montes de Oca Rickes, *Mediating the Past: Continuity and Diversity in the Chicano Literary Tradition,* Ph.D. dissertation, (University of South Carolina, 1991), p. 97–98.

21. All citations in this paragraph are from "La Prieta," in *This Bridge Called My Back,* ed. Anzaldúa and Moraga (New York: Kitchen Table Press, 1981): 198–209.

22. Anzaldúa herself never uses the term "hysterectomy" but Ana Castillo does, in "Un Tapiz: The Poetics of Concientización," in *The Massacre of the Dreamers: Essays on Xicanisma* (New York: Plume, 1995): 163–179, p. 172.

23. For the purposes of this reading, I will provide an English translation of the text, with the request that English speakers bear in mind the implications of its original language.

24. See Erich Neumann, *The Great Mother: An Analysis of an Archetype,* trans. Ralph Manheim (Princeton: Princeton University Press, 1955), p. 77.

25. For more on Tlazolteotl, see Todorov, *The Conquest of America,* trans. Richard Howard (New York: HarperPerennial, 1992), p. 231; and Markman

and Markman, *The Flayed God: The Mythology of Mesoamerica* (San Francisco: Harper, 1992), pp. 166–167.

26. Neumann, pp. 182–183 and 301.

27. For more on these aspects of Tlazolteotl, see Gene S. Stuart, *The Mighty Aztecs* (Washington, D.C.: National Geographic Society, 1981), p. 137; and Tey Diana Rebolledo, *Women Singing in the Snow: A Cultural Analysis of Chicana Literature* (Tucson: University of Arizona Press, 1995), pp. 51 and 68.

28. Neumann, pp. 158 and 187. Buffie Johnson also writes that for the Aztecs the west was the "womb of death," the place where the sun died each night; see *Lady of the Beasts: Ancient Images of the Goddess and Her Sacred Animals* (San Francisco: Harper Row, 1988), p. 163.

29. From J. E. Circot, *A Dictionary of Symbols,* 2nd ed., trans. from the Spanish by Jack Sage (New York: Philosophical Library, 1971), p. 233.

30. As Ellen S. Zinner and Mary Beth Williams write in their conclusion to *When a Community Weeps: Case Studies in Group Survivorship,* "rituals play a healing role as *symbolic communal responses* to an event that goes beyond any one individual or family in its impact and consequence" (252).

31. The origins of shamanism are addressed by Mircea Eliade in *Shamanism: Archaic Techniques of Ecstasy,* trans. William R. Trask (Princeton: Princeton University Press, 1964), p. 333.

Chapter Seven

1. Alicia Ostriker writes that Sexton is committed to the erotic view of life in "Anne Sexton and the Seduction of the Audience," in *Sexton: Selected Criticism,* ed. Diana Hume George (Urbana, IL: University of Illinois Press, 1988): 3–18, p. 7. Estella Lauter praises Sexton's refusal to cover up and her refusal to be shamed into silence in *Women as Mythmakers: Poetry and Visual Art by Twentieth-Century Women* (Bloomington, IN: Indiana University Press, 1984), p. 25. Brian Gallagher claims that it was "on matters of overt sexuality" that Sexton made the most significant contributions to a proto-feminist dialogue. See his "A Compelling Case," *Denver Quarterly* 21:2 (Fall 1986): 95–111, p. 105. Finally, Liz Porter Hankins argues that despite Sexton's Puritan background, she attempts to achieve a sense of identity through the body, in "Summoning the Body: Anne Sexton's Body Poems," *Midwest Quarterly: A Journal of Contemporary Thought* 28:4 (Summer 1987): 511–524.

2. Brian Gallagher, in the essay cited above, calls Sexton a "major religious poet," a poet of "belief in belief" (111), while Estella Lauter, also cited above, claims Sexton's work from 1970–74 as a prophetic body of work (23). Further, Louise Calio writes that Sexton and Plath are "modern pioneers" of goddess poetry in "A Rebirth of the Goddess in Contemporary Women Poets of the Spirit," *Studia Mystica* 7:1 (Spring 1984): 50–59, p. 51.

For more on Sexton as a spiritual poet, see David J. Johnson, "Anne Sexton's The Awful Rowing Toward God: A Jungian Perspective of the Individuation Process," *Journal of Evolutionary Psychology* 7:1–2 (March 1986): 117–126; Kevin Lewis, "A Theologian on the Courtly Lover Death in Three Poems by Emily Dickinson, Anne Sexton, and Sylvia Plath," *Lamar Journal of the Humanities* 8:1 (Spring 1982): 13–21; Diane Wood Middlebook, "Poet of Weird Abundance," *Parnassus: Poetry in Review* 12–13:2–1 (Spring–Winter 1985): 293–315 (cited hereafter as Middlebrook "Poet"); William Shurr, "Mysticism and Suicide: Anne Sexton's Last Poetry," *Soundings: An Interdisciplinary Journal* 68:3 (Fall 1985): 335–356.

3. Alicia Ostriker writes that after *Transformations* Sexton sees herself as "the heroine on a spiritual quest . . . [while the] woman question . . . deepens and darkens" in "'That Story: Anne Sexton and Her Transformations," *The American Poetry Review* 11:4 (July–Aug. 1982): 11–16, p. 13 (cited hereafter as "That Story"). See also Diana Huma George, "Is It True? Feeding, Feces, and Creativity in Anne Sexton's Poetry," *Soundings: An Interdisciplinary Journal* 68:3 (Fall 1985): 357–371.

4. "Reconstructing the Impact of Trauma on Personality," *Personality and Psychopathology: Feminist Reappraisals,* ed. Laura S. Brown and Mary Ballou (New York: The Guilford Press, 1992): 229–265, p. 238.

5. *The Second Sex,* trans. H. M. Parshley (New York: Knopf, 1953); rpt. (New York: Vintage Books, 1974), p. 188–189; originally published as *Le deuxième sexe* (Paris: Gallimard, 1949).

6. Elizabeth Waites, *Trauma and Survival: Post-Traumatic and Dissociative Disorders in Women* (New York, Norton, 1993), p. 4.

7. I know "goodness" is not a very precise word for what I am trying to convey here, but interestingly, the synonyms for this word imply an absence of the sexual: chastity, purity, morality, and decency among them. Further, I have decided to use the word "goodness" throughout this chapter on healing since, according to Arthur Green, sexually abused children often feel a profound sense of "badness" about themselves. See "Childhood Sexual and Physical Abuse," *International Handbook of Traumatic Stress Syndromes,* ed. John P. Wilson and Beverley Raphael (New York: Plenum Press, 1993): 577–592, p. 579. See also Finkelhor and Browne, "Initial and long-term effects: A conceptual framework," in *A Sourcebook on Child Sexual Abuse,* ed. D. Finkelhor (Beverly Hills: Sage Publications, 1986): 180–198.

8. Cynthia Eller, *Living in the Lap of the Goddess: The Feminist Spirituality Movement in America,* (New York: Crossroad Press, 1993). I have chosen this work among many for several reasons: it provides not only explanation but criticism of the movement; it attempts to convey the differences as well as the commonalities among those who call themselves "spiritual feminists;" it does not rely only upon first-person narratives in the present but rather attempts to interpret the stories of women in the light of the double his-

tory of our society and the movement's development. What has been labeled the feminist spirituality movement began in the early 1970's when (mostly white) women began to form small groups to share and discuss their experiences as women in what was called "consciousness raising," or CR groups (3; 44). During these discussions, many women began to talk openly, not only of their daily experiences, but also of their spiritual yearnings: their growing dissatisfaction with patriarchal religion, their desires to be priests, their visions of a female god. From this beginning and into various forms—such as retreats, workshops, and individual study—a pattern began to emerge under the rubric of feminist spirituality, defined by, above all, an emphasis on the need for empowerment and healing, which is accomplished by the valorization of nature and women, and which includes a reconstruction of history (3).

9. Such groundbreaking works include, in order of publication, Elizabeth Gould Davis, *The First Sex* (Baltimore: Penguin, 1971); Mary Daly, *Beyond God the Father* (Boston: Beacon Press, 1973); M. Esther Harding, *Woman's Mysteries, Ancient and Modern: A Psychological Interpretation of the Feminine Principle as Portrayed in Myth, Story, and Dreams* (New York: Bantam, 1973); Marija Gimbutas, *The Gods and Goddesses of Old Europe—7000–3000 B.C., Myths Legends and Cult Images* (London: Thames and Hudson, 1974), rpt. as *Goddesses and Gods of Old Europe—6500–3500 B.C.* (Berkeley: University of California Press, 1982); Rosemary R. Ruether, *Religion and Sexism* (New York: Simon and Schuster, 1974); Merlin Stone, *When God Was A Woman* (New York: Harcourt Brace Jovanovich, 1978).

10. Gimbutas' work is cited in the footnote above. Gimbutas is listed as one of the fellowship recipients in the press release from Radcliffe, in the Sexton Collection, Box 31, HRHRC.

11. The poem is the first in "The Jesus Papers" series, which makes up the third part of *The Book of Folly* in the original publication, and the second part of the book in *Anne Sexton: The Complete Poems.* All citations are from *The Book of Folly* in *Anne Sexton: The Complete Poems* (Boston: Houghton Mifflin, 1981): 297–345. Diana Hume George describes "The Jesus Papers" as "Sexton's radical retelling of the story of humanity's creation, fall and renewal," in *Oedipus Anne* (Urbana, IL: University of Illinois Press, 1987), p. 80.

12. Diane Wood Middlebrook writes in "The Poet of Weird Abundance," cited above, that "The experience of separation or the creation of the selfish ego becomes in these poems ["The Jesus Papers"] *the* principal human experience needing spiritual cure" (304).

13. All citations are from *All My Pretty Ones* in *Anne Sexton: The Complete Poems* (Boston: Houghton Mifflin, 1981): 47–92.

14. Debora Ashworth remarks that many women poets in the United States use Mary as a way to address God in "Madonna or Witch: Women's Muse in Contemporary American Poetry," *Women's Culture: The Women's Renaissance*

of the Seventies, ed. Gayle Kimball (Metuchen, NJ: Scarecrow, 1981):
178–186, p. 180.

15. All citations are from *Live or Die* from *Anne Sexton: The Complete Poems*
(Boston: Houghton Mifflin, 1981): 93–170.

16. Diane Wood Middlebrook, "The Poet of Weird Abundance," cited above,
p. 300.

17. Interestingly, such a statement is also made by the French feminist theorist,
Hélène Cixous, in her essay, "The Laugh of the Medusa," from 1975.
Reprinted in David H. Richter, ed. *The Critical Tradition* (Boston: Bedford,
1998): 1454–1466. Sexton's connection to French feminism will be exam-
ined later in the chapter.

18. From page 15 of the page proofs for the interview, for which Sexton her-
self typed the original transcription. From the Sexton Collection, Box 16,
HRHRC.

19. "Housewife into Poet: The Apprenticeship of Anne Sexton," *The New Eng-
land Quarterly: A Historical Review of New England Life and Letters* 56: 4 (Dec.
1983): 483–503, p. 502.

20. "Anne Sexton's 'Motherly' Poetics," *Original Essays on the Poetry of Anne Sex-
ton,* ed. Francis Bixler (Conway, AR: University of Central Arkansas Press,
1988): 92–101, p. 100.

21. All citations are from *The Awful Rowing Toward God* in *Anne Sexton: The
Complete Poems* (Boston: Houghton Mifflin, 1981): 415–474.

22. Kathleen Nichols, "The Hungry Beast Rowing Toward God: Anne Sexton's
Later Religious Poetry," *Sexton: Selected Criticism,* ed. Diana Hume George
(Urbana, IL: University of Illinois Press, 1988): 165–170, p. 165.

23. "Anne Sexton's Island God," *Original Essays on the Poetry of Anne Sexton,* ed.
Francis Bixler (Conway, AR: University of Central Arkansas Press, 1988):
169–183, p. 179.

24. Stephanie Demetrakopoulos, "Goddess Manifestations as Stages in Femi-
nine Metaphysics in the Poetry and Life of Anne Sexton," *Sexton: Selected
Criticism,* ed. Diana Hume George (Urbana, IL: University of Illinois Press,
1988): 117–144, p. 436.

25. "That Story: Anne Sexton and Her Transformations," cited above, p. 16.

26. Citations are from *Love Poems* in *Anne Sexton: The Complete Poems* (Boston:
Houghton Mifflin, 1981): 171–220.

27. Rise B. Axelrod, "'I Dare to Live': The Transforming Art of Anne Sexton,"
Concerning Poetry 7 (Spring 1974): 6–13. Rpt. in *Critical Essays on Anne Sex-
ton,* ed. Linda Wagner-Martin (Boston: Hall, 1989): 177–185, p. 181.

28. Citations are from *The Death Notebooks* in *Anne Sexton: The Complete Poems*
(Boston: Houghton Mifflin, 1981): 347–413.

29. Sexton's poetry thus predates the contemporary reinterpretations of sexu-
ality in feminist spirituality characterized by feminist theologian, Rosemary
Radford Ruether: "Sin is not a fall into sexuality, but a fall into oppression

and injustice. Salvation is not a flight from the body, nature, and history, but a reordering of the social systems by which we live our embodied historical lives so that the full value and dignity of all persons can be realized." See "Asceticism and Feminism: Strange Bedmates?" *Sex and God: Some Varieties of Women's Religious Experience,* ed. Linda Hurcombe (London: Routledge Kegan Paul, 1987): 229–250, p. 245.

30. *A New Species of Trouble: Explorations in Disaster, Trauma, and Community* (New York: Norton, 1994), p. 231.

31. Lynette McGrath, "Anne Sexton's Poetic Connections: Death, God, and Form," *Original Essays on the Poetry of Anne Sexton,* ed. Frances Bixler (Conway, AR: University of Central Arkansas Press, 1988): 138–163, p. 146. Italics mine.

32. As Hilary Clark writes of the poem cited from *The Death Notebooks,* "The death wish in 'Seven Times' involves a desire to return to a lost maternal nurturing, a lost mother-daughter intimacy." See "Depression, Shame, and Reparation: The Case of Anne Sexton," *Scenes of Shame: Psychoanalysis, Shame, and Writing,* eds. Joseph Adamson and Hillary Clark (Albany, NY: State University of New York Press, 1999): 189–206, p. 200.

33. Jennifer L. Manlowe, *Faith Born of Seduction: Sexual Trauma, Body Image, and Religion* (New York: New York University Press, 1995), p. 62.

34. All citations are from *45 Mercy Street* in *Anne Sexton: The Complete Poems* (Boston: Houghton Mifflin, 1981): 476–555. I should note that although this volume was published posthumously, Sexton herself considered the manuscript "complete," according to Linda Gray Sexton in her Editor's Note to the volume (479).

35. *Trauma and Survival: Post-Traumatic and Dissociative Disorders in Women* (New York, Norton, 1993), p. 47.

36. Monica Sjöö and Barbara Mor note that in ancient times, "Spinning and weaving were imbued with magic powers, and inscribed spindle-whorls are found in innumerable Neolithic sacrificial pits sacred to the goddess." See *The Great Cosmic Mother: Rediscovering the Religion of the Earth* (San Francisco: Harper, 1991), p. 51. See also Marta Weigle, *Spiders and Spinsters: Women and Mythology* (Albuquerque, NM: University of New Mexico Press, 1982), which is a good sourcebook for myths, images, and literature on both European and North and South American meanings of spider and spinster archetypes.

37. From *This Sex Which Is Not One,* trans. Catherine Porter with Carolyn Burke (Ithaca, NY: Cornell University Press, 1985): 205–218; pages 205 and 214. Originally published as "Quand nos lèvres se parlent," in *Cahiers du grif,* no. 12. English translation: "When Our Lips Speak Together," trans. Carolyn Burke, *Signs* 6:1 (Fall 1980): 69–79.

38. Waltraud Mitgutsch characterizes "The Consecrating Mother" as a poem in which women's sexuality becomes cosmic, as the "earth opens like a cave,

like a womb to receive the persona, to mother her, to heal her fragmented self." See "Women in Transition: The Poetry of Anne Sexton and Louise Gluck," *Arbeiten aus Anglistik und Amerikanistik* 9:2 (1984): 131–145, p. 141. Another critic, Estella Lauter, echoes this statement when she remarks that the goddess image of this poem is both maternal and sexual and that all of Sexton's poems about the female deity have sexual as well as religious energy. See *Women as Mythmakers: Poetry and Visual Art by Twentieth-Century Women* (Bloomington, IN: Indiana University Press, 1984), pp. 33 and 37. Finally, Diana Hume George writes that in "The Consecrating Mother," ". . . the ocean is a source of nurture, power, force, and comfort . . . a solid sense of feminine strength is imagined in the bodied, naked power of the ocean [where all of the] damning and beloved mothers of other poems . . . are incorporated and transcended." See *Oedipus Anne: The Poetry of Anne Sexton* (Urbana, IL: University of Illinois Press, 1987) p. 73.

39. *Oedipus Anne,* p. 54, my emphasis.

Chapter Eight

1. From Lorde's Forward to *Showing Our True Colors:Afro-German Women Speak Out,* ed. May Opitz and Katharina Oguntoye, trans. Anne V. Adams (Amherst: University of Massachusetts Press, 1992): viii.

2. *Black Feminist Thought* (New York: Routledge, 1990), pp. 72 and 78. See also K. Sue Jewell, *From Mammy to Miss America and Beyond: Cultural Images and the Shaping of U.S. Social Policy* (New York: Routledge, 1993).

3. The first quote is from Collins, p. 77; the second is from Barbara Christian, *Black Women Novelists: The Development of a Tradition, 1892–1976* (Westport, Conn: Greenwood Press, 1980), p. 15.

4. Beverly Guy-Sheftall, "The History of Black Women's Liberation," Lecture, September 7, 1994, Emory University, Atlanta, Georgia. See also Guy-Sheftall, ed. *Words of Fire: An Anthology of African-American Feminist Thought* (New York: The New Press, 1995), pp. 3–4.

5. The speech can be found in *Maria S. Stewart: America's First Black Woman Political Writer, Essays and Speeches,* ed. with Intro. Marilyn Richardson (Bloomington: Indiana University Press, 1987): 65–74.

6. The speech has been anthologized many times, including in *Crossing the Danger Water: Three Hundred Years of African-American Writing,* ed. with Intro. Deirdre Mullane (New York: Anchor Books, 1993): 186.

7. From *Major Speeches by Negroes in the U.S., 1797–1971,* ed. Eric Foner (New York: Simon and Schuster, 1972): 345–346. Reprinted in *Words of Fire,* pages 37–38, p. 38.

8. *Black Women's Autobiography: A Tradition Within a Tradition* (Philadelphia: Temple University Press, 1989), p. 73.

9. Fannie Barrier Williams, "The Intellectual Progress of the Colored Women of the United States Since the Emancipation Proclamation," *World's Congress of Representative Women,* ed. May Wright Sewell (Chicago, 1893): 696–711.

10. bell hooks, *Ain't I A Woman: Black Women and Feminism* (Boston: South End Press, 1981), p. 166. Biographical information is from Beverly Guy-Sheftall, *Words of Fire,* p. 43.

11. Anna Julia Cooper, *A Voice from the South* (New York: Oxford University Press, 1988): 48–79, p. 59.

12. Barbara Smith's essay is discussed in chapter two. Lorde's essay was originally published as a pamphlet by Out & Out Books, reprinted in *Sister/Outsider* (Freedom, CA: The Crossing Press, 1984): 53–59; cited as Erotic. Although this is the first complete essay Lorde writes on the subject, the theme can be seen in her work from the beginning. In an interview on April 23, 1976, she says of her first volume of poetry, *New York Head Shop and Museum,* "I have gotten a lot of really weird reviews and I think this happens whenever you have poetry that has a lot of juice, that has the *erotic* in it, you are going to have people react not only to the poetry but to their own fear of their own feelings" (18, italics mine). From an interview with Deborah Wood from *In the Memory and Spirit of Francis, Zora, and Lorraine: Essays and Interviews on Black Women and Writing,* ed. Juliette Bowles (Washington, D.C.: Institute for the Arts and the Humanities, Howard University, 1979): 11–22.

13. Lorde is credited with being the major influence on the theology of the erotic by Anne Bathurt Gilson in *Eros Breaking Free: Interpreting Sexual Theo-Ethics* (Cleveland: Pilgrim Press, 1995), esp. pp. 66–68. Lorde's theory of the erotic has also influenced the work of many black lesbian writers; see *Afrekete: An Anthology of Black Lesbian Writing,* eds. Catherine E. McKinley and L. Joyce Delaney (New York: Doubleday, 1995).

14. Even though Ana Louise Keating notes that Lorde' address was given to a group of women historians, Keating's own lack of historical contextualization about Lorde's erotic in the face of black women's history is striking. See *Women Reading / Women Writing: Self-Invention in Paula Gunn Allen, Gloria Anzaldúa, and Audre Lorde* (Philadelphia: Temple University Press, 1996), pp. 51–54.

15. See Alison M. Jaggar, "Love and Knowledge: Emotion in Feminist Epistemology," in *Inquiry* 32: 151–176, for a discussion of the role of emotion in Western epistemology and the (mostly Anglo) feminist argument that "the ideal of the dispassionate investigator is a classist, racist, and especially masculinist myth" (165).

16. *The Cancer Journals* (San Francisco: Spinsters/Aunt Lute, 1980); cited as Cancer. *The Black Unicorn* (New York: Norton, 1978); cited as BU. *Zami: A New Spelling of My Name* (San Francisco, The Crossing Press, 1982); cited as Zami. "Eye to Eye: Black Women, Hatred, and Anger" in *Sister Outsider* (Freedom, CA: Crossing Press, 1984): 145–175; cited as Eye.

17. See "An Interview: Audre Lorde and Adrienne Rich," from August 30, 1979 in Montague, Massachusetts; reprinted in *Sister Outsider,* 81–109, p. 99. Cited hereafter as Interview.

18. In an interview in October 1978, one month after the "erotic" address, Lorde emphasizes the need for black women's history: "We need the archives. We need to have access to Alicia Johnson . . . to these Black women who wrote forty, fifty years ago. I never knew Anne Spencer. I never knew these women's writings even when I read about the Harlem Renaissance because their experience wasn't underlined, as Barbara Smith so aptly says. . . ." (12). See Karla M. Hammond, "Audre Lorde: Interview," Denver Quarterly 16:1 (Spring 1981): 10–27.

19. See Christian, Georgoudaki, Ostriker, and Zimmerman.

20. Such a focus on the positive aspects of the *figural* mother can be found in DiBernard and Lauter. In focusing on the positive lessons Audre's *own mother* teaches, I do not mean to downplay the many painful aspects of their relationship discussed by Ana Louise Keating in her excellent analysis of *Zami* in *Women Reading / Women Writing:* Audre's mother "would not openly acknowledge her own 'blackness'"; would not discuss "the differences in skin tone between herself, her husband, and her three daughters"; hit and chastised Audre when she lost for class president; and "ignored or condemned her anger" when she confronted racism (148–149). However, by focusing on the positive aspects of Audre's mother, I am going beyond other critics by showing that Lorde not only takes the model for Afrekete from her research into West African mythology, but also from her own reclamation of the positive lessons about sexuality and spirituality that she learned from her mother.

21. Similarly to Keating (see note above), Jennifer Browdy de Hernandez contrasts the "disappointment and even anger with their biological mothers" that both Lorde and Anzaldúa express with the "idealized images they present of the mother-goddesses who serve as role models for their independent, emergent sense of self." As my readings make clear, I want to trace the sources of these "mother-goddesses" in the writers' personal as well as cultural biographies. See "Mothering the Self: Writing the Lesbian Sublime in Audre Lorde's *Zami* and Gloria Anzaldúa's *Borderlands/La Frontera,*" in *Other Sisterhoods: Literary Theory and U.S. Women of Color,* ed. Sandra Kumamoto Stanley (Urbana, IL: University of Illinois Press, 1998): 244–62, p. 246.

22. Chinosole similarly traces Lorde's text through the "matrilineal diaspora" back to slave narratives but does not treat the issue of sexual abuse in her essay.

23. In this section I rely upon the work of anthropologists Smith and Hill to whom Lorde could have referred for her research; she explicitly mentions Donald Hill in her Acknowledgments, while Hill cites M. G. Smith as the expert on Carriacou. Further evidence that Lorde relied upon these sources

can be found in the similarity between Hill's observation that "One man believed that women get the drive to become zami from their mother's blood" (Hill 281) and Lorde's last line of her narrative: "There it is said that the desire to lie with other women comes from the mother's blood" (256).

24. From Griaule, p. 95; quoted in Raynaud, p. 238.

25. It is interesting to note the connection between Lorde's mention of the songs "for everything" in Carriacou (11) and Hill's description of calypso, a form of music/poetry that expresses feelings about slavery, government, history, and community relations (209). Hill also notes that the songs at festivals are in call and response pattern and are African in style (330).

26. Chinosole writes that "'zami' is *patois* for 'lesbian,' based on the French expression, les amies" (385, 393).

27. See Mbiti, Karenga, and Richards.

28. See Awiakta.

29. Suzette A. Henke, in her *Shattered Subjects: Trauma and Testimony in Women's Life Writing,* writes of the encounter with Afrekete: "Virtually eating the Mother / Nature-Goddess, Audre/Zami breaks down the barriers that separate mother and daughter, humankind and nature, Demeter and Persephone, child and MawuLisa, male and female, East and West, body and spirit" (111).

Chapter Nine

1. Ana Castillo, in *Massacre of the Dreamers: Essays on Xicanisma,* writes, "In much the same way that the [White Woman's Movement] sought an affirmation of womanhood through European goddess worship, the mestiza resurrects her own pantheon of indigenous goddesses, particularly Guadalupe/Tonantzin, and Coatlicue. This desire . . . is a most necessary process for self-healing . . . from the devastating blows we receive from society for having been born poor, non-white, and female." (New York: Plume, 1994), p. 152.

2. Tey Diana Rebolledo writes that her book, *Women Singing in the Snow: A Cultural Analysis of Chicana Literature,* examines women who have been "a *witness* to the historical, social, and cultural processes that formed" them (x, italics mine). She goes on to say that after *Borderlands/La Frontera,* "Chicanas breathed a sigh of relief because the tensions, the conflict, the shiftings had finally been articulated. And Anzaldúa not only defined what Chicanas had been feeling for some time, but she presented it in a positive way" (103). (Tucson: University of Arizona Press, 1995).

3. Roberta H. and Peter T. Markman, *The Flayed God: The Mesoamerican Mythological Tradition* (San Francisco: Harper, 1992), p. 190. The myth of origin appears on pp. 76–77.

4. From Rachel Phillips, "Marina / Malinche: Masks and Shadows," in *Women in Hispanic Literature: Icons and Fallen Images,* ed. Beth Miller (Berkeley: University of California Press, 1983): 97–114. Cited in Ricks, p. 165.

5. Miguel Léon-Portilla, ed. with Intro. *The Broken Spears: The Aztec Account of the Conquest of Mexico,* trans. from Nahuatl into Spanish, Angel Maria Garibay K. English trans., Lysander Kemp (Boston: Beacon, 1992), p. 35. Cited hereafter as *Account.*

6. From Phillips, cited in Ricks, p. 165.

7. Bernal Diaz del Castillo, *The Conquest of New Spain,* trans. J. M. Cohen (New York: Penguin, 1963), p. 85.

8. Rebelledo, *Women Singing in the Snow,* p. 62; del Castillo, *The Conquest of New Spain,* pp. 85–87.

9. La Malinche's role as a scapegoat for the Mexican male's fear of failure is discussed by Jean Franco in *Plotting Women: Gender and Representation in Mexico* (New York: Columbia University Press, 1989), pp. 91–101.

10. See Franco, *Plotting Women,* p. 131.

11. Rebelledo, *Women Singing in the Snow,* cited above, p. 125.

12. The similarities between the appearance of the Virgin of Guadalupe and appearances of the Virgin in Europe are discussed by Enrique Florescano, *Memory, Myth, and Time in Mexico: From the Aztecs to Independence,* trans. Albert G. Bork and Kathryn G. Bork (Austin: University of Texas Press, 1994), p. 143.

13. From Bernadino de Sahagún, *Historia general de las cosas Nueva España,* 4 vols., ed. Angel Maria Garibay K. (Mexico: Editorial Porrúa, 1956). Cited in Ricks, p. 163.

14. See Florescano, pp. 134–136 and 192.

15. Tey Diana Rebelledo and Eliana S. Rivero, "Introduction," *Infinite Divisions* (Tucson: University of Arizona Press, 1993): 1–33, p. 31.

16. Rebelledo includes a good discussion of the significance of the myth of La Llorona and Anzaldúa's revisioning of it in *Women Singing in the Snow,* pp. 62–64; 78.

17. Miguel Léon-Portilla, *The Aztec Image of Self and Society: An Introduction to Nahua Culture,* trans. J. Jorge Klor de Alva (Salt Lake City: University of Utah Press, 1992), p. 114. Cited as *Aztec.*

18. "Traddutora, Traditora: A Paradigmatic Figure of Chicana Feminism," *Cultural Critique* 13 (Fall 1989): 57–87, p. 61. Alarcón also writes that throughout history, Our Lady has been "evoked by utopically inspired movements" (61). Indeed: in 1991, after the fall of the "Iron Curtain," I received a letter from my devout Catholic grandmother who wrote, "Russia's problems showed us what can happen. Thank God our Blessed Mother turned them around. Those people have been suffering since 1917."

19. Ferdinand Anton, *Women in Pre-Columbian America* (New York: Abner Schram, 1973), p. 58–59.

20. Gene S. Stuart, *The Mighty Aztecs* (Washington, D.C.: The National Geographic Society, 1981), p. 136.

21. These aspects of Tlazolteotl are addressed by Markman and Markman in *The Flayed God*, p. 187; by Stuart in *The Mighty Aztecs*, p. 137; and by Rebolledo in *Women Singing in the Snow*, p. 68.

22. See Rebelledo, *Women Singing in the Snow*, pp. 50 and 93.

23. Debra D. Andrist writes that for Anzaldúa, "La serpiente entonces no solamente simboliza la natalidad y la función creativa por su aspecto divino, sino que también ofrece una esperanza para el futuro [The serpent then not only symbolizes birth and the creative function by its divine aspect, but also offers a hope for the future]" (245, my translation). See "La semiotica de la chicana: La escritura de Gloria Anzaldúa," *Mujer y literatura mexicana y chicana: Culturas en contacto, II,* ed. Aralia Lopez Gonzalez, Amelia Malagamba, and Elena Urrutia (Mexico City; Tijuana: Colegio de Mexico; Colegio de la Frontera Norte, 1990): 243–247.

24. See Rebelledo, *Women Singing in the Snow*, pp. 214–215.

25. See Markman and Markman, *The Flayed God*, pp. 221–222.

26. This aspect of Mesoamerican belief is addressed in Markman and Markman, p. 4.

27. Neumann, *The Great Mother*, pp. 190–191.

28. For more on the conceptions of history and time in Aztec civilization, see Tzvetan Todorov, *La Conquête de l'Amérique* (Paris: Editions du Seuil, 1982) and Roberta H. Markman and Peter T. Markman, *The Flayed God:The Mythology of Mesoamerica* (New York: HarperCollins Publishers, 1992): 164–179.

29. See Buffie Johnson, *Lady of the Beasts: Ancient Images of the Goddess and Her Sacred Animals* (San Francisco: Harper Row: 1988), pp. 163.

30. See Justino Fernández, *Mexican Art* (Middlesex: The Hamlyn Publishing Group Ltd., 1965, rev.ed. 1967), p. 33.

31. The figure of fire as a sign of loss by death and the ignition of mourning can be seen in Lacan's reading of Freud's dream of the burning child from *The Interpretation of Dreams,* in *Les Quatre Concepts Fondamentaux de la Psychanalyse* (Paris: Editions du Seuil, 1973).

32. This can be traced in Freud's "Mourning and Melancholia" and "Negation," both from *General Psychological Theory* (New York: Collier, 1963): 164–179 and 213–217; and in Melanie Klein, "A Contribution to the Psychogenesis of Manic-Depressive States" and "Mourning And Its Relation to Manic-Depressive States" both from *Contributions to Psycho-analysis 1921–1945* (London: Hogarth Press, 1948): 282–310 and 311–338.

33. Keating calls Coatlicue's fall in this poem a "decision to jump," but, as we will see, the fall is not determined to be either suicide or murder. See Ana Louise Keating, *Women Reading / Women Writing: Self-Invention in Paula*

Gunn Allen, Gloria Anzaldúa, and Audre Lorde (Philadelphia: Temple University Press, 1996), p. 40.

34. Cherríe Moraga writes of this particular piece of Anzaldúa's writing that "the imagery seems to float, disconnected from its point of reference," which, although intended to be a criticism of Anzaldúa's writing, is actually a perfect description of Anzaldúa's effectiveness in conveying the impossibility of reference in traumatic history. Ana Louise Keating seems to understand this when she writes that "Anzaldúa adopts this mythic figure to invent an ethnic specific yet transcultural symbol; . . . the disorienting prose that Moraga finds so objectionable furthers Anzaldúa's metaphor, for it replicates the fragmentation that characterizes the Coatlicue state." See Moraga, "Algo secretamente amado," *The Sexuality of Latinas,* ed. Norma Alarcón, Ana Casillo, and Cherríe Moraga (Berkeley: Third Women Press, 1993): 151–156, p. 152; and Keating, *Women Reading / Women Writing,* p. 35.

35. See *Remembering: A Phenomenological Study* (Bloomington: Indiana University Press, 1987), p. 255.

36. Casey, *Remembering,* pp. 244–245, his emphasis.

37. Bessel A. van der Kolk, "The Role of the Group in the Origin and Resolution of the Trauma Response," *Psychological Trauma,* ed. Bessel A. van der Kolk, M.D. (Washington, D.C.: American Psychiatric Press, 1987): 153–171, p. 162.

38. From *The Florentine Codex,* Book Six. Cited in Stuart, *The Mighty Aztecs,* p. 124.

39. See Sufi Order of the West, *Spiritual Retreat Guide* (New Lebanon, NY: Omega Press, 1985). The practice is spelled "La illaha illa 'la hu." It literally means "There is no god but God." Thanks to Karen Murphy for sharing this information with me.

40. From *Webster's New Twentieth Century Dictionary,* unabridged, 2nd ed. (Williams Collins, 1980), p. 1763.

41. From J. E. Circot, *A Dictionary of Symbols,* 2nd ed., trans. from the Spanish by Jack Sage (New York: Philosophical Library, 1971), p. 8.

42. From Webster's *New Twentieth Century Dictionary,* unabridged, 2nd ed. (Williams Collins, 1980), p. 402.

43. Circot writes that the sword's "primary symbolic meaning . . . is of a wound and the power to wound" (323), while Noble writes of the sword as a symbol of "mental activity and the powers of the mind" as well as "the Aryan race . . . aggression, 'power over,'" and "spiritual 'transcendence'" (154).

44. From *The New World Spanish-English and English-Spanish Dictionary,* ed. Salvatore Ramondino (New York: Signet, 1969), p. 285.

45. *The New World Spanish-English and English-Spanish Dictionary,* ed. Salvatore Ramondino (New York: Signet, 1969), p. 220.

46. *Everything In Its Path* (New York: Simon and Schuster, 1976), p. 154.

47. Lourdes Torres, "The Construction of the Self in U.S. Latina Autobiographies," *U.S. Third World Women and the Politics of Feminism,* ed. Chandra T. Mohanty, Anne Russo and Lourdes Torres (Bloomington, IN: Indiana University Press, 1991): 271–287, p. 283.

48. Jessica Benjamin, as well, contributes to the understanding of intersubjectivity in the light of loss and destruction in "The Shadow of the Other (Subject): Intersubjectivity and Feminist Theory," *Constellations* vol. 1, no. 2 (1994): 231–254.

49. It is interesting to note that Lawrence Langer, as well, valorizes the "multiple identities" that he observes in the testimonies of Holocaust survivors: "It would be more honest and accurate, when confronting their testimony, if we were to pluralize identity and address the question of multiple identities, not of course in a pathological sense but as a historical result of the value-dispersion that characterizes their experience" (203).

50. Sidonie Smith, "The Autobiographical Manifesto: Identities, Temporalities, Politics," *Autobiography and Questions of Gender,* ed. Shirley Neuman (London: Cass, 1992): 186–212, p. 203. See also Diane L. Fowlkes, "Moving from Feminist Identity Politics to Coalition Politics through a Feminist Materialist Standpoint of Intersubjectivity in Gloria Anzaldúa's Borderlands/La Frontera: The New Mestiza," *Hypatia: A Journal of Feminist Philosophy* 12:2 (Spring 1997): 105–24, for further discussion of how Anzaldúa's work presents a theory of the "intersubject."

51. "Feminism on the Border: From Gender Politics to Geopolitics," *Criticism in the Borderlands,* ed. Hector Calderon and José David Saldívar (Durham, NC: Duke University Press, 1991): 203–220, p. 216, my emphasis.

Bibliography

Anne Sexton

Alkalay-Gut, Karen. "'For We Swallow Magic and We Deliver Anne': Anne Sexton's Use of Her Name." *The Anna Book: Searching for Anna in Literary History,* ed. Mickey Pearlman. Westport, CT: Greenwood, 1992. 139–49.

Ashworth, Debora. "Madonna or Witch: Women's Muse in Contemporary American Poetry." *Women's Culture: The Women's Renaissance of the Seventies,* ed. Gayle Kimball. Metuchen: Scarecrow, 1981. 178–186.

Axelrod, Rise B. "'I Dare to Live': The Transforming Art of Anne Sexton." *Concerning Poetry* 7 (Spring 1974): 6–13. Rpt. *Critical Essays on Anne Sexton,* ed. Linda Wagner-Martin. Boston: Hall, 1989. 177–185.

Banerjee, Jacqueline. "Grief and the Modern Writer." *English: The Journal of the English Association* 43:175 (Spring 1994): 17–36.

Barry, Ann Marie Seward. "In Praise of Anne Sexton's The Book of Folly: A Study of the Woman/Victim/Poet." *Original Essays on the Poetry of Anne Sexton,* ed. Francis Bixler. Conway: University of Central Arkansas Press, 1988. 46–65.

Bechtolsheim, Barbara von. "Uber Anne Sexton." *Akzente: Zeitschrift fur Literatur* 33:4 (August 1986): 366–370.

Bixler, Francis. "Anne Sexton's 'Motherly' Poetics." *Original Essays on the Poetry of Anne Sexton,* ed. Francis Bixler. Conway: University of Central Arkansas Press, 1988. 92–101.

———, ed. *Original Essays on the Poetry of Anne Sexton.* Conway, AR: University of Central Arkansas Press, 1988.

Blake, Nancy. "'Anne, Anne,/Fuis sur ton ane': Image and Psychotic Experience in the Poetry of Anne Sexton." In *Twelfth International Conference on Literature and Psychoanalysis,* ed. Frederico Pereira. Lisbon, Portugal: Instituto Superior de Psicologia Aplicada, 1996. 111–15.

Blanton, Smiley. *The Healing Power of Poetry.* New York: Thomas Y. Crowell, 1960.

Bobolas, Eniko. "Woman and Poet? Conflicts in the Poetry of Emily Dickinson, Sylvia Plath, and Anne Sexton." In *The Origins an Originality of American Culture,* ed. Tibor Frank. Budapest: Akademiai Kiado, 1984: 375–383.

Braham, Jeanne. *Crucial Conversations: Interpreting Contemporary Literary Autobiographies by Women.* New York: Teachers College, Columbia University Press, 1995.

Burns, Michael. "Confession as Sacrament." In *Original Essays on the Poetry of Anne Sexton,* ed. Francis Bixler. Conway, AR: University of Central Arkansas Press, 1988. 130–137.

Calio, Louise. "A Rebirth of the Goddess in Contemporary Women Poets of the Spirit." *Studia Mystica* 7:1 (Spring 1984): 50–59.

Capo, Kay Ellen Merriman. "'I Have Been Her Kind': Anne Sexton's Communal Voice." In *Original Essays on the Poetry of Anne Sexton,* ed. Francis Bixler. Conway, AR: University of Central Arkansas Press, 1988. 22–45.

———. "Redeeming Words." In *Anne Sexton: Telling the Tale,* ed. Steven E. Colburn. Ann Arbor: University of Michigan Press, 1988. 88–102.

Cixous, Hélène. "The Laugh of the Medusa." Reprinted in *The Critical Tradition,* ed. David H. Richter. Boston: Bedford, 1998: 1454–1466.

Clark, Hilary. "Depression, Shame, and Reparation: The Case of Anne Sexton." In *Scenes of Shame: Psychoanalysis, Shame, and Writing,* eds. Joseph Adamson and Hillary Clark. Albany, NY: State University of New York Press, 1999. 189–206.

Colburn, Steven E. "Anne Sexton: A Supplemental Bibliography, 1945–1990." *Bulletin of Bibliography* 48:2 (June 1991): 109–15.

———, ed. *No Evil Star: Selected Essays, Interviews, and Prose.* Ann Arbor: University of Michigan Press, 1985.

———, ed. *Anne Sexton: Telling the Tale.* Ann Arbor: University of Michigan Press, 1988.

———. "'This Is My Tale Which I Have Told': Anne Sexton as Storyteller." In *Critical Essays on Anne Sexton,* ed. Linda Wagner-Martin. Boston: Hall, 1989: 166–177.

Cunci, Marie Christine Lemardeley. "Anne Sexton (1928–1974), ou comment faire taire Jocaste." *Revue Francaise d'Etudes Americaines* 7:15 (November 1982): 383–394.

———. "Crises exquises: Persistance de la douleur dans la poesie de Anne Sexton." In *Eclats de Voix: Crises en représentation dans la litterature nord-americaine.* ed. Christine Raguet Bouvart. La Rochelle: Rumeur des Ages, 1995: 137–146.

Davani, Maria Carmela Coco. "Anne Sexton: The Scene of the Disordered Senses." *RSA Journal* 2 (1991): 53–71.

Davis, Elizabeth Gould. *The First Sex.* Baltimore: Penguin, 1971.

Daly, Mary. *Beyond God the Father.* Boston: Beacon Press, 1973.

de Beauvoir, Simone. *The Second Sex,* trans. H. M. Parshley. New York: Vintage Books, 1974. Rpt. New York: Knopf, 1953. Originally published as *Le deuxième sexe.* Paris: Gallimard, 1949.

Demetrakopoulos, Stephanie. "Goddess Manifestations as Stages in Feminine Metaphysics in the Poetry and Life of Anne Sexton." In *Sexton: Selected Criticism,* ed. Diana Hume George. Urbana, IL: University of Illinois Press, 1988. 117–144.

———. "The Nursing Mother and Feminine Metaphysics: An Essay on Embodiment." *Soundings: An Interdisciplinary Journal* 65:4 (Winter 1982): 430–443.

DeSalvo, Louise. *Virginia Woolf: The Impact of Childhood Sexual Abuse on Her Life and Work.* Boston: Beacon, 1989.

de Souza, Eunice. "Kamala Das." In *Indian Poetry in English: A Critical Assessment,* ed. Vasant A Shahane and M. Sivaramkrishna. Atlantic Highlands, NJ: Humanities, 1981. 41–47.

Dickey, James. "Five First Books." *Poetry* XCVII:5 (February 1961): 318–319. Rpt. *Anne Sexton: The Artist and her Critics,* ed. J. D. McClatchy. Bloomington, IN: Indiana University Press, 1978: 117–118.

Eller, Cynthia. *Living in the Lap of the Goddess: The Feminist Spirituality Movement in America.* New York: Crossroad Press, 1993.

FitzGerald, Margot. "Using Sexton to Read Freud: The Pre-Oedipal Phase and the Etiology of Lesbianism in Sexton's 'Rapunzel'." *Journal of Homosexuality* 19:4 (1990): 55–65.

Freedman, William. "Sexton's 'The Legend of the One-Eyed Man'." *Explicator* 51:4 (Summer 1993): 248–52.

Gallagher, Brian. "A Compelling Case." *Denver Quarterly* 21:2 (Fall 1986): 95–111.

George, Diana Hume. "Anne Sexton's Island God." In *Original Essays on the Poetry of Anne Sexton,* ed. Francis Bixler. Conway, AR: University of Central Arkansas Press, 1988. 169–183.

———. "Anne Sexton's Suicide Poems." *Journal of Popular Culture* 18:2 (Fall 1984): 17–31.

———. "Beyond the Pleasure Principle: Anne Sexton's 'The Death Baby'." *University of Hartford Studies in Literature: A Journal of Interdisciplinary Criticism* 15:2 (1983): 75–92.

———. "Death Is a Woman, Death Is a Man: Anne Sexton's Green Girls and the Leaves That Talk." *University of Hartford Studies in Literature: A Journal of Interdisciplinary Criticism* 18:1 (1986): 31–44.

———. "How We Danced: Anne Sexton on Fathers and Daughters." *Women's Studies: An Interdisciplinary Journal* 12:2 (1986): 179–202.

———. "Is It True? Feeding, Feces, and Creativity in Anne Sexton's Poetry." *Soundings: An Interdisciplinary Journal* 68:3 (Fall 1985): 357–371.

———. "Itinerary of an Obsession: Maxine Kumin's Poems to Anne Sexton." In *Original Essays on the Poetry of Anne Sexton,* ed. Francis Bixler. Conway, AR: University of Central Arkansas Press, 1988. 243–266.

———. "Kumin on Kumin and Sexton: An Interview." *Poesis: A Journal of Criticism* 6:2 (1985): 1–18.

———. *Oedipus Anne: The Poetry of Anne Sexton.* Urbana: University of Illinois Press, 1987.

———. "The Poetic Heroism of Anne Sexton." *Literature and Psychology* 33:3–4 (1987): 76–88.

Georgoudaki, E. "Portrait of the Poet as a Woman in the Writings of Anne Sexton, Adrienne Rich and Denise Levertov." *Working Papers in Linguistics and Literature,* ed. A. Kakouriotis and Gounelas R. Parkin. Thessaloniki: Aristotle University, 1989. 165–184.

Gimbutas, Marija. *The Gods and Goddesses of Old Europe—7000–3000 B.C., Myths Legends and Cult Images.* London: Thames and Hudson, 1974. Rpt. as *Goddesses and Gods of Old Europe-6500–3500 B.C.* Berkeley: University of California Press, 1982.

Goodman, Jenny. "Anne Sexton's Live or Die: The Poem as the Opposite of Suicide." In *Original Essays on the Poetry of Anne Sexton,* ed. Francis Bixler. Conway, AR: University of Central Arkansas Press, 1988. 71–80.

Green, Kate. "Inventory of Loss." Review of *45 Mercy Street. Moons and Lion Tails* 2:2 (1976). Rpt. *Anne Sexton: Telling the Tale,* ed. Steven E. Colburn. Ann Arbor: University of Michigan Press. 376–380.

Hall, Caroline King Barnard. *Anne Sexton.* Boston: Twayne, 1989.

———. "Transformations: A Magic Mirror." In *Original Essays on the Poetry of Anne Sexton,* ed. Francis Bixler. Conway, AR: University of Central Arkansas Press, 1988. 107–129.

Hankins, Liz Porter. "Summoning the Body: Anne Sexton's Body Poems." *Midwest Quarterly: A Journal of Contemporary Thought* 28:4 (Summer 1987): 511–524.

Harding, M. Esther. *Woman's Mysteries, Ancient and Modern: A Psychological Interpretation of the Feminine Principle as Portrayed in Myth, Story, and Dreams.* New York: Bantam, 1973.

Hartman, Geoffrey. "Les Belles Dames Sans Merci." *Kenyon Review* XXII.4 (Autumn 1960): 696–99. Rpt. *Anne Sexton: The Artist and Her Critics,* ed. J. D. McClatchy. Bloomington: Indiana University Press, 1978. 118–121.

Irigaray, Luce. "When Our Lips Speak Together." In *This Sex Which Is Not One,* trans. Catherine Porter with Carolyn Burke. Ithaca, NY: Cornell University Press, 1985. 205–218.

Johnson, David J. "Anne Sexton's The Awful Rowing Toward God: A Jungian Perspective of the Individuation Process." *Journal of Evolutionary Psychology* 7:1–2 (March 1986): 117–126.

Juhasz, Suzanne. *Naked and Fiery Forms: Modern American Poetry by Women, A New Tradition.* New York: Harper Colophon, 1976.

———. "Seeking the Exit or the Home: Poetry and Salvation in the Career of Anne Sexton." In *Shakespeare's Sisters: Feminist Essays on Women Poets,* ed. Sandra M. Gilbert and Susan Gubar. Bloomington: Indiana University Press, 1979. 261–68. Rpt. in *Sexton: Selected Criticism,* ed. Diana Hume George. Urbana: University of Illinois Press, 1988. 303–311.

Kavaler-Adler, Susan. "Ann Sexton and the Daemonic Lover." *The American Journal of Psychoanalysis* 49:2 (June 1989):105–14.

————. *The Creative Mystique: From Red Shoes Frenzy to Love and Creativity.* New York: Routledge, 1996.

Keenan, James F. "Sexton's Last Tapes: Breaking the Seal of the Therapist's Code." *Commonweal* 118:19 (November 8, 1991): 635–37.

Kerr, Walter. "A Woman upon the Altar." Review of *Mercy Street.* New York Times. November 2, 1969. Rpt. *Anne Sexton: Telling the Tale,* ed. Steven E. Colburn. Ann Arbor: University of Michigan Press, 1988. 211–212.

Lauter, Estella. *Women as Mythmakers: Poetry and Visual Art by Twentieth-Century Women.* Bloomington, IN: Indiana University Press, 1984.

Leedy, Jack J., ed. *Poetry Therapy: The Use of Poetry in the Treatment of Emotional Disorders.* Philadelphia: J. B. Lippincott, 1969.

————, ed. *Poetry as Healer.* New York: The Vanguard Press, 1985.

Leventen, Carol. "Transformations's Silencings." In *Critical Essays on Anne Sexton,* ed. Linda Wagner-Martin. Boston: Hall, 1989. 136–149.

Lewis, Kevin. "A Theologian on the Courtly Lover Death in Three Poems by Emily Dickinson, Anne Sexton, and Sylvia Plath." *Lamar Journal of the Humanities* 8:1 (Spring 1982): 13–21.

Locke, Maryel F. "Anne Sexton Remembered." In *Rossetti to Sexton: Six Women Poets at Texas,* ed. Dave Oliphant and Robin Bradford. Austin: Harry Ransom Humanities Research Center, University of Texas at Austin, 1992. 155–63.

Long, Mihhail Ann. "As If Day Had Rearranged into Night: Suicidal Tendencies in the Poetry of Anne Sexton." *Literature and Psychology* 39:1–2 (1993): 6–41.

Lucas, Rose. "A Witch's Appetite: Anne Sexton's Transformations." *Southern Review: Literary and Interdisciplinary Essays* 26:1 (March 1993): 73–85.

Luedtke, Janet E. "'Something Special for Someone': Anne Sexton's Fan Letters from Women." In *Rossetti to Sexton: Six Women Poets at Texas,* ed. Dave Oliphant and Robin Bradford. Austin: Harry Ransom Humanities Research Center, University of Texas at Austin, 1992. 165–89.

Martin, Carrie. "'There Are More Important Things Than Judgment Involved': James Dickey's Criticism of Anne Sexton and the Search for Self." *James Dickey Newsletter* 13:2 (Spring 1997): 17–24.

Mc Cabe, Jane. "'A Woman Who Writes': A Feminist Approach to the Early Poetry of Anne Sexton." In *Anne Sexton: The Artist and Her Critics,* ed. J. D. McClatchy. Bloomington: Indiana University Press, 1978. 216–243.

McClatchy, J. D., ed. *Anne Sexton: The Artist and Her Critics.* Bloomington, IN: Indiana University Press, 1978.

————. "Anne Sexton: Somehow to Endure." In *Sexton: Selected Criticism,* ed. Diana Hume George. Urbana, IL: University of Illinois Press, 1988. 29–72.

McGrath, Lynette. "Anne Sexton's Poetic Connections: Death, God, and Form." *Original Essays on the Poetry of Anne Sexton,* ed. Francis Bixler. Conway, AR: University of Central Arkansas Press, 1988. 138–163.

Middlebrook, Diane Wood. *Anne Sexton: A Biography.* New York: Vintage, 1991.

————. "Anne Sexton: The Making of 'The Awful Rowing Toward God'." In *Ros-*

setti to Sexton: Six Women Poets at Texas, ed. Dave Oliphant and Robin Bradford. Austin: Harry Ransom Humanities Research Center, University of Texas at Austin, 1992. 223–37.

———. "1957: Anne Sexton's Bedlam." *Pequod: A Journal of Contemporary Literature and Literary Criticism* 23:24 (1987): 131–143.

———. "Becoming Anne Sexton." *Denver Quarterly* 18:4 (Winter 1984): 24–34.

———. "Housewife into Poet: The Apprenticeship of Anne Sexton." *The New England Quarterly: A Historical Review of New England Life and Letters* 56:4 (December 1983): 483–503.

———. "I tapped my own head': The Apprenticeship of Anne Sexton." In *Coming to Light,* ed. Diane Wood Middlebrook. Ann Arbor: University of Michigan Press, 1985. 195–213.

———. "Poet of Weird Abundance." *Parnassus: Poetry in Review* 12–13:2–1 (Spring-Winter 1985): 293–315.

———. "Seduction in Anne Sexton's Unpublished Play Mercy Street." In *Sexton: Selected Criticism,* ed. Diana Hume George. Urbana, IL: University of Illinois Press, 1988. 19–26.

———. "Spinning Straw Into Gold." In *The Literary Biography: Problems and Solutions,* ed. Dale Salwak. Iowa City: University of Iowa Press, 1996. 86–90.

———. "What Was Confessional Poetry?" In *The Columbia History of American Poetry,* ed. Jay Parini, Jay and Brett C. Miller. New York: Columbia University Press, 1993. 632–49.

Mitgutsch, Waltraud. "Women in Transition: The Poetry of Anne Sexton and Louise Gluck." *Arbeiten aus Anglistik und Amerikanistik* 9:2 (1984): 131–145.

Monteiro, George. "Anne Sexton's Radio Days." *Notes on Contemporary Literature* 25:5 (November 1995): 4–5.

Nelson, Deborah. "Penetrating Privacy: Confessional Poetry and the Surveillance Society." In *Homemaking: Women Writers and the Politics and Poetics of Home,* ed. Catherine Wiley and Fiona R. Barnes. New York: Garland, 1996. 87–114.

Nichols, Kathleen. "The Hungry Beast Rowing Toward God: Anne Sexton's Later Religious Poetry." In *Sexton: Selected Criticism,* ed. Diana Hume George. Urbana, IL: University of Illinois Press, 1988. 165–170.

Nucifora, Joan Ellen. "'The awful babble of that calling'." In *Anne Sexton: Telling the Tale,* ed. Steven E. Colburn. Ann Arbor: University of Michigan Press, 1988. 311–319.

Ostriker, Alicia. "Anne Sexton and the Seduction of the Audience." In *Sexton: Selected Criticism,* ed. Diana Hume George. Urbana, IL: University of Illinois Press, 1988. 3–18.

———. "That Story: Anne Sexton and Her Transformations." *The American Poetry Review* 11:4 (July–August 1982): 11–16.

———. " 'What Are Patterns For?' Anger and Polarization in Women's Poetry." *Feminist Studies* 10:3 (Fall 1984): 485–503.

Rose, Ellen Cronan. "Through the Looking Glass: When Women Tell Fairy Tales." In *The Voyage In: Fictions of Female Development,* ed. Elizabeth Abel, Marianne Hirsch, and Elizabeth Langland Elizabeth. Hanover, NH: University Press of New England for Dartmouth College, 1983. 209–227.

Ross, Virginia. "The Posthumous Confession of Anne Sexton." *Dionysos: The Literature and Intoxication TriQuarterly* 3:2 (Fall 1991): 31–35.

Ross-Bryant, Lynn. "Imagination and the Re-Valorization of the Feminine." *Journal of American Academy of Religious Thematic Studies* 48:2 (1981): 105–117.

Ruether, Rosemary Radford. "Asceticism and Feminism: Strange Bedmates?" In *Sex and God: Some Varieties of Women's Religious Experience,* ed. Linda Hurcombe. London: Routledge Kegan Paul, 1987. 229–250.

———. *Religion and Sexism.* New York: Simon and Schuster, 1974.

Scarborough, Margaret. "Anne Sexton's 'Otherworld Journey'." In *Original Essays on the Poetry of Anne Sexton,* ed. Francis Bixler. Conway, AR: University of Central Arkansas Press, 1988. 184–202.

Schechter, Ruth Lisa, C.P.T. "Poetry: A Therapeutic Tool in the Treatment of Drug Abuse." In *Poetry as Healer,* ed. Jack J. Leedy. New York: The Vanguard Press, 1985. 287–293.

Sexton, Anne. *Anne Sexton: The Complete Poems.* Boston: Houghton Mifflin, 1981.

———. Unpublished papers in the Sexton Collection. Harry Ransom Humanities Research Center, University of Texas, Austin.

Sexton, Linda. *Searching for Mercy Street: My Journey Back to My Mother, Anne Sexton.* Boston: Little, Brown, 1994.

Sexton, Linda Gray and Lois Ames. *Anne Sexton: A Self-Portrait in Letters.* Boston: Houghton Mifflin, 1977.

Shurr, William. "Mysticism and Suicide: Anne Sexton's Last Poetry." *Soundings: An Interdisciplinary Journal* 68:3 (Fall 1985): 335–356.

Sjöö, Monica and Barbara Mor. *The Great Cosmic Mother: Rediscovering the Religion of the Earth.* San Francisco: Harper, 1991.

Skorczewski, Dawn. "What Prison Is This? Literary Critics Cover Incest in Anne Sexton's 'Briar Rose.'" *Signs* 21:21 (Winter 1996): 309–342.

Stone, Merlin. *When God Was A Woman.* New York: Harcourt Brace Jovanovich, 1978.

Vossekuil, Cheryl. "Embracing Life: Anne Sexton's Early Poems." *Critical Essays on Anne Sexton,* ed. Linda Wagner-Martin. Boston: Hall, 1989. 120–127.

Wagner-Martin, Linda, ed. *Critical Essays on Anne Sexton.* Boston: Hall, 1989.

———. "Introduction: Anne Sexton, Poet." In *Critical Essays on Anne Sexton,* ed. Linda Wagner-Martin. Boston: Hall, 1989. 1–18.

———. "45 Mercy Street and Other Vacant Houses." In *American Literature: The New England Heritage,* ed. James Nagel and Richard Astro. New York: Garland, 1981. 145–165.

Weigle, Marta. *Spiders and Spinsters: Women and Mythology.* Albuquerque: University of New Mexico Press, 1982.

Audre Lorde

Alexander, Elizabeth. *Collage: An Approach to Reading African American Women's Writing.* University of Pennsylvania Dissertation, 1992.

———. " 'Coming Out Blackened and Whole': Fragmentation and Reintegration in Audre Lorde's Zami and The Cancer Journals." *American Literary History* 6:4 (Winter 1994): 695–715.

Annas, Pamela. "A Poetry of Survival: Unnaming and naming in the Poetry of Audre Lorde, Pat Parker, Sylvia Plath, and Adrienne Rich." *Colby Library Quarterly* 18 (March 1982): 9–25.

Avi-ram, Amittai F. "Apo Koinou in Audre Lorde and the Moderns: Defining the Differences." *Callaloo* 9:1 (Winter 1986): 193–208.

Awiakta, Marilou. *Selu: Seeking the Corn Mother's Wisdom.* Golden, CO: Fulcrum Publishing, 1993.

Bambara, Toni Cade. *Preface to The Black Woman,* ed. Toni Cade Bambara (New York: Penguin, 1970): 7–12.

Beale, Francis. "Double Jeopardy: To Be Black and Female." In *The Black Woman,* ed. Toni Cade Bambara. New York: Penguin, 1970. 90–100.

Bennett, Lerone, Jr. *Before the Mayflower: A History of Black America,* 6th ed. New York: Penguin, 1988.

Branch, Taylor. *Parting the Waters: America in the King Years, 1954–63.* New York: Simon and Schuster, 1988.

Braxton, Joanne M. *Black Women's Autobiography: A Tradition Within a Tradition.* Philadelphia: Temple University Press, 1989.

Brice-Baker, Janet R. "West Indian Women of Color: The Jamaican Woman." In *Women of Color: Integrating Ethnic and Gender Identities in Psychotherapy,* ed. Lillian Comas-Díaz and Beverly Greene. New York: The Guilford Press, 1994. 139–160.

Browdy de Hernandez, Jennifer. "The Plural Self: The Politicization of Memory and Form in Three American Ethnic Autobiographies." In *Memory and Cultural Politics: New Approaches to American Ethnic Literatures,* ed. Amriitjit Singh and Joseph T. Skerrett. Boston: Northeastern University Press, 1996. 41–59.

Carlston, Erin G. "Zami and the Politics of Plural Identity." In *Sexual Practice, Textual Theory: Lesbian Cultural Criticism,* ed. Susan J. Wolfe and Julian Penelope. Cambridge, MA: Blackwell, 1993. 226–236.

Carr, Brenda. " 'A Woman Speaks . . . I Am Woman and Not White': Politics of Voice, Tactical Essentialism, and Cultural Intervention in Audre Lorde's Activist Poetics and Practice." *College Literature* 20:2 (June 1993): 133–53.

Carrillo, Karen. "A Litany for Survival." *Cineaste* 22:2 (1996): 37.

Carruthers, Mary J. "The Re-Vision of the Muse: Adrienne Rich, Audre Lorde, Judy Grahn, Olga Broumas." *The Hudson Review* 36:2 (Summer 1983): 293–322.

Chinosole. "Audre Lorde and Matrilineal Diaspora: 'moving history beyond nightmare into structures for the future . . .' " In *Wild Women in the Whirlwind: Afra-American Culture and the Contemporary Literary Renaissance,* ed. Joanne M. Braxton and Andrée Nicola McLaughlin. New Brunswick: Rutgers University Press, 1990. 379–394.

Christian, Barbara. *Black Women Novelists: The Development of a Tradition, 1892–1976.* Westport, CT: Greenwood Press, 1980.

———. "No More Buried Lives: The theme of lesbianism in Audre Lorde's *Zami,* Gloria Naylor's *Women of Brewster Place,* Ntozake Shange's *Sassafras, Cypress, and Indigo,* and Alice Walker's *The Color Purple.*" In *Black Feminist Criticism.* New York: Pergamon Press, 1985. 187–204.

Collins, Patricia Hill. *Black Feminist Thought.* New York: Routledge, 1990.

Combahee River Collective. "A Black Feminist Statement." In *This Bridge Called My Back: Writings by Radical Women of Color,* ed. Cherríe Moraga and Gloria Anzaldúa. New York: Kitchen Table Press, 1981. 210–218.

Cooper, Anna Julia. *A Voice from the South.* New York: Oxford University Press, 1988. 48–79.

Couser, G. Thomas. "Autopathography: Women, Illness, and Lifewriting." *A/B: Autobiography* 6:1 (Spring 1991): 65–75.

Davis, Angela. "Reflections on the Black Woman's Role in the Community of Slaves." In *The Black Scholar* (December 1971). Rpt. *Words of Fire: An Anthology of African-American Feminist Thought,* ed. Beverly Guy-Sheftall. New York: The New Press, 1995. 200–218.

De Hernandez, Jennifer Browdy. "Mothering the Self: Writing the Lesbian Sublime in Audre Lorde's *Zami* and Gloria Anzaldúa's *Borderlands/La Frontera.*" In *Other Sisterhoods: Literary Theory and U.S. Women of Color,* ed. Sandra Kumamoto Stanley. Urbana, IL : University of Illinois Press, 1998. 244–62.

DeShazer, Mary K. *Inspiring Women: Reimagining the Muse.* New York: Pergamon Press, 1986.

Dhairyam, Sagri. "'Artifacts for Survival': Remapping the Contours of Poetry with Audre Lorde." *Feminist Studies* 18:2 (Summer 1992): 229–256.

DiBernard, Barbara. "*Zami:* A Portrait of an Artist as a Black Lesbian." *The Kenyon Review* 13:4 (Fall 1991): 195–213.

Dilworth, Thomas. "Lorde's 'Power'." *Explicator* 57:1 (Fall 1998): 54–57.

Dyson, Michael. "Remembering Emmett Till." In *Reflecting Black: African American Cultural Criticism.* Minneapolis: University of Minnesota Press, 1993. 194–198.

Foster, Thomas. " 'The Very House of Difference': Gender as 'Embattled' Standpoint." *Genders* 8 (Summer 1990): 17–37.

Fox-Genovese, Elizabeth. "My Statue, My Self: Autobiographical Writings of African American Women." In *Reading Black, Reading Feminist,* ed. Henry Louis Gates, Jr. New York: Meridian, 1990. 176–203.

Friedman, Alfred B. "Ballad." In *The Princeton Encyclopedia of Poetry and Poetics,* ed. Alex Preminger. Princeton: Princeton University Press, 1965. 62–64.

Gillan, Jennifer. "Relocating and identity in *Zami: A New Spelling of My Name.*" In *Homemaking: Women Writers and the Politics and Poetics of Home,* ed. Catherine Wiley and Fiona R. Barnes. New York: Garland, 1996. 209–221.

Ginzberg, Ruth. "Audre Lorde's (Nonessentialist) Lesbian Eros." *Hypatia* 7:4 (Fall 1992): 73–90.

Gougordaki, Ekaterini. "Audre Lorde: Revising Stereotypes of Afro-American Womanhood." *Arbeiten aus Anglistik und Amerikanistik* 16:1 (1991): 47–66.

Grahn, Judy. *Another Mother Tongue: Gay Words, Gay Worlds.* Boston: Beacon, 1984.

———. *The Highest Apple: Sappho and the Lesbian Poetic Tradition.* San Francisco: Spinsters Ink, 1985.

Griaule, Marcel. *Conversations with Ogotemmêli.* London: Oxford University Press, 1967.

Guy-Sheftall, Beverly. "The History of Black Women's Liberation." Lecture. September 7, 1994. Emory University, Atlanta, Georgia.

———. "The Impact of Slavery On Black Women." Lecture. September 22, 1994. Emory University, Atlanta, Georgia.

———. "The Women of Bronzeville." In *Sturdy Black Bridges: Visions of Black Women in Literature,* ed. Roseann P. Bell, Bettye J. Parker, and Beverly Guy-Sheftall. Garden City, NY: Anchor/Doubleday, 1979. 157–170.

———, ed. *Words of Fire: An Anthology of African-American Feminist Thought.* New York: The New Press, 1995.

Hammond, Karla M. "Audre Lorde: Interview." *Denver Quarterly* 16:1 (Spring 1981): 10–27.

Harper, Margaret Mills. "First Principles and Last Things: Death and the Poetry of Eavan Boland and Audre Lorde." *Representing Ireland: Gender, Class, Nationality. Susan Shaw Sailer,* ed. Gainesville, FL: University Press of Florida, 1997. 181–93.

Henderson, Mae Gwendolyn. "Speaking in Tongues: Dialogics, Dialectics, and the Black Woman Writer's Literary Tradition." In *Changing Our Words: Essays on Criticism, Theory, and Writing by Black Women,* ed. Cheryl A. Wall. New Brunswick, NJ: Rutgers University Press, 1989. Rpt. *Reading Black, Reading Feminist,* ed. Henry Louis Gates. New York: Meridian, 1990. 116–142.

Henderson, Stephen, ed. *Understanding the New Black Poetry: Black Speech and Black Music as Poetic References.* New York: William Morrow, 1973.

Henke, Suzette A. *Shattered Subjects: Trauma and Testimony in Women's Life Writing.* New York: St. Martin's Press, 1998.

Herman, Judith, and Lisa Hirschman. "Father-Daughter Incest." *Signs* 2:4 (1977): 735–756.

Hill, Donald. *The Impact and Migration on the Metropolitan and Folk Society of Carriacou, Grenada. Anthropological Papers of the American History Museum.* Vol. 54, Part 2. New York, 1977.

Hine, Darlene Clark. "Rape and the inner lives of Black women in the Middle West: Preliminary thoughts on the culture of dissemblance." *Signs* 14:4 (1989). Rpt. *Words of Fire: An Anthology of African-American Feminist Thought,* ed. Beverly Guy-Sheftall. New York: The New Press, 1995. 380–387.

Holland, Sharon Patricia. "'Which Me Will Survive': Audre Lorde and the Development of a Black Feminist Ideology." *Critical Matrix* Special Issue, No. 1 (1988): 1–30.

hooks, bell. *Ain't I A Woman: Black Women and Feminism.* Boston: South End Press, 1981.

Hughes, Langston. "Harlem." In *Six American Poets,* ed. Joel Conarroe. New York: Random House, 1991. 257.

Hull, Gloria T. "Living on the Line: Audre Lorde and Our Dead Behind Us." In *Changing Our Own Words: Essays on Criticism, Theory and Writing by Black Women,* ed. Cheryl A. Wall. New Brunswick: Rutgers, 1989. 150–173.

Jewell, K. Sue. *From Mammy to Miss America and Beyond: Cultural Images and the Shaping of U.S. Social Policy.* New York: Routledge, 1993.

Jordan, Winthrop D. *The White Man's Burden: Historical Origins of Racism in the United States.* London: Oxford University Press, 1974.

Kader, Cheryl. "'The Very House of Difference': *Zami,* Audre Lorde's Lesbian-Centered Text." In *Critical Essays: Gay and Lesbian Writers of Color,* ed. Emmanuel S. Nelson. New York: Haworth, 1993. 181–194.

Karenga, Maulanga. *Introduction to Black Studies.* Los Angeles: Kawaida Publications, 1982.

Keating, Ana Louise. *Women Reading / Women Writing: Self-Invention in Paula Gunn Allen, Gloria Anzaldúa, and Audre Lorde.* Philadelphia: Temple University Press, 1996.

———. "(De)Centering the Margins?: Identity Politics and Tactical Renaming." In *Other Sisterhoods: Literary Theory and U.S. Women of Color,* ed. Sandra Kumamoto Stanley. Urbana, IL: University of Illinois Press, 1998. 23–43.

Keating, AnnLouise. "Making 'our shattered faces whole': The Black Goddess and Audre Lorde's Revision of Patriarchal Myth." *Frontiers* 13:1 (1992): 20–33.

———. "Myth Smashers, Myth Makers: (Re) Visionary Techniques in the Works of Paula Gunn Allen, Gloria Anzaldúa and Audre Lorde." In *Critical Essays: Gay and Lesbian Writers of Color,* ed. Emmanuel S. Nelson. New York: Haworth, 1993. 73–95.

———. "Reading 'Through the Eyes of the Other': Self, Identity, and the Other in the Works of Paula Gunn Allen, Gloria Anzaldúa, and Audre Lorde." *Readerly Writerly Texts* 1:1 (Fall–Winter 1993): 161–86.

Kimmich, Allison. "Writing the Body: From Abject to Subject." *A/B: Auto-Biography Studies* 13:2 (Fall 1998): 223–34.

King, Deborah K. "Multiple Jeopardy, Multiple Consciousness: The Context of a Black Feminist Ideology." *Signs* 14:1 (Autumn 1988): 265–295.

Klein, Yvonne M. "Myth and Community in Recent Lesbian Autobiographical Fiction." In *Lesbian Texts and Contexts: Radical Revisions,* ed. Karla Jay and Joanne Glasgow. New York: New York University Press, 1990. 330–338.

Lauter, Estella. "Re-visioning Creativity: Audre Lorde's Refiguration of Eros as the Black Mother Within." *Writing the Woman Artist: Essays on Poetics, Politics, and Portraiture,* ed. Suzanne W. Jones. Philadelphia: Temple University Press, 1991. 398–418.

Lemons, Gary L. " 'Young Man, Tell Our Stories of How We Made It Over': Beyond the Politics of Identity." In *Teaching What You're Not: Identity Politics in Higher Education,* ed. Katherine J. Mayberry. New York: New York University Press, 1996. 259–284.

Lorde, Audre. *Between Our Selves.* Point Reyes, CA: Eidolon Editions, 1976.

———. *The Black Unicorn.* New York: Norton, 1978.

———. *A Burst of Light.* Ithaca, NY: Firebrand Books, 1988.

———. *The Cancer Journals.* San Francisco: Spinsters/Aunt Lute, 1980.

———. *Chosen Poems, Old and New.* New York: Norton, 1982.

———. *Coal.* New York: Norton, 1976.

———. "Eye to Eye: Black Women, Hatred, and Anger." *Sister Outsider.* Freedom, CA: Crossing Press, 1984. 145–175.

———. Forward to *Showing Our True Colors: Afro-German Women Speak Out,* ed. May Opitz and Katharina Oguntoye, trans. Anne V. Adams. Amherst: University of Massachusetts Press, 1992. vii–xiv.

———. "An Interview: Audre Lorde and Adrienne Rich." August 30, 1979 in Montague, Massachusetts. *Sister Outsider.* Freedom, CA: The Crossing Press, 1984. 81–109.

———. "My Words Will Be There." *Black Women Writers 1950–1980,* ed. Mari Evans. New York: Anchor Books, 1984. 261–268.

———. *New York Head Shop and Museum.* Detroit: Broadside Press, 1974.

———. "Revolutionary Hope: A Conversation Between James Baldwin and Audre Lorde." *Essence* (December 1984): 73–74; 129–130.

———. "Sisterhood and Survival." *The Black Scholar* (March/April 1986): 5–7.

———. "The Uses of Anger: Women Responding to Racism." Keynote presentation at the National Women's Studies Association Conference, Storrs, Connecticut, June 1981. *Sister Outsider.* Freedom, CA: The Crossing Press, 1984. 124–133.

———. "Uses of the Erotic: The Erotic as Power." Originally published as a pamphlet by Out & Out Books. Rpt. *Sister/Outsider.* Freedom, CA: The Crossing Press, 1984. 53–59.

———. *Zami: A New Spelling of My Name.* San Francisco: The Crossing Press, 1982.

Mbiti, J. *African Religions and Philosophies.* New York: Anchor Press, 1969.

Ostriker, Alicia. *Stealing the Language: The Emergence of Women's Poetry in America.* Boston: Beacon, 1986.

Parrinder, Geoffrey. *African Mythology.* London: Paul Hamlyn, 1967.

Perreault, Jeanne. " 'that the pain not be wasted': Audre Lorde and the Written Self." *A/B: Autobiography Studies* 4:1 (Fall 1988): 1–16.

Portilla, Miguel León and Gary Gossen. *South and Meso-American Native Spirituality: From the Cult of the Feathered Serpent to The Theology of Liberation.* New York: Crossroad Press, 1993.

Provost, Kara. "Becoming Afrekete: The Trickster in the Work of Audre Lorde." *MELUS* 20:4 (Winter 1995): 45–59.

Raynaud, Claudine. "'A Nutmeg nestled inside Its covering of mace': Audre Lorde's *Zami.*" In *Life/lines: Theorizing Women's Autobiography,* ed. Bella Brodski and Celeste Schenck. Ithaca, NY: Cornell University Press, 1988. 221–242.

Rich, Adrienne. "Interview with Matthew Rothschild." *The Progressive* (January 1994): 31–35.

Richards, Dona. "The Implications of African American Spirituality." In *African Culture,* ed. M. K. Asante and K. W. Asante. Trenton: Africa World Press, 1990. 207–231.

Smith, Barbara. "Toward a Black Feminist Criticism." *Conditions Two* 1:2 (October 1977): 25–44.

———. "The Truth That Never Hurts: Black Lesbians in Fiction in the 1980s." *Feminisms: An Anthology of Literary Theory and Criticism,* eds. Robyn R. Warhol and Diane Price Herndl. New Brunswick, NJ : Rutgers University Press, 1997. 784–806.

Smith, M. G. *Kinship and Community in Carriacou.* New Haven: Yale University Press, 1962.

Spillers, Hortense. "Interstices: A Small Drama of Words." In *Pleasure and Danger: Exploring Female Sexuality,* ed. Carol Vance. London: Pandora, 1984. 73–100.

Stewart, Maria S. "Farewell Address to Her Friends in the City of Boston." In *Maria S. Stewart: America's First Black Woman Political Writer, Essays and Speeches,* ed. with Intro. Marilyn Richardson. Bloomington, IN: Indiana University Press, 1987. 65–74.

Thomas, Laurence Mordecai. *Vessels of Evil: American Slavery and the Holocaust.* Philadelphia: Temple University Press, 1993.

Thomson, Rosemarie Garland. "Disabled Women as Powerful Women in Petry, Morrison, and Lorde: Revising Black Female Subjectivity." In *The Body and Physical Difference: Discourses of Disability,* eds. David T. Mitchell and Sharon L. Snyder. Ann Arbor: University of Michigan Press, 1997. 240–66.

Truth, Sojourner. "Address to the Ohio Women's Rights Convention." In *Crossing the Danger Water: Three Hundred Years of African-American Writing,* ed. with Intro. Deirdre Mullane. New York: Anchor Books, 1993. 186.

———. "When Woman Gets Her Rights Man Will Be Right." *Major Speeches by Negroes in the U.S., 1797–1971,* ed. Eric Foner. New York: Simon and Schuster, 1972. 345–346. Reprinted in *Words of Fire: An Anthology of African-American Feminist Thought,* ed. Beverly Guy-Sheftall. New York: The New Press, 1995. 37–38.

Waldrep, Shelton. "'Building Bridges': Cleaver/Baldwin/Lorde and African-American Sexism and Sexuality." In *Critical Essays: Gay and Lesbian Writers of Color,* ed. Emmanuel S. Nelson. New York: Haworth, 1993. 167–180.

Wells-Barnett, Ida B. "Lynch Law in America." *Arena* (January 1900): 15–24. Rpt. *Words of Fire: An Anthology of African-American Feminist Thought,* ed. Beverly Guy-Sheftall. New York: The New Press, 1995. 70-76.

Williams, Fannie Barrier. "The Intellectual Progress of the Colored Women of the United States Since the Emancipation Proclamation." In *World's Congress of Representative Women,* ed. May Wright Sewell. Chicago, 1893. 696–711.

Wilson, Anna. "Audre Lorde and the African-American Tradition: When the Family is Not Enough." In *New Lesbian Criticism,* ed. Sally Munt. New York: Harvester Wheatsheaf, 1992. 75–93.

———. "Rites/Rights of Canonization: Audre Lorde as Icon." In *Women Poets of the Americas: Toward a Pan-American Gathering,* eds. Jacqueline Vaught Brogan and Candelaria Cordelia Chavez. Notre Dame, IN: University of Notre Dame Press, 1999. 17–33.

Wood, Deborah. "Interview with Audre Lode on April 23, 1976." In *In the Memory and Spirit of Francis, Zora, and Lorraine: Essays and Interviews on Black Women and Writing,* ed. Juliette Bowles. Washington, D.C.: Institute for the Arts and the Humanities, Howard University, 1979. 11–22.

Worsham, Fabian Clements. "The Poetics of Matrilineage: Mothers and Daughters in the Poetry of African American Women, 1965–1985." In *Women of Color: Mother-Daughter Relationships in 20th-Century Literature,* ed. Elizabeth Brown-Guillory. Austin: University of Texas Press, 1996. 177–31.

Zimmerman, Bonnie. *The Safe Sea of Women: Lesbian Fiction 1969–1989.* Boston: Beacon, 1990.

Gloria Anzaldúa

Adams, Kate. "Northamerican Silences: History, Identity and Witness in the Poetry of Gloria Anzaldúa, Cherríe Moraga, and Leslie Marmon Silko." In *Listening to Silences: New Essays in Feminist Criticism,* ed. Elaine Hedges and Shelley Fisher Fishkin. New York: Oxford University Press, 1994. 130–145.

Alarcón, Norma. "Chicana's Feminist Literature: A Re-Vision Through Malintzin/ or Malintzin: Putting Flesh Back on the Object." *This Bridge Called My Back,* ed. Cherrie Moraga and Gloria Anzaldúa. New York: Kitchen Table, 1983. 182–190.

———. "Making Familia from Scratch: Split Subjectivities in the Work of Helena Maria Viramontes and Cherrie Moraga." *Chicana Creativity and Criticism: Charting New Frontiers in American Literature,* ed. Maria Herrera-Sobek and Helena Maria Viramontes. Houston: Arte Publico Press, 1988. 147–159.

———. "The Theoretical Subject(s) of *This Bridge Called My Back* and Anglo-American Feminism." In *Criticism in the Borderlands.* Durham, NC: Duke University Press, 1991. 28–39.

———. "Traddutora, Traditora: A Paradigmatic Figure of Chicana Feminism." *Cultural Critique* 13 (Fall 1989): 57–87.

Allen, Paula Gunn. " 'Border Studies': The Intersection of Gender and Color." In *The Ethnic Canon: Histories, Institutions, and Interventions,* ed. David Palumbo-Liu. Minneapolis: University of Minnesota Press, 1995. 31–47.

Andrist, Debra D. "La semiotica de la chicana: La escritura de Gloria Anzaldúa." *Mujer y literatura mexicana y chicana: Culturas en contacto, II,* ed. Aralia Lopez Gonzalez, Amelia Malagamba, and Elena Urrutia. Mexico City; Tijuana: Colegio de Mexico; Colegio de la Frontera Norte, 1990. 243–247.

Anton, Ferdinand. *Women in Pre-Columbian America.* New York: Abner Schram, 1973.

Anzaldúa, Gloria. *Borderlands/La Frontera.* San Francisco: Aunt Lute, 1987.

———. "Metaphors in the Tradition of the Shaman." In *Conversant Essays: Contemporary Poets on Poetry,* ed. James McCorkle. Detroit: Wayne State University Press, 1990. 99–100.

———. "La Prieta." In *This Bridge Called My Back,* ed. Anzaldúa and Moraga. New York: Kitchen Table Press, 1981, 1983. 198–209.

Arteaga, Alfred. *"Heterotextual Reproduction."* theory@buffalo (Fall 1996): 61–85.

Barnard, Ian. "Gloria Anzaldúa Queer Mestisaje." *MELUS: The Journal of the Society for the Study of the Multi-Ethnic Literature of the United States* 22:1 (Spring 1997): 35–53.

Basabe, Enrique Alejandro. "Una migracion aparente: El sujeto y el genero en 'Atravesando fronteras/Crossing Borders' de Gloria Anzaldúa." *Anclajes: Revista del Instituto de Analisis Semiotico del Discurso* 2:2 (Dec 1998): 29–43.

Behar, Ruth. "A Life Story to Take across the Border: Notes on an Exchange." In *Storied Lives: The Cultural Politics of Self-Understanding,* ed. George C. Rosenwald and Richard L. Ochberg. New Haven: Yale University Press, 1992. 108–123.

———. *Translated Woman: Crossing the Border with Esperanza's Story.* Boston: Beacon Press, 1993.

Bickford, Susan. "In the Presence of Others: Arendt and Anzaldúa on the Paradox of Public Appearance." In *Feminist Interpretations of Hannah Arendt,* ed. Bonnie Honig. University Park: Pennsylvania State University Press, 1995. 313–335.

Blom, Gerdien. "Divine Individuals, Cultural Identities: Post-Identitarian Representations and Two Chicana/o Texts." *Thamyris: Mythmaking from Past to Present* 4:2 (Autumn 1997): 295–324.

Branche, Jerome. "Anzaldúa: El ser y la nacion." *Entorno* 34 (Winter 1995): 39–44.

Browdy de Hernandez, Jennifer. "The Plural Self: The Politicization of Memory and Form in Three American Ethnic Autobiographies." In *Memory and Cultural Politics: New Approaches to American Ethnic Literatures,* ed. Amriitjit Singh and Joseph T. Skerrett. Boston: Northeastern University Press, 1996. 41–59.

Bruce-Novoa, Juan D. *Retrospace: Collected Essays on Chicano Literature, Theory, and History.* Houston, Texas: Arte Publico Press, 1990.

Calderón, Hector. "Texas Border Literature: Cultural Transformation and Historical Reflection in the Works of Americo Paredes, Rolando Hinojosa and Gloria Anzaldúa." *Dispositio: Revista Americana de Estudios Semioticos y Culturales* 16:41 (1991): 13–27. Rpt. as "Literatura fronteriza tejana: El compromiso con la historia en Americo Paredes, Rolando Hinojosa y Gloria Anzaldúa." *Mester* 22–23:2–1 (Fall 1993–Spring 1994): 41–61.

Calderón, Hector and José David Saldívar. "Editors' Introduction." *Criticism in the Borderlands.* Durham: Duke University Press, 1991. 1–7.

Castillo, Ana. *Massacre of the Dreamers: Essays on Xicanisma.* New York: Plume, 1994.

Circot, J. E. *A Dictionary of Symbols.* 2nd ed. trans. from the Spanish by Jack Sage. New York: Philosophical Library, 1971.

Concannon, Kevin. "The Contemporary Space of the Border: Gloria Anzaldúa's *Borderlands* and William Gibson's *Neuromancer.*" *Textual Practice* 12:3 (Winter 1998): 429–42.

Daniel, G. Reginald. "Black and White Identity in the New Millennium: Unsevering the Ties That Bind." In *The Multiracial Experience: Racial Borders as the New Frontier,* ed. Maria P. P. Root. Thousand Oaks, CA.: Sage, 1996. 121–139.

Davis, Jingle. "Martyrs or Contributors to Genocide?" *The Atlanta Journal Constitution* (Saturday, April 2, 1994): E6.

De Hernandez, Jennifer Browdy. "Mothering the Self: Writing the Lesbian Sublime in Audre Lorde's *Zami* and Gloria Anzaldúa's *Borderlands/La Frontera.*" In *Other Sisterhoods: Literary Theory and U.S. Women of Color,* ed. Sandra Kumamoto Stanley. Urbana, IL: University of Illinois Press, 1998. 244–62.

———. "The Plural Self: The Politicization of Memory and Form in Three American Ethnic Autobiographies." In *Memory and Cultural Politics: New Approaches to American Ethnic Literatures,* eds. Amritjit Singh and Joseph T. Skerrett, Jr. Boston: Northeastern University Press, 1996. 41–59.

Diaz del Castillo, Bernal. *The Conquest of New Spain,* trans. J. M. Cohen. New York: Penguin, 1963.

Eliade, Mircea. *Shamanism: Archaic Techniques of Ecstasy,* trans. William R. Trask. Princeton: Princeton University Press, 1964.

Erikson, Kai T. *Everything In Its Path.* New York: Simon and Schuster, 1976.

Espinoza, Dionne. "Women of Color and Identity Politics: Translating Theory, Haciendo Teoria." In *Other Sisterhoods: Literary Theory and U.S. Women of Color,* ed. Sandra Kumamoto Stanley. Urbana, IL : University of Illinois Press, 1998. 44–62.

Florescano, Enrique. *Memory, Myth, and Time in Mexico: From the Aztecs to Independence,* trans. Albert G. Bork and Kathryn G. Bork. Austin: University of Texas, 1994.

Fowlkes, Diane L. "Moving from Feminist Identity Politics to Coalition Politics through a Feminist Materialist Standpoint of Intersubjectivity in Gloria Anzaldúa's *Borderlands/La Frontera: The New Mestiza.*" *Hypatia: A Journal of Feminist Philosophy* 12:2 (Spring 1997): 105–24.

Fox-Genovese, Elizabeth. "The Claims of Common Culture: Gender, Race, Class and the Canon." *Salmagundi* 72 (1986): 131–143.

Franco, Jean. *Plotting Women: Gender and Representation in Mexico.* New York: Columbia University Press, 1989.

Freedman, Diane P. "Writing in the Borderlands: The Poetic Prose of Gloria

Anzaldúa and Susan Griffin." In *Constructing and Reconstructing Gender: The Links among Communication, Language, and Gender,* ed. Linda A. M. Perry, Lynn H. Turner, and Helen Sterk. Albany: State University of New York Press, 1992. 211–17.

Fregoso, Rosa Linda. *The Bronze Screen: Chicana and Chicano Film Culture.* Minneapolis: University of Minnesota Press, 1993.

Gal, Susan. "Language and Political Economy." *Annual Review of Anthropology* 18 (1989): 345–367.

Garcia-Serrano, Maria Victoria. "Gloria Anzaldúa y la politica de la identidad." *Revista Canadiense de Estudios Hispanicos* 19:3 (Spring 1995): 479–494.

Gomez-Hernandez, Adriana. "Gloria Anzaldúa: Enfrentando el desafio." *Cuadernons Americanos* 59 (September–October 1996): 57–63.

Grewal, Inderpal. "Autobiographic Subjects and Diasporic Locations: Meatless days and Borderlands." In *Scattered Hegemonies: Postmodernity and Transnational Feminist Practices,* ed. Inderpal Grewal and Caren Kaplan. Minneapolis: University of Minnesota Press, 1994. 231–254.

Gutiérrez-Jones, Carl. *Rethinking the Borderlands: Between Chicano Culture and Legal Discourse.* Berkeley: University of California Press, 1995.

Halifax, Joan. *Shamanic Voices: A Survey of Visionary Narratives.* New York: E. P. Dutton, 1979.

Hedley, Jane. "Neplantist Poetics: Narrative and Cultural Identity in the Mixed-Language Writings of Irena Klepfisz and Gloria Anzaldúa." *Narrative* 4:1 (January 1996): 36–54.

Herrera-Sobek, Maria. "The Politics of Rape: Sexual Transgression in Chicana Fiction." In *Chicana Creativity and Criticism: Charting New Frontiers in American Literature,* ed. Maria Herrera-Sobek and Helena María Viramontes. Houston: Arte Publico Press, 1988. 171–181.

Hillman, James. *Re-visioning Psychology.* New York: Harper and Row, 1975.

Johnson, Buffie. *Lady of the Beasts: Ancient Images of the Goddess and her Sacred Symbols.* San Francisco: Harper and Row, 1988.

Kaup, Monika. "Crossing Borders: An Aesthetic Practice in Writings by Gloria Anzaldúa." In *Cultural Difference and the Literary Text: Pluralism and the Limits of Authenticity in North American Literatures,* eds. Winfried Siemerling and Katrin Schwenk. Iowa City, IA: University of Iowa Press, 1996. 100–11.

Keating, Ana Louise. *Women Reading / Women Writing: Self-Invention in Paula Gunn Allen, Gloria Anzaldúa, and Audre Lorde.* Philadelphia: Temple University Press, 1996.

———. "(De)Centering the Margins? Identity Politics and Tactical (Re)Naming." In *Other Sisterhoods: Literary Theory and U.S. Women of Color,* ed. Sandra Kumamoto Stanley. Urbana, IL: University of Illinois Press, 1998. 23–43.

Keating, AnnLouise. "Reading 'Through the Eyes of the Other': Self, Identity, and the Other in the Works of Paula Gunn Allen, Gloria Anzaldúa, and Audre Lorde." *Readerly Writerly Texts* 1:1 (Fall–Winter 1993): 161–86.

———. "Writing, Politics, and las Lesberadas: Platicando con Gloria Anzaldúa." *Frontiers* 14:1 (1993): 105–130.

Lauter, Paul. "The Literatures of America: A Comparative Discipline." In *Redefining American Literary History.* New York: MLA, 1990. 9–34.

Leal, Luis. "Mexican American Literature: A Historical Perspective." In *Modern Chicano Writers,* eds. Joseph Sommers and Tomas Ybarra-Frausto. Englewood Cliffs: Prentice Hall, 1979. 18–30.

———. "The Rewriting of American Literary History." In *Criticism in the Borderlands.* Durham, NC: Duke University Press, 1991. 21–27.

Leland, Dorothy. "La formacion de la identidad en Borderlands/La Frontera, de Gloria Anzaldúa." In *La seduccion de la escritura: Los discursos de la cultura hoy, 1996,* eds. Rosaura Hernandez Monroy and Manuel F. Medina. Mexico City, Mexico: (no publisher), 1997. 170–75.

Léon-Portilla, Miguel. *The Aztec Image of Self and Society: An Introduction to Nahua Culture,* trans. J. Jorge Klor de Alva. Salt Lake City: University of Utah Press, 1992.

———. ed. with Intro. *The Broken Spears: The Aztec Account of the Conquest of Mexico,* trans. from Nahuatl into Spanish, Angel Maria Garibay K., Eng. trans. Lysander Kemp. Boston: Beacon, 1992.

Limon, Jose E. "Oral Tradition and Poetic Influence: Two Poets from Greater Mexico." In *Redefining American Literary History.* New York: MLA, 1990: 124–141.

Markman, Roberta H. and Peter T. Markman. *The Flayed God: The Mesoamerican Mythological Tradition.* San Francisco: HarperCollins, 1992.

Martínez, Oscar J. *Border People: Life and Society in the U.S.–Mexico Borderlands.* Tucson: University of Arizona Press, 1994.

Meier, Matt S. and Feliciano Ribera. *Mexican Americans/American Mexicans: From Conquistador to Chicano.* Rev. ed. Chicanos (1972). San Francisco: HarperCollins, 1993.

Mignolo, Walter D. "Linguistic Maps, Literary Geographies, and Cultural Landscapes: Languages, Languaging and (Trans)Nationalism." *Modern Language Quarterly* 57:2 (June 1996): 181–196.

Miller, Alice. *Thou Shalt Not Be Aware: Society's Betrayal of the Child,* trans. Hildegarde and Hunter Hannum. New York: Meridian, 1986.

Moraga, Cherríe. "Algo secretamente amado." In *The Sexuality of Latinas,* ed. Norma Alarcón, Ana Castillo, and Cherríe Moraga. Berkeley: Third Woman Press, 1993, 151–156.

Murphy, Patrick D. "Grandmother Borderland: Placing Identity and Ethnicity." *Isle: Interdisciplinary Studies in Literature and Environment* 1:1 (Spring 1993): 35–41.

Nakashima, Cynthia. "Voices from the Movement: Approaches to Multiraciality." In *The Multiracial Experience: Racial Borders as the New Frontier,* ed. Maria P. P. Root. Thousand Oaks, CA: Sage, 1996. 79–97.

Neely, Carol Thomas. "Women/Utopia/Fetish: Disavowal and Satisfied Desire in Margaret Cavendish's *New Blazing World* and Gloria Anzaldúa's *Borderlands/La*

Frontera." In *Heterotopia: Postmodern Utopia and the Body Politic,* ed. Tobin Siebers. Ann Arbor: University of Michigan Press, 1995. 58–95.

Neumann, Erich. *The Great Mother,* trans. Ralph Manheim. Princeton: Princeton University Press, 1955, 1963, 1991.

Noble, Vicki. *Motherpeace: A Way to the Goddess.* San Francisco: Harper Press, 1983.

Ortega, Eliana and Nancy Saporta Sternbach. "At the Threshold of the Unnamed: Latina Literary Discourse in the Eighties." *Breaking Boundaries: Latina Writing and Critical Readings,* ed. Asuncion Horno-Delgado, E. Ortega, N. M. Scott, and N. S. Sternbach. Amherst: University of Massachusetts Press, 1989. 2–23.

Oxford English Dictionary, The Compact Edition. Vols. I and II. Oxford: Oxford University Press, 1971.

Perry, Donna. "Gloria Anzaldúa." In *Backtalk: Women Writers Speak Out.* New Brunswick: Rutgers University Press, 1993. 19–42.

Phillips, Rachel. "Marina / Malinche: Masks and Shadows." In *Women in Hispanic Literature: Icons and Fallen Images,* ed. Beth Miller. Berkeley: University of California Press, 1983. 97–114.

Raiskin, Judith. "Inverts and Hybrids: Lesbian Rewritings of Sexual and Racial Identities." In *The Lesbian Postmodern,* ed. Laura Doan and Robyn Wiegman. New York: Columbia University Press, 1994. 156–172.

Ramirez, Arturo. "El feminismo y la frontera: Gloria Anzaldúa." *A Ricardo Gullon: Sus discipulos,* ed. Adelaida Lopez de Martinez. Erie, PA: Pub. de la Asociation Licenciados y Doctores Epanoles en Estados Unidos, 1995. 203–209.

Ramondino, Salvatore, ed. *The New World Spanish-English and English-Spanish Dictionary.* New York: Signet, 1969.

Rebolledo, Tey Diana. "The Politics of Poetics: or What Am I, A Critic, Doing in this Text Anyhow." In *Chicana Creativity and Criticism: Charting New Frontiers in American Literature,* ed. Maria Hererra-Sobek and Helena Maria Viramontes. Houston: Arte Publico Press, 1988: 129–138.

———. *Women Singing in the Snow: A Cultural Analysis of Chicana Literature.* Tucson: University of Arizona Press, 1995.

Rebolledo, Tey Diana and Eliana S. Rivero. "Introduction." In *Infinite Divisions,* ed. Tey Diana Rebolledo and Eliana S. Rivero. Tucson: University of Arizona Press, 1993. 1–33.

Reuman, Ann E. "'Wild Tongues Can't Be Tamed': Gloria Anzaldúa's (R)Evolution of Voice." In *Violence, Silence, and Anger: Women's Writing as Transgression,* ed. Deirdre Lashgari. Charlottesville: University Press of Virginia, 1995. 305–319.

Ricard, Serge. "'La Fiancee de Frankenstein' aux pays des Azteques: La nouvelle metisse selon Gloria Anzaldúa." *Annales du Centre de Recherches sur l'Amerique Anglophone* 20 (1995): 143–55, 237.

Rickes, Maria Montes de Oca. *Mediating the Past: Continuity and Diversity in the Chicano Literary Tradition.* Ph.D. dissertation. University of South Carolina, 1991.

Rives, George Lockhart. *The United States and Mexico, 1821–1848: A History of the*

Relations Between the Two Countries from the Independence of Mexico to the Close of the War with the United States. 2 vols. New York: Charles Scribner's Sons, 1913.

Root, Maria P. P., ed. *The Multiracial Experience: Racial Borders as the New Frontier.* Thousand Oaks, CA: Sage, 1996.

Sahagún, Bernadino de. *Historia general de las cosas Nueva España.* 4 vols, ed. Angel Maria Garibay K. Mexico: Editorial Porrúa, 1956.

Saldívar, Ramón. *Chicano Narrative: The Dialectics of Difference.* Madison, WI: University of Wisconsin Press, 1990.

———. "Narrative, Ideology, and the Reconstruction of American Literary History." In *Criticism in the Borderlands.* Durham, NC: Duke University Press, 1991. 11–27.

Saldivar-Hull, Sonia. "Feminism on the Border: From Gender Politics to Geopolitics." In *Criticism in the Borderlands.* Durham: Duke University Press, 1991: 203–220.

Segala, Amos. "Literatura nahuatl." *Cuadernos Americanos* 6: 24 (November–December 1990): 9–29.

Smith, Sidonie. "The Autobiographical Manifesto: Identities, Temporalities, Politics." *Autobiography and Questions of Gender,* ed. Shirley Neuman. London: Cass, 1992. 186–212.

Spitta, Silvia. "Gloria Anzaldúa: The New Mestiza Rides/Writes; Proceedings of the IV International Conference on the Hispanic Cultures of the United States." In *Gender, Self, and Society,* ed. Renate von Bardeleben. Frankfurt, Germany : Peter Lang, 1993. 75–85.

Streeter, Carolina A. "Ambiguous Bodies: Locating Black/White Women in Cultural Representations." In *The Multiracial Experience: Racial Borders as the New Frontier,* ed. Maria P. P. Root. Thousand Oaks, CA: Sage, 1996. 305–320.

Stuart, Gene S. *The Mighty Aztecs.* Washington, D.C.: The National Geographic Society, 1981.

Sufi Order of the West. *Spiritual Retreat Guide.* New Lebanon, NY: Omega Press, 1985.

Tafolla, Carmen. "La Malinche." In *Infinite Divisions,* ed. Tey Diana Rebolledo and Eliana S. Rivero. Tucson: University of Arizona Press, 1993. 198–199.

Takaki, Ronald. *A Different Mirror: A History of Multicultural America.* Boston: Little, Brown and Company, 1993.

Todorov, Tzvetan. *The Conquest of America: The Question of the Other,* trans. Richard Howard. New York: Harper and Row, 1984.

Torres, Lourdes. "The Construction of the Self in U.S. Latina Autobiographies." In *U.S. Third World Women and the Politics of Feminism,* ed. Chandra T. Mohanty, Anne Russo and Lourdes Torres. Bloomington, IN: Indiana University Press, 1991. 271–287.

Turner, Mike. "Relearning Ancient Lessons." *The Atlanta Journal Constitution* (Saturday, March 19, 1994): E1, E8.

Webster's New Twentieth Century Dictionary Unabridged. 2nd ed. USA: William Collins Publishers, 1980.

Yarbro-Bejarano, Yvonne. "Chicana Literature from a Chicana Feminist Perspective." *Chicana Creativity and Criticism: Charting New Frontiers in American Literature,* ed. Maria Hererra-Sobek and Helena Maria Viramontes. Houston: Arte Publico Press, 1988. 139–145.

———. "Gloria Anzaldúa's *Borderlands / La Frontera:* Cultural Studies, 'Difference,' and the Non-Unitary Subject." *Cultural Critique* 28 (Fall 1994): 5–28.

———. "The Lesbian Body in Latina Cultural Production." In *?Entiendes? Queer Readings, Hispanic Writings,* ed. Emilie L. Bergmann and Paul Julian Smith. Durham, NC: Duke University Press, 1995. 181–197.

Zavella, Patricia. "Reflections on Diversity Among Chicanas." *Frontiers* 12:2 (1991): 73–85.

Trauma Studies

Abraham, Nicolas and Maria Torok. "Deuil ou mélancholie: Introjecter-incorporer." In *L'Ecorce et Le Noyau.* Paris: Flammarion, 1987. 259–275.

Alcoff, Linda and Laura Gray. "Survivor discourse: Transgression or recuperation?" *Signs* 18:2 (Winter 1993): 260–290.

Armstrong, Louise. *Rocking the Cradle of Sexual Politics: What Happened When Women Said Incest.* Reading, MA: Wesley Publishing Group, 1994.

Benjamin, Jessica. *The Bonds of Love: Psychoanalysis, Feminism, and the Problem of Domination.* New York: Pantheon, 1988.

———. "The Shadow of the Other (Subject): Intersubjectivity and Feminist Theory." *Constellations* 1:2 (1994): 231–255.

Bertrand, Michèle. *La pensée et le trauma.* Paris: Harmattan, 1990.

Breuer, Josef and Sigmund Freud. *Studies on Hysteria,* trans. James Strachey. New York: Basic Books. Reprint of Volume II of the Standard Edition of the Complete Psychological Works of Sigmund Freud. London: Hogarth Press, 1955.

Brice-Baker, Janet R. "West Indian Women of Color: The Jamaican Woman." In *Women of Color: Integrating Ethnic and Gender Identities in Psychotherapy,* ed. Lillian Comas-Díaz and Beverly Greene. New York: The Guilford Press, 1994. 139–160.

Brown, Laura S. "Not Outside the Range: One Feminist Perspective on Trauma." In *Trauma: Explorations in Memory,* ed. Cathy Caruth. Baltimore: Johns Hopkins University Press, 1995. 100–112.

Burris, Ada, M.D. "Somatization as a Response to Trauma." In *Victims of Abuse: The Emotional Impact of Child and Adult Trauma,* ed. Alan Sugarman, Ph.D. Madison: International Universities Press, Inc., 1994. 131–137.

Caruth, Cathy. "Départs traumatiques: La survie et l'histoire chez Freud." *Le passage des frontières: Autour du travail de Jacques Derrida.* Colloque de Cerisy. Paris: Editions Galilée, 1994. 435–439.

———. *Introduction to Trauma: Explorations in Memory.* Baltimore: Johns Hopkins University Press, 1995. 3–12.

————. "Traumatic Departures: Survival and History in Freud." Lecture. February 3, 1994. Emory University, Atlanta, Georgia.

————. *Unclaimed Experience: Trauma, Narrative, and History.* Baltimore: Johns Hopkins University Press, 1996.

Casey, Edward S. *Remembering: A Phenomenological Study.* Bloomington, IN: Indiana University Press, 1987.

Champagne, Rosaria M. *The Politics of Survivorship: Incest, Women's Literature, Feminist Theory.* New York: New York University Press, 1996.

Culbertson, Roberta. "Embodied Memory, Transcendence, and Telling: Recounting Trauma, Re-establishing the Self." *New Literary History* 26 (1995): 169–195.

Danieli, Yael. "Treating Survivors and Children of Survivors of the Nazi Holocaust." In *Post-Traumatic Therapy and Victims of Violence,* ed. Frank M. Ochberg, M.D. New York: Brunner/Mazel, 1988. 278–294.

Erikson, Kai T. *Everything In Its Path.* New York: Simon and Schuster, 1976.

————. *A New Species of Trouble: Explorations in Disaster, Trauma, and Community.* New York: Norton, 1994.

Espin, Olivia M. and Mary Ann Gawelek. "Women's Diversity: Ethnicity, Race, Class, and Gender in Theories of Feminist Psychology." In *Personality and Psychopathology: Feminist Reappraisals,* ed. Laura S. Brown and Mary Ballou. New York: The Guilford Press, 1992. 88–107.

Finkelhor, D., ed. *A Sourcebook on Child Sexual Abuse.* Beverly Hills: Sage Publications, 1986.

Fresco, Nadine. "Remembering the Unknown," trans. Alan Sheridan. *International Review of Psycho-Analysis* 11:417 (1984): 417–426. Originally published in *Nouvelle Revue de Psychanalyse* 24 (1981).

Freud, Sigmund. *Beyond the Pleasure Principle,* trans. James Strachey. New York: Norton, 1961.

————. "Further Recommendations on the Technique of Psychoanalysis: Recollection, Reconstructing, Working Through" (1914). In *Therapy and Technique,* ed. Philip Rieff. New York: Macmillan, 1963. 157–166.

————. *Moses and Monotheism,* trans. Katharine Jones. New York: Knopf, 1949.

————. "Mourning and Melancholia." In *General Psychological Theory.* New York: Collier, 1963. 164–179.

————. "Negation." In *General Psychological Theory.* New York: Collier, 1963. 213–217.

————. "The Psychopathology of Hysteria." *Project for a Scientific Psychology.* 405–416.

Freyd, Jennifer J. *Betrayal Trauma: The Logic of Forgetting Childhood Abuse.* Cambridge: Harvard University Press, 1996.

Green, Arthur. "Childhood Sexual and Physical Abuse." In *International Handbook of Traumatic Stress Syndromes,* ed. John P. Wilson and Beverley Raphael. New York: Plenum Press, 1993. 577–592.

Green, Beverly. "African American Women." In *Women of Color: Integrating Ethnic and Gender Identities in Psychotherapy,* ed. Lillian Comas-Díaz and Beverly Greene. New York: The Guilford Press, 1994. 10–29.

Haaken, Janice. "The Recovery of Memory, Fantasy, and Desire: Feminist Approaches to Sexual Abuse and Psychic Trauma." *Signs* 21:4 (Summer 1996): 1069–1094.

Halbwachs, Maurice. *The Collective Memory,* trans. Francis J. Ditter, Jr. and Vida Yazdi Ditter. New York: Harper and Row, 1980.

Hartman, Geoffrey H. "On Traumatic Knowledge and Literary Studies." *New Literary History* 26 (1995): 537–563.

Herman, Judith Lewis. *Trauma and Recovery.* New York: Basic Books, 1992.

Herman, Judith and Lisa Hirschman. "Father-Daughter Incest." *Signs* 2: 4 (1977): 735–756.

Janet, Pierre. *Psychological Healing* [1919]. Vol. 1, trans. E. Paul and C. Paul. New York: Macmillan, 1925.

Janis, Irving L. *Stress and Frustration.* New York: Harcourt Brace Jovanovich, 1971.

Kestenberg, Judith S., M.D. and Ira Brenner, M.D. *The Last Witness: The Child Survivor of the Holocaust.* Washington, D.C.: American Psychiatric Press, 1996.

Klein, Melanie. *Contributions to Psycho-analysis 1921–1945.* London: Hogarth Press, 1948. 282–338.

Krugman, Steven, Ph.D. "Trauma in the Family: Perspectives on the Intergenerational Transmission of Violence," In *Psychological Trauma,* ed. Bessel A. van der Kolk, M.D. Washington, D.C.: American Psychiatric Press, 1987. 127–151.

Krystal, Henry. "Trauma and Aging: A Thirty-Year Follow-Up." In *Trauma: Explorations In Memory,* ed. Cathy Caruth. Baltimore: Johns Hopkins University Press, 1995. 76–99.

Lacan, Jacques. *Les Quatre Concepts Fondamentaux de la Psychanalyse.* Paris: Editions du Seuil, 1973.

Langer, Lawrence. *Holocaust Testimonies: The Ruins of Memory.* New Haven: Yale University Press, 1991.

Laplanche, Jean. *New Foundations for Psychoanalysis,* trans. David Macey. Oxford: Basil Blackwell, 1989.

Laub, Dori. "Truth and Testimony: The Process and the Struggle." In *Trauma: Explorations in Memory,* ed. Cathy Caruth. Baltimore: Johns Hopkins University Press, 1995. 61–75.

Lifton, Robert Jay. Interview with Cathy Caruth. In *Trauma: Explorations in Memory,* ed. Cathy Caruth. Baltimore: Johns Hopkins University Press, 1995. 128–147.

Luc-Nancy, Jean. "The Unsacrificeable." In *Yale French Studies 79, Literature and the Ethical Question,* ed. Claire Nouvet (1991): 20–38.

Lyotard, Jean-François. Lecture: "Time in Augustine's Confessions." Emory University, Atlanta, Georgia. March 29, 1995.

Manlowe, Jennifer L. *Faith Born of Seduction: Sexual Trauma, Body Image, and Religion.* New York: New York University Press, 1995.

McEvoy, Maureen and Leah Minuk. "Repairing Personal Boundaries: Group Therapy with Survivors of Sexual Abuse." In *Healing Voices: Feminist Approaches to Therapy with Women,* ed. Toni Ann Laidlaw, Cheryl Malmo and Associates. San Francisco: Jossey-Bass Publishers, 1990. 62–79.

Miller, Alice. *Thou Shalt Not be Aware: Society's Betrayal of the Child,* trans. Hildegarde and Hunter Hannum. New York: Meridian, 1986.

Paul, Robert M. "Freud's Anthropology: A reading of the 'cultural books.'" In *The Cambridge Companion to Freud,* ed. Jerome Neu. Cambridge: Cambridge University Press, 1991. 267–286.

Root, Maria P. P. "Reconstructing the Impact of Trauma on Personality." In *Personality and Psychopathology: Feminist Reappraisals,* ed. Laura S. Brown and Mary Ballou. New York: The Guilford Press, 1992. 229–265.

Rose, Jacqueline. "'Where Does the Misery Come From?' Psychoanalysis, Feminism, and the Event." In *Why War?—Psychoanalysis, Politics, and the Return to Melanie Klein.* Oxford: Blackwell, 1993. 89–109.

Schacter, Daniel L. *Searching for Memory.* New York: Basic Books, 1996.

Shengold, Leonard. *Soul Murder: The Effects of Childhood Abuse and Deprivation.* New Haven: Yale University Press, 1989.

———. *Soul Murder Revisited: Thoughts about Therapy, Hate, Love, and Memory.* New Haven: Yale University Press, 1999.

Starzecpyzel, Eileen. "The Persephone Complex." In *Lesbian Psychologies,* ed. Boston Lesbian Psychologies Perspective. Urbana, IL: University of Illinois Press, 1987. 261–282.

Sugarman, Alan, Ph.D. "Trauma and Abuse: An Overview." In *Victims of Abuse: The Emotional Impact of Child and Adult Trauma,* ed. Alan Sugarman, Ph.D. Madison, WI: International Universities Press, Inc., 1994. 1–24.

Terr, Lenore. *Unchained Memories: True Stories of Traumatic Memories Lost and Found.* New York: Basic Books, 1994.

van der Kolk, Bessel A. "The Role of the Group in the Origin and Resolution of the Trauma Response," In *Psychological Trauma,* ed. Bessel A. van der Kolk, M.D. Washington, D.C.: American Psychiatric Press, 1987. 153–171.

van der Kolk, Bessel A. and Onno van der Hart. "The Intrusive Past: The Flexibility of Memory and the Engraving of Trauma." In *Trauma: Explorations in Memory,* ed. Cathy Caruth. Baltimore: Johns Hopkins University Press, 1995. 158–182.

van der Kolk, Bessel A. and José Saporta. "Biological Responses to Trauma." *International Handbook of Traumatic Stress Syndromes,* ed. John P. Wilson and Beverley Raphael. New York: Plenum Press, 1993. 25–33.

Vasquez, Melba J. T. "Latinas." In *Women of Color: Integrating Ethnic and Gender Identities in Psychotherapy,* ed. Lillian Comas-Díaz and Beverly Greene. New York: The Guilford Press, 1994. 114–138.

Vegh, C. *I Didn't Say Goodbye,* trans. R. Schwartz. New York: E. P. Dutton, 1984.

Waites, Elizabeth. *Trauma and Survival: Post-Traumatic and Dissociative Disorders in Women.* New York: Norton, 1993.

Walker, Lenore. *The Battered Woman.* New York: Harper and Row, 1979.

Wigrin, Jodie. "Narrative Completion in the Treatment of Trauma." *Psychotherapy* 31.3 (Fall 1994): 415–423.

Young, Allan. *The Harmony of Illusions: Inventing Post-Traumatic Stress Disorder.* Princeton: Princeton University Press, 1995.

Zerubavel, Yael. "The Death of Memory and the Memory of Death: Masada and the Holocaust as Historical Metaphors." *Representations* 45 (Winter 1994): 72–100.

Zinner, Ellen S. and Mary Beth Williams, eds. *When a Community Weeps: Case Studies in Group Survivorship.* Philadelphia: Brunner/Mazel, 1999.

Index